D0108367

THE ANALOGY OF LEARNING

THE
ANALOGY
OF
LEARNING

*An essay toward a Thomistic psychology
of learning*

by TAD W. GUZIE, S.J.

SHEED AND WARD · NEW YORK

CONTENTS

Contents

To my mother and father

PREFACE

IT IS AN HONOR and a pleasure to write a few words of introduction for this first major work of a young American Thomist. Let no one take fright at the term "Thomist." The reader will not find here a dry rehash of textbook Thomism or even a scholarly investigation of issues crucial in the thirteenth century but no longer of interest or importance in the world of learning.

To be sure, this is a work in which the writings of Saint Thomas Aquinas are approached with the finest instruments and methods of scholarship. Its sound Thomistic scholarship is one of its primary virtues. I have myself given a great deal of time to the development of a truly scholarly approach to the "reading" of Saint Thomas; I have pointed out, in a sharply critical way, how difficult Thomistic exegesis is and how little genuinely fundamental and permanently valuable research has been done on the *littera* of Saint Thomas.[1] It is then a pleasure to say that here is an author who knows what is required to "read" a Thomistic text. This is not a man who picks and chooses tag-ends of texts in the traditional manner. He presents over

1. See particularly: "St. Thomas' Methodology in the Treatment of 'Positiones' with Particular Reference to 'Positiones Platonicae,'" *Gregorianum,* XXXVI (1955), 391–409; "A Note on Certain Textual Evidence in Fabro's *La Nozione Metafisica di Participazione,*" *Modern Schoolman,* XXXIV (May, 1957), 265–82.

and over again the example of a modern scholar truly trying to understand the mind of Saint Thomas.

Under this approach the thought of Saint Thomas becomes vibrantly alive. Thomistic epistemology has so often been presented both in textbooks and in more advanced philosophical discussions in a rigid and truncated form. Here we recapture at least a glimpse of the incredible wealth of insight Saint Thomas has given us on problems of knowledge. Not only is there an unsuspected richness of developed doctrine but, as our author points out, there are, scattered through the works and apropos of a wide variety of subjects, creative clues which point the way to profounder understandings. Thus, instead of a formalized and closed system, we find a theory of knowledge, characterized indeed by nuanced precisions which yet, for all its firmness, remains fluid and open. The text of Saint Thomas, then, presents not only finished doctrine but challenge and inspiration.

But this book is not just an excursion in Thomistic scholarship, however important we must admit this to be. The discussion is wholly relevant to contemporary problems in Catholic thought and in education and epistemology generally. In a sense our author has himself established the need for this book through his careful review (in the Introduction) of modern Catholic works in the field of educational philosophy and learning theory. But he is not addressing himself just to "Catholic" problems; the substantive investigation is carried on in the closest contact with contemporary problems and with full awareness of the results of recent research.

Nor is it simply another essay on that ill-defined subject called "learning" theory. It presents itself as a *philosophical* work, in which the author is consciously and clearly aware of the difference between "philosophical" knowledge and "scientific" knowledge. The discussion moves forward without being caught in the kind of confusion which results when these two types of knowledge are naively and unwittingly mixed. Yet the author's understanding of this difference is such that he can maintain fruitful contact with all the modes of knowing and make use of all their results. This regulation of philosophical and scientific knowledge is one of the most important contributions of this study.

On the philosophical side, all modern theories of knowledge have been caught in the now hardened dichotomy between rationalism and empiricism, or between idealism and naturalism. Even when it is recognized that we are here within a dilemma that is culturally parochial and historically dated, our philosophers seem unable to rise above the dilemma or to push back to its prehistory. I dare assert that nothing could be more effective in freeing us from this incubus of dated assumptions than the independent study of Saint Thomas' insights into human knowledge. Saint Thomas' philosophy of knowledge escapes these categories since it simply does not make the assumptions—erroneous ones, I would maintain—which gave rise to the rationalist-empiricist tension.

One of the most important sources of this tension was the inability, common to those in both traditions, to understand the integrated functioning of sense and intellect in human knowing. Kant saw that precisely here his predecessors had entangled themselves in hopeless dilemmas; yet he was himself enclosed within their horizons, and his solution—a genial tour de force—rests still upon their assumptions. To recapture the broad and inclusive vision of Saint Thomas is like emerging in flight from the clouds when all is rain and storm at ground level. Here again our author makes a notable contribution since a central part of his study is devoted to the rehabilitation of forgotten functions of both sense and intellect. This reintroduction of lost insights into contemporary discussion may well have an effect comparable to that produced by the reintroduction of the lost notion of "intentionality" by Brentano and the phenomenologists.

On the scientific side, we have had, in the study of "learning," a flood of material experimentation and a confusion of ineffective theories.[1] The philosophical clarifications presented in this book will perhaps suggest new directions for our experimental work and a

---

1. See "Philosophy of Knowledge and Theory of Learning," *Educational Theory,* VIII (October, 1958), 193–99.

possible reintegration of our experimental and theoretical understanding of human learning.

Finally, this study is most fruitful in pointing out problems and
suggesting needed research. Undoubtedly it will itself be revised and
improved after maturer reflection and broader research, for it contains its share of lacunae and mistakes.

Most important of all, Mr. Guzie has shown us how to be truly a
contemporary philosopher, a man of today, while yet making full
use of the perennial insights of Thomism and of the Western tradition.

SAINT LOUIS UNIVERSITY
FEBRUARY, 1960

R. J. HENLE, S.J.
PROFESSOR OF PHILOSOPHY
DEAN OF THE GRADUATE SCHOOL

ACKNOWLEDGMENTS

MANY of this book's merits are due to the excellent criticisms and helpful suggestions contributed by the Reverend John E. Blewett, Messrs. William J. Weiler, Roland J. Teske, and Martin D. O'Keefe, all of the Society of Jesus; and by John J. O'Brien and Andrew M. Doyle, both of the Department of Education at Saint Louis University. No author can express adequately enough his thanks for the assistance received from such generous hands. I am also grateful to Very Reverend John J. Foley, S.J., and the Reverend Joseph J. Labaj, S.J., my superiors at Creighton Preparatory School, Omaha, Nebraska, who saw to it that I had time to revise and complete the manuscript during a busy school year. Thanks are also due to Dr. Vincent E. Smith, who kindly consented to my using in the Introduction essentially the same materials I offered to *The New Scholasticism*.

There are two men to whom I am grateful in a very special way. The Reverend Robert J. Henle, S.J., Dean of the Graduate School at Saint Louis University, first suggested this study, encouraged me in the writing of it, saw to its publication, and completed it with his most kind preface. And without the aid of the Reverend George P. Klubertanz, S.J., Dean of the College of Philosophy and Letters, this book could never have been competently written; to him I am indebted for countless hours of discussion on many aspects of learning theory, philosophy, and science. But my gratitude to these two men extends far beyond the limits of this book. For, through their solid scholarship and inspired teaching, they have illustrated for me what it really means to be a truly contemporary philosopher in the tradition reaching back through Aquinas to Aristotle and Plato.

INTRODUCTION

THE GROWTH AND DEVELOPMENT of scholarship on the philosophy of St. Thomas Aquinas in the last half-century has included a rather large number of textual studies connected with educational and especially learning theory, considered from a Thomistic point of view. These studies, like their companions in the area of strictly speculative philosophy, exhibit the numerous problems involved in the development of Aquinas' thought. For, understanding of such things as Thomas' method of presentation, his terminology, and in general the historical setting and context of his writings has necessarily been gradual.

Consequently, the aim of the survey included in this Introduction is not to criticize the inaccuracies of those who have written on Aquinas and learning theory, simply for criticism's sake. Rather, the approach and direction actually taken in this essay toward a philosophical psychology of learning has been very largely determined by the conclusions that emerge from the survey.

AQUINAS AND LEARNING THEORY: A BIBLIOGRAPHICAL SURVEY

Numerous books and articles have been written on Catholic educational theory in which are delineated principles that have their sources in Thomistic philosophy or theology; various authors of educational works, moreover, have been inspired by Aquinas' thought, though they do not refer to him explicitly; finally, some works on different aspects of Thomas' philosophy (psychology and ethics in particular) include brief references to questions of education and learning. Studies of the sorts just mentioned, however, are not included in the following survey. Its scope has been limited as precisely as possible to writings on Aquinas and education that make a more or less direct use of the Thomistic texts themselves.[1]

The various books and articles have been grouped into two classifications, the first consisting of works of a more general character, the second (and larger) group comprising studies explicitly devoted to learning theory. It may be noted, especially with regard to the first group of studies, that the term *education* is used by various authors in different senses. In American usage, the word primarily means intellectual formation, while foreign writers generally use the term to mean moral formation, reserving the term *instruction* to designate intellectual training.[2]

GENERAL STUDIES

The works in this classification cover a range of subjects from McCormick's appreciative study of Aquinas the teacher and scholar[3] to more technical collections of general educational principles taken from Aquinas' works. Kocourek's commentary on the maxims contained in Thomas' letter "De Modo Studendi"[4] stresses order in obtaining knowledge and the instrumentality of the teacher in learning.[5] Another brief study is that of Jacobs and Bishop,[6] who comment on the virtue of studiousness and the vice of curiosity as one basis for a Thomistic pedagogical theory.[7] DeBeaurecueil[8] traces the second part of the *Summa Theologiae* for the fundamental Thomistic principles of moral formation; a rather interesting basis for "child psychology" is suggested by the author in his comments on Thomas' treatment of the state of the infant before original sin.[9]

Several articles have dealt with the problem of a Thomistic definition of education. Calà-Ulloa's analysis of Aristotelian and Thomistic principles results in a causal and logical definition of education.[10] Leoncio da Silva and Dufault are concerned more with finality alone; the former states the end of education as the actualization of all human capacities,[11] while the latter summarizes its goal as the perfect integration of the moral and intellectual virtues.[12] Leoncio da Silva has also written a lengthy volume on educational practice.[13]

In an article on "Dualism in Education,"[14] C. L. Maloney calls attention to the spirituality of the soul and the necessity of drilling into students the fundamental principle that man is not merely matter; he attributes the present educational evils almost totally to the lack of a dualist view on the part of educators. However, one receives the impression amid the polemics that the author is talking about the dualism of Descartes rather than the philosophy of St. Thomas. A recent article by Bednarski includes a good number of Aquinas' remarks on the biological, psychological, and pedagogical growth of the child; doctrinal rather than inductive, this study is one of the more complete summaries of a general nature.[15]

There remain nine further studies which appear to be concerned with general Thomistic principles of education. All are foreign (with South America making a substantial contribution) and none were located.[16]

The difficulties connected with studies of a general character are perhaps already evident from the preceding sketch of their contents. Such studies have more a hortatory than a scholarly value, since Aquinas' precepts are generally stated with little or no indication of the experiential philosophy upon which their truth-value rests. Hence, these precepts are effectively normative only insofar as the reader personally understands their true meaning. General studies, of course, are valuable as more or less detailed surveys of Aquinas' thought, provided that accuracy is not sacrificed to generalization. Kuničić's article, a more recent one of this type, is perhaps the best general survey of Thomistic educational principles that has yet appeared.[17] The author treats four topics—the teacher, the student, knowledge-values, and method—and does not restrict his selection of texts to any particular work of St. Thomas. Although he goes into very little detail on the philosophical foundations of Thomas' teachings, the author's emphasis on the fact that general principles must be interpreted anew in each concrete teaching situation is significant. For, the majority of studies give the impression that Thomistic principles are rigidly univocal in their application.

Though the terms *habit* and *virtue* are used a great deal in many of the preceding studies, no studies of any length have been *specifically* devoted to the subject of habit-formation as an aim of education. Mlle. Chabrol's brief and largely non-technical article points out the rather evident importance of the development of habits for effective learning.[18] Castiello's study of "The Psychology of Habit in St. Thomas Aquinas"[19] includes a brief application of Aquinas' thought to the educational question of transfer of training. The author points out how, in St. Thomas' view, ideals and methods would be considered transferable, but not the material and specific elements involved. A few other studies on habit are listed in the various bibliographies in the context of educational theory;[20] but since these studies of Aquinas's teaching are not devoted explicitly to habits in an educational setting, the two articles listed above complete our survey in this area.

STUDIES ON LEARNING THEORY

The greater majority of textual studies listed in the various bibliographies under the heading of educational theory pertain more directly to the psychology of the learning process. A chronological arrangement may provide the most effective way of surveying these works.

M. B. Schwalm's article on "L'action intellectuelle d'un maître d'après s. Thomas,"[21] which appeared in 1900 and is apparently the earliest study explicitly on Thomistic educational principles, is also one of the better studies. The author does not make learning through teaching (*doctrina* in the Thomistic texts) a process totally different from learning through personal discovery (*inventio*); a divorce of this type is implied by some later writers. Nor does he treat the "De Magistro" (question 11 of the *De Veritate*) as though it were Thomas' explicit and final treatise on the psychology of learning. Originality is combined with fidelity to Aquinas' thought in a somewhat wordy presentation of the efficient causality exercised by the teacher (instrumentally) and by the student (principally) in the process of learning. E. A. Pace's study,[22] which appeared shortly after Schwalm's, introduces us to some of the major faults to be committed in the following fifty years by scholars of Thomistic learning theory. The "De Magistro" is handled as an *ex professo* treatment of educational theory; hence, the author is led to wonder why Thomas has not discussed memory more fully. No reference is made to the historical context of the "De Magistro," where Aquinas is presenting his own teaching largely in answer to St. Augustine and sometimes in terms borrowed from Augustine. Thus, Pace has difficulty explaining the meaning of "seminal reasons," a phrase which Aquinas applies to first principles; and "light," spoken of frequently throughout Thomas' works in connection with the agent intellect. Unless these terms are understood as analogies drawn from Augustine's teaching (and possibly in deference to St. Augustine), it is easy to misconstrue Aquinas' own teaching.[23]

Three further articles on the subject of learning appeared in the first two decades of the century; one of these, by Willmann, is the only satisfactory encyclopedic treatment of Aquinas' teaching that is to be found.[24]

The work of the Italian Neoscholastics on learning theory, which began to appear in the 1920's, deserves a separate discussion. This school of philosophers found in the principles of Aquinas an answer to Actual Idealism and the philosophy of education represented by Giovanni Gentile, whose educational reforms[25] had begun taking place under Mussolini. Within less than ten years, four separate commentaries on the "De Magistro" were printed, in addition to other articles drawing their precepts from Thomas' works.[26] Although the position of Guzzo is a more radical brand of Neoscholasticism, in that he attempts to present Thomistic principles while clinging to the Idealist tradition, most of these Italian scholars reveal definite influences from Rationalism and from the Rosminian school as well as from St. Thomas.

Mario Casotti, a professor in the Catholic University of the Sacred Heart at Milan, is the author of the most detailed Neoscholastic works directed against the Actual Idealists. *Maestro e scolaro,*[27] his first book, takes issue with one of Gentile's basic tenets (though the latter is not mentioned by name). Gentile had affirmed that teaching either obstructs a pupil's progress or else "hurries him along the way which he would have chosen of his own accord, but along which he would have liked to advance freely, calmly, joyously . . . and without unwelcome compulsion."[28] Hence, the dualism of pupil and teacher must vanish in the synthesis of the two activities into the unity of mind, a union which is to be achieved through the identity of the two wills in the act of spiritual love.[29] Casotti counters polemically with a treatment of the part of the teacher in the learning process and the transfer of knowledge from teacher to student. Heavily metaphysical and wordy, the book goes into detail on the substantial distinction between teacher and pupil and the problem of unity and multiplicity, with few references to the existential basis for these distinctions. Since Gentile identifies the problems of education with philosophy,[30] Casotti tends to make St. Thomas a philosopher of education and to treat the "De Magistro" as an explicit work on that subject.[31] Aquinas' thought is distorted, insofar as the role of the teacher is discussed in isolation from the principal efficient causality exercised by the learner. Moreover, a theory of knowledge which the author considers Thomistic is presented without a clear distinction being made between the thing known and the mode of knowing, the relational as opposed to the immanent character of cognition.

In an equally wordy series of articles published after the appearance of Casotti's book, G. Busnelli[32] takes issue with the former on his interpretation of the Cartesian *cogito* and on the knowledge of first principles, which Casotti interprets as a priori categories.[33]

The role of habits in learning is not clearly presented, and the author's entire treatment is harmed by the fact that he seems more interested in taking issue with Casotti on numerous points than in giving a unified and orderly exposition of any single point.

A year after the appearance of *Maestro e scolaro,* Casotti published *La pedagogia di s. Tommaso d'Aquino,*[34] in which is found an even harsher criticism of assumptions attributed to the Italian Idealists. Gentile's school was an extreme and perhaps inevitable reaction to the formalism of the late nineteenth century. But his emphases on teacher-pupil relations, considered apart from their philosophical framework, are on the whole perhaps more valuable to educators than the abstruse metaphysical discussions of the Neo-scholastics. The reader is inclined to doubt the value of an investigation (suggested by Casotti)[35] into the work of other Italian Neo-scholastics as a rebuttal against "non-Scholastics." The lesson to be learned from the Italians seems to be that little advancement in Thomistic educational scholarship is possible as long as a negative and even polemical approach to and selection of Thomas' texts is maintained. Aquinas' critique of Augustinian illuminism, for instance, which Casotti employs in his second book, cannot be an effective critique of Idealist theories unless it is first accurately presented in its historical setting and then very carefully and precisely adapted to the present situation. The historical presentation is certainly not of necessity in itself; but if the actual texts of St. Thomas are employed, their meaning cannot be unfolded in any other way.

Although Thomistic educational scholarship was dominated in the 1920's by the work of the Italians,[36] the closing of that decade saw the publication of the only *book* in English specifically treating the learning process according to Aquinas. Mary Helen Mayer's work, *The Philosophy of Teaching of St. Thomas Aquinas,*[37] in spite of its title gives more emphasis to the learner. E. A. Fitzpatrick's introduction to the book gives a good summary of some of Thomas' basic psychology and general philosophical principles. Following a rather latinized translation of the "De Magistro" is a lengthy commentary. Since, once again, no reference is made to the historical setting of this work, the interpretation often becomes distorted; basic principles become lost in a treatment that gives generally equal emphasis to all the points discussed. The book labors under many of the same difficulties that are met in the Italian writings. Many scattered remarks are directed against the American counterpart of the then dominant Gentilists, namely, progressive education and the theories (or supposed theories) of John Dewey. The result, consequently, is a rather unorganized, often inaccurate, and incomplete presentation of Aquinas' theories. The book contains a good random selection of key texts from other works of St. Thomas which indicate the manifold problems that must be handled if Aquinas' theory is to be made manifest. However, although some of Thomas' ideas are aptly expressed, the real meaning of many texts is not unfolded, the author rather often allowing texts to speak for themselves. This approach evidently has its difficulties when the texts are fraught with technical terminology or when they are extremely laconic summaries of some of the more elaborate teachings of St. Thomas.

The 1930's saw the appearance of four further articles on Aquinas and learning theory. The first of these, which again employs a rather negative approach, points out the significance of Thomistic principles for the modern *science* of education; this paper by Woroniecki[38] is one of the few that implies the difference that exists between a philosophical and a scientific approach to learning theory. A second article, "Traité sommaire d'éducation d'après la psychologie thomiste,"[39] discusses the operations of the will in learning with hardly any reference to the functions of the sensory emotions; the anonymous author's rigid opposition between intellect and will results in a voluntarism that is certainly not "according to Thomistic psychology."

Keller's study[40] takes us back once more to the "De Magistro," which this time is properly handled in its Augustinian setting. Fitting emphasis is laid on the importance of sense experience and the function of signs in learning. However, the impression is given that knowledge is in some way deduced from first principles, since the author tends to isolate and misinterpret Thomas' analogous use of the Augustinian "seminal reasons" as applied to first principles. R. J. Slavin's article, "The Essential Features of the Philosophy of Education of St. Thomas,"[41] labors under this same difficulty. Although this author summarizes well the objective truths of being and knowledge, a deductive theory of learning is implied. The principle of finality, for instance, is derived from the principle of sufficient reason, according to Father Slavin; and the truth that the intellect seeks is "that which can be deduced from principles furnished by the virtue of understanding."[42] Thus, it would seem that education must be rigidly logical; no reference is made to the way of discovery (*inventio*), which might lead to a more psychological view of the learning process. The over-all impression given the reader is that a Thomistic theory of learning is in the last analysis quite rationalistic. A later study of Father Slavin involves some clarifications and a little rewording of the matter concerning first principles; but it is largely the same in content as his 1937 paper, except that the discussion is placed in the setting of the causality involved in education.[43]

During the war years, there was published one of the finest books that has come from the American presses on the subject of Christian liberal education. Jacques Maritain's discussion of educational aims in *Education at the Crossroads*[44] is perhaps the best treatment of goals in education that has appeared in English. His emphasis on the importance of sense experience provides a welcome contrast to some of the studies considered above. It would seem that a direct analysis of texts from St. Thomas (particularly those from the "De Magistro") leads writers to a rationalistic interpretation of the learning process; while Maritain's study, which involves only oblique or implicit references to Aquinas, contains a sound psychological interpretation of the way we learn. The principal difficulty with the former studies seems to be that individual texts from Thomas' writings are frequently not considered in the light of his whole philosophy; whereas, Maritain's knowledge of Aquinas' philosophy prevents him from making this basic error. However, when he turns to a deeper analysis of the learning process, M. Maritain introduces his personal theories of the pre-conscious life of the intellect and intuitive power, which are difficult to interpret in any context and which spring from the author's rather restricted view of the intellect's operations.[45]

The studies of Thomistic learning theory that have appeared since the early 1940's have in general been written in a more literary and less highly technical vein; and yet they have often presented the psychology of St. Thomas with more accuracy and reference of texts to their context than the works of previous decades. Corbishley's article on "St. Thomas and Educational Theory"[46] and Shannon's study, "Aquinas on the Teacher's Art,"[47] give fresh emphasis to the use of signs in teaching and to the importance of sense experience in learning. Francis Wade's two studies handle the problem of the teaching-learning process in a manner that is both colorful and meaningful. The first of these articles[48] defines more precisely the instrumentality of the teacher in learning and includes an enlightening discussion of the meaning of "indoctrination," which Father Wade defines as teaching divorced from first principles. The second study, appearing in the recent book *Some Philosophers on Education,*[49] makes more direct use of texts from St. Thomas. A well-handled and cleverly exemplified treatment of the nature of teaching is prefaced with a discussion of the intellect's need for recourse to and cooperation with the senses. This essay, which handles in a more organized and intelligible fashion many of the significant problems raised in Mary Helen Mayer's book, is the only work in our entire bibliography which treats explicitly the unity of man as a foundation for learning theory. Wade concludes with some remarks on the nobility of teaching, a subject which Etienne Gilson has discussed in a recent lecture. Both scholarly and inspiring, Gilson's essay is one of the best presentations of the role of the teacher in learning.[50]

It may be noted that the more recent studies, from the mid-forties to the present, move away from the exaggerated intellectualism of earlier decades in giving greater consideration to the function of the senses in learning. Mention should also be made of the fact that American scholars have contributed relatively little to the problem of a Thomistic educational theory.[51]

CONCLUSIONS FROM THE SURVEY

The problem of learning psychology would seem to be central to any philosophy of education. Questions of method and curriculum certainly depend directly upon the position one takes concerning how we learn. Ethical questions of discipline, "academic freedom," democracy, "indoctrination," and the like all involve the teacher more or less directly and find their answers in terms of the teacher's role in learning. One might go so far as to suggest that the development of a Thomistic philosophy of education at present depends on the elaboration of a Thomistic psychology of learning. This may be an overstatement. However, if the school is child-centered and if its primary aim is to contribute to the intellectual formation of the student, it seems to be within the context of the learning process and the teacher's place in learning that solutions to tangent pedagogical problems are most meaningful. The place of moral formation as contributed to by the school would also find its meaning in this context; for, learning psychology must embrace questions of motivation and goals.

Now the fact is that, with the exception of a few good treatments of the "De Magistro," almost no thorough scholarly work has been published on Thomistic psychology as related specifically to learning. Various notions, true enough, have been handled frequently and fully, if not always accurately. Among these, as has been indicated, are the doctrines of the intellect as an active power, the agent intellect, and first principles as the foundation of all knowledge—all of which are discussed at some length in the "De Magistro," as one would expect of a treatise handling the theory of divine illumination or the Averroist separated intellect.[52] The causality exercised by the teacher, a natural correlate to the doctrines just mentioned, has also been discussed; and the function of signs in learning has received some minimal attention.

However, in very many cases, these doctrines are stated in a doctrinal fashion. That is to say, the theories are presented as St. Thomas' teaching, while little or none of the evidence of experience upon which their truth rests is given. It is true that the role of the teacher has been handled more or less inductively in a number of studies. This is to be expected, since Aquinas himself gives the experiential basis for the role of the teacher in the "De Magistro" article and in question 117 of the *Summa Theologiae;* and these have been the most popular texts chosen for commentary in previous studies. But, however carefully the teacher's place in the learning process be discussed, the exposition cannot find cogency apart from a more complete discussion of the learning process itself. And, if we may sound another dissonant note, most present-day educational theorists would be inclined to reject an exposition of a philosophical psychology of learning right from the start. For does not this whole area of thought belong to the experimental learning theorist?

A possible solution to the problems involved can be centered around a series of suggestions that will serve as general conclusions drawn from the bibliographical survey. The particular issues to be taken up in the present study will then be stated in the light of these conclusions.

First, St. Thomas did not have a theory of learning or a philosophy of education as such. This is not to say that development of these areas of practical philosophy from a Thomistic point of view is not possible. But, except for the two texts mentioned above, Aquinas' references to learning and teaching are to be found primarily in obiter dicta which generally imply a highly developed psychology. Hence, if texts from Thomas' writings are directly employed in the elaboration of a philosophical learning theory, they may profitably be taken from other works than "De Magistro," which in no way supplies a complete theory of learning. The thorough textual studies done by accomplished scholars on various aspects of Aquinas' psychology have made possible a fruitful textual approach to a Thomistic learning theory. In whatever way Thomistic texts be used, studies of the sort just mentioned will prove to be most suggestive concerning such things as the internal senses, the psychology of judgment and reasoning, and the operations of the sensory emotions and will. But the problem will be to explain not simply how the mind works, but how the mind works in *learning*.

Secondly, these remarks imply that a clear distinction be made between a *logical* classification of the operations of the mind and a *psychological* explanation of cognitive and motivational processes. This distinction seems to be particularly important in view of the fact that a good number of previous studies have allowed a logical analysis of first principles to stand for a psychological explanation of learning. The first principles have thus lost the *re*ductive function that Aquinas gave them and acquired a rationalistic *de*ductive function. The precise role of the senses in learning, moreover, has only begun to be explored in a Thomistic context.

Thirdly, the metaphysics and psychology of knowledge, or whatever other philosophical principles are involved, would be most effectively presented according to the proper method of a philosophical inquiry, which involves a lengthy analytic and inductive process. If one is writing for professional Thomists, it is generally sufficient merely to restate the principles, or rather, conclusions that are brought to bear upon a particular issue. But if the presentation is to be made meaningful for anyone who is not thoroughly acquainted with Aquinas' philosophy, one cannot dispense with the inductive analysis.

Fourthly, the question of philosophical method raises a further problem. Though a few of the previous studies of Thomistic learning theory imply a difference between a philosophical and an experimental approach, none discuss this fundamental matter. When the question at hand is a strictly philosophical one such as the end of education, there is no pressing need to consider the differences between philosophical and scientific method. But when one proposes to treat from a philosophical point of view many of the same problems that are specifically handled by experimental science, a careful distinction between scientific and philosophical inference and forms of knowledge seems imperative. It is fundamental particularly to any presentation of philosophical learning psychology to indicate precisely what sort of question the philosophical approach plans to answer, what its limitations are, and how the knowledge thus acquired differs from experimental laws and fits into the scheme of learning theory as a whole.

All of the suggestions just offered imply that really nothing should be presumed in the elucidation of any aspect of a philosophical learning theory. For, the bibliographical survey indicates at least this, that too much has been presumed for too long. The suggestions concerning philosophical method are based on historical factors that have contributed to today's philosophical situation. In itself, there is nothing wrong with demonstrative exposition in terms of resolution to first principles. However, such an approach does not illustrate sufficiently the type of question which a philosophical psychology of learning would be intent upon answering. On the other hand, an experiential and inductive philosophical analysis of learning activity might have real force for the contemporary educational theorist.[53]

THE AIM OF THE PRESENT STUDY

In an effort to lay the foundations for a philosophical psychology of learning, it is the aim of the present study to explore the *cognitive aspects of learning*. The reason for this choice will become more evident as the analysis itself proceeds. It will be sufficient to remark here that questions of motivation and other problems involving volition and emotion presuppose cognition of some sort, as do problems of habit and behavioral modification resulting from a process of learning.

The conclusions drawn from the bibliographical survey will be kept in mind throughout the study. Thus, Chapter One will take up the question of philosophical method. Though innumerable problems can be raised in this area, our discussion will be restricted chiefly to illustrating the type of problem, the kind of evidence, and the form of conceptual organization proper to a philosophical analysis. An effort will also be made to show relationships between philosophical and scientific psychology. The sketch of methodology contained in this chapter, together with differences between experimental and philosophical questions, will be concretely illustrated throughout the remainder of the work.

Chapter Two traces the fundamental psychology of knowledge. Beginning with a consideration of knowledge as a total experience, the analysis proceeds inductively through the psychological structure of the human knower. Symbolic communication, a theme which will keep recurring throughout the study, is introduced here as a means of establishing the unity of cognitive experience as well as the nature of thought. Pursuing the close relationship between sensation and intellection brought to light in the second chapter, Chapter Three goes on to consider the precise function of the senses in intellectual knowledge, in terms of the role of the image in behavior and more specifically in intellection. Chapter Four then traces the psychological nature of judgment and the causal roots of differences in understanding.

Discussion of learning as a more distinct type of activity begins with Chapter Five. The nature of human learning is investigated in the light of the psychological principles established in the preceding chapters. The cognitive causes of behavioral modification are considered in terms of the structure of knowledge, and an analysis of verbal symbols is used to determine the types and characteristics of intellectual learning. Chapter Six serves as a judgmental summary of all the preceding inductions, and learning is explicitly defined in its cognitive aspects.

The final chapter begins the work of drawing out the practical implications of the real nature of human learning. Various academic subjects are investigated in the light of a philosophical psychology of learning, and the act of teaching is finally considered in its total reality.

It is important to note that this essay toward a philosophical learn-

ing theory is meant to be an *exposition* and not a *confrontation*. Historical questions and philosophical problems raised in various contemporary schools of thought are not formally discussed. Historical
considerations are sometimes introduced with a view to clarifying
or focusing attention upon some point, but these matters are invariably restricted to the footnotes. We are not ignoring or dismissing
these various problems as inconsequential. But they must be prescinded from in a work of this nature, which is oriented toward a
positive presentation of the matters sketched above.

A NOTE ON THE USE OF AQUINAS' WRITINGS

We have remarked that St. Thomas did not elaborate a theory of
learning as such. This point, in addition to the fact that Aquinas
generally states his teachings in judgmentally organized form, thus
presupposing the inductive moments of philosophical reasoning, indicates that extensive *direct* use of texts will not be immediately
helpful for our own presentation. Moreover, Thomas uses his own
terminology, presenting his ideas in terms of the problems current
in his own day. Extensive quotations from his writings, consequently,
would raise further historical and semantic questions quite unrelated
to the matter at hand.

However, St. Thomas' writings have been immediately helpful in
developing the points taken up in this study; and hence copious
references are given to his works. Though Aquinas' own analyses
are directly used in a few instances, all textual matters are generally
confined to the footnotes. The notes are intended to summarize and
clarify Aquinas' teaching on certain points as well as to amplify
and elucidate in a more technical fashion some of the matters discussed in the body of the work.

Where there exist competent textual studies on various aspects
of Aquinas' psychology, these are cited rather than the writings of
Thomas himself, since his teaching on many matters must often be
culled from many works in order to be seen as a whole. Our own

study, in fact, is quite dependent upon textual studies of this sort. The *Summa Theologiae* is otherwise used as a primary source, since, as one of St. Thomas' most personal and mature writings, it contains some of his most succinct statements on psychological matters.[54]

This essay toward a philosophical psychology of learning, then, is not "Thomistic" in the sense of being an historical or a strictly textual study. Rather, it is an attempt to use, in the area of learning theory, the realistic philosophical *method* that Thomas Aquinas carefully developed and applied to the philosophical issues current in his own day.[55] Thomas' own insights will not be seen here apart from the evidence which validates them. In this way, we hope to erect the framework of a psychology of learning founded on the evidence of experience.

NOTES

1. The bibliographical sources employed were:
   Vernon J. Bourke, *Thomistic Bibliography: 1920–1940* (St. Louis: Modern Schoolman, 1945).
   G. A. DeBrie (ed.), *Bibliographia philosophica: 1934–1945* (Bruxelles: Editiones Spectrum, 1950).
   P. Mandonnet and J. Destrez, *Bibliographie thomiste* [1800–1920] (Kain: Le Saulchoir, 1921).
   Répertoire bibliographique de la philosophie (Louvain: Editions de l'Institut Supérieur de Philosophie), Vol. 1 (1949) to the present.
   Also consulted, especially for more recent studies, were the bibliographies published in the *Modern Schoolman* (St. Louis) and in the *Bulletin thomiste* (Paris).
   If the Mandonnet-Destrez listing is complete, the present survey includes all that has been published on St. Thomas and educational theory since 1800, though the first article on the subject did not appear until 1900. Although this survey is certainly subject to further augmentation with regard to more recent works that have not yet appeared in the reviews as well as older works that may have been overlooked, it attempts to include all that has been published on the subject in German, French, Italian, Spanish, Portuguese, and Eng-

lish. Wholly popular discussions and book reviews have not been included.

   Inter-library services were made use of, with the kind cooperation of the Saint Louis University reference library staff, who consulted the Union Lists of Serials for the location of periodicals and the National Union Catalogue and other catalogues in the Library of Congress for that of books. In order to indicate the nature and scope of scholarship on St. Thomas and educational philosophy, I have listed also those (apparently) pertinent works which were included in the various bibliographies, but which I was unable to obtain. The designation "not located" after a work indicates either that its location is not given in the Union Lists or National Catalogue, or that though located the work is not available for inter-library loan. Hence, for all practical purposes, works accompanied by this designation are unavailable to the American researcher.

2. St. Thomas, too, uses the word *educatio* (to my knowledge) only in reference to the "education" of a child to a proper moral character. E.g., see *Commentary on the Sentences,* Bk. IV, distinction 26, question 1, article 1, where *educatio* is defined as "promotio [prolis] usque ad perfectum statum hominis inquantum homo est, qui est virtutis status." This usage is thus much broader than the usual American meaning of the term.

3. John F. McCormick, S.J., *Saint Thomas and the Life of Learning* ("Aquinas Lecture"; Milwaukee: Marquette University Press, 1937). A brief study of the man Thomas and his views on and devotion to learning and scholarship.

4. P. Mandonnet (ed.), *Opuscula Omnia* (Paris: Lethielleux, 1927) IV, 535, no. 44. Listed by Bourke (*Thomistic Bibliography,* p. 19) as of doubtful authenticity.

5. R. A. Kocourek, "St. Thomas on Study," *Thomistic Principles in a Catholic School* (St. Louis: Herder, 1943), pp. 14–38. Based on the 17th-century commentary of the Dominican John Paul Nazarius on the letter.

6. J. F. Jacobs, O.P., and J. Bishop, O.P., "Learning Humanly," *Reality,* I (1950–51), 37–43.

7. Based on *Summa Theologiae,* Second Division of Part II, questions 166–67.

8. S. deBeaurecueil, O.P., "S. Thomas d'Aquin et la pédagogie," *Cahiers, Cercle thomiste,* II (1949), 3–30.

9. *Summa Theologiae,* Part I, questions 99–101.

10. The causal definition includes God, teacher, and pupil as the efficient

causes, the educand as the material cause, the formation of a humane and Christian personality as the formal and final cause. The logical definition designates education as a practical art (quasi proximate genus) leading to the formation of a humane and Christian personality (quasi specific difference). Guglielmo Calà-Ulloa, "Il concetto della pedagogia alla luce dell' aristotelismo tomistico," *Sapienza*, III (1950), 28–45.

11. C. Leoncio da Silva, S.D.B., "Il fine dell' educazione secondi i principi di s. Tommaso," *Salesianum*, IX (1947), 207–39.
12. L. Dufault, O.M.I., "The Aristotelian-Thomistic Concept of Education," *New Scholasticism*, XX (1946), 239–57.
13. *Pedagogia speciale pratica*, Vol. I: *L'educando* (Torino: Soc. ed. internaz., 1948). Not located.
14. *Catholic Educational Review*, XLIV (1946), 335–41.
15. F. Bednarski, O.P., "Animadversiones S. Thomae Aquinatis de iuvenibus eorumque educatione," *Angelicum*, XXXV (1958), 375–411.
16. A. L. Barthélemy, O.P., *L'éducation: Les bases d'une pédagogie thomiste* (Bruxelles, 1925).

    J. Engert, "Die Pädagogik des hl. Thomas von Aquin," *Pharus*, VI (1925), 321–31.

    B. Navarro, *Commentario filosofico-teologico a la carta de s. Tomás sobre el modo de estudiar fructuosamente* (Almagro: Dominicos de Andalucia, 1925).

    V. Devy, "La pédagogie de s. Thomas d'Aquin," *Revue de l'Université d'Ottawa*, II (1932), 139*–62*.

    P. Boullay, O.P., *Thomisme et éducation* (Bruxelles, 1933).

    S. Tauzin, O.P., "S. Tomás e la pedagogía moderna," *Revista Brasileira de Pedagogía*, XXXVIII–IX (1937), 118–29.

    A. Alves de Siqueira, *Filosofia da educação* (Petrópolis: Vozes, 1942).

    Alberto García Vieyra, *Ensayos sobre pedagogía según la mente de s. Tomás de Aquino* (Buenos Aires: Desclée, 1949).

    Rosa T. diSisto, "El concepto de pedagogía según s. Tomás," *Anales del Instituto de Investigaciones Pedagógicas* (San Luis, Argentina), II (1952–53), 234. [Possibly a review of García Vieyra's book.]
17. Jordanus Kuničić, "Principia didactica s. Thomae," *Divus Thomas* (Piacenza), LVIII (1955), 398–411. Apparently the same article appears in *Sapienza*, VIII (1955), 316–36, as "Principi pedagogici di s. Tommaso."

18. J. Chabrol, "Habitus et éducation," *Cahiers, Cercle Sainte-Jeanne* (1932), 60–67.
19. Jaime Castiello, S.J., *Modern Schoolman*, XIV (1936), 8–12.
20. The studies listed are B. Roland-Gosselin, *L'habitude* (Paris: Beauchesne, 1920) and Jacques Chevalier, *L'habitude: Essai de métaphysique scientifique* (Paris: Boivin, 1929). The latter work is particularly good on the physiological and neurological aspects of habit; the author's denial of habits with no foundations in the senses is especially noteworthy.
21. *Revue thomiste*, VIII (1900), 251–72.
22. "St. Thomas' Theory of Education," *Catholic University Bulletin*, VIII (1902), 290–303.
23. The first article of the "De Magistro" (which is the most important of the four articles in this question, insofar as it presents the basic psychological and epistemological principles of learning) is a direct answer to a distinctly Augustinian question: "whether one man can teach another or whether only God can be called a teacher." The question as thus stated is not meaningful outside the context of a theory of divine illumination.

   Later in his life, when he had become more thoroughly acquainted with the doctrines of Plato and Averroes, St. Thomas placed the same question in a somewhat different historical context. In the *Summa Theologiae*, Part I, question 117, article 1, Aquinas asks "whether one man can teach another." His arguments in this article are parallel to (and more mature than) those given in the "De Magistro." However, by omitting the phrase concerning God as a teacher in his statement of the question, Thomas prescinds from St. Augustine, going directly to the Platonic and Averroist theories (though Augustine's doctrine of divine illumination finds its roots in Platonic thought). Averroes had held that there is only one possible intellect and one set of intelligible *species* for all men; hence, a teacher merely guides his students in organizing their phantasms so that they can receive the single knowledge that is common to all men, by reason of a single intellect. According to the Platonists, the soul has always possessed knowledge through participation in the separated Forms, but it forgets this knowledge upon becoming united with a body; hence, learning is nothing but remembering, and the teacher's function is to lead the student to recall what he already knows.

   Aquinas' discussions in the above-mentioned articles thus center principally around the nature of the human intellect and by no means give all the principles necessary for a complete theory of learning. Two commentaries which consider the "De Magistro" in its proper historical setting are:

William L. Wade, S.J., "A Comparison of the 'De Magistro' of St. Augustine with the 'De Magistro' of St. Thomas" (unpublished Ph.D. dissertation, Dept. of Philosophy, St. Louis University, 1935), especially pp. 81–163.

Wilhelm Schneider, *Die Quaestiones Disputatae De Veritate des Thomas von Aquin in ihrer philosophie-geschichtlichen Beziehung zu Augustinus,* Vol. XXVII, Part III of *Beiträge zur Geschichte der Philosophie und Theologie des Mittelalters,* ed. Martin Grabmann (Münster: Aschendorffschen Verlagsbuchhandlung, 1930).

24. O. Willmann, "Thomas von Aquin," *Lexikon der Pädagogik* (Freiburg im B.: Roloff, 1917), Vol. V, cols. 105–21. Contains a section "Lehren und Lernen" and one on "Die Quaestio de Magistro." The former emphasizes basic psychological doctrines; the latter gives a general summary of the "De Magistro," putting it in its proper historical setting. The recent *Lexikon der Pädagogik* (Bern: A. Franke, 1952), III, 31, refers the reader to Willmann's article.

The remaining two articles of this period were not located:

O. Willmann, "Des hl. Thomas von Aquin Untersuchungen über dem Lehrer," *W. aus Hörsaal und Schulstube, gesammelte kleinere Schriften zur Erziehungs und Unterrichtslehre* (Freiburg im B.: Herder, 1904), pp. 40–45.

Martin Grabmann, "Die Psychologie des Lehrens und Lernens nach dem hl. Thomas von Aquin," *Die Christliche Schule* (1910), 145–51.

25. On Gentile's educational reforms, see Ugo Spirito, "Education in Italy," tr. H. Marraro, *Educational Yearbook: International Institute of Teachers' College* (New York: Columbia University Press, (1924), pp. 329–51. The principles behind the Gentilian reform are traced in Peter J. Roebrocks, M.S.F., "Giovanni Gentile: A Critical Analysis of His Actual Idealism and His Educational Philosophy" (unpublished Master's thesis, Dept. of Philosophy, St. Louis University, 1936), pp. 91–98. See also P. Romanelli, *Gentile* (New York: S. F. Vanni, 1938), pp. 13–14.

26. The "De Magistro" commentaries are:

R. Rung, "Studio sulla Quaestio disputata 'De Magistro' di s. Tommaso d'Aquino," *Rivista di filosofia neoscolastica,* XIV (1922), 109–65.

G. Muzio, *S. Tommaso d'Aquino: Il maestro* (Torino: Soc. ed. internaz., 1928).

A. Guzzo, *Tommaso d'Aquino: Il maestro* (Firenze: Vallechi, 1930).

D. Morando, "Sul 'De Magistro' di s. Tommaso," *Rivista Rosminiana di filosofia e di coltura* (Torino), XXV (1931). Not located.

Articles of this period other than the above direct commentaries are the following (not located):

G. Tincani, "L'azione intellettuale del maestro secondo s. Tommaso d'Aquino," *Scuola Cattolica*, Vol. XIX, ser. V (1920), 37–50, 115–29, 173–85.

E. Chiochetti, "La pedagogia de s. Tommaso," *S. Tommaso d' Aquino: Pubblicazione commemorativa del sesto centenario della canonizazione* (Milano: Vita e Pensiero, 1923), pp. 280–93.

The most recent Italian translation of the "De Magistro" (under that title) with introduction and notes is by Giovanni di Napoli (Torino: Soc. ed. internaz., 1954).

27. M. Casotti, *Maestro e scolaro: Saggio di filosofia dell' educazione* (Milano: Vita e Pensiero, 1930).

28. G. Gentile, *The Reform of Education*, tr. D. Bigongiari (New York: Harcourt, Brace & Co., 1922), pp. 39–40.

29. Compare Gentile's desire to eliminate the distinction between teacher and student on the affective level with Averroes' elimination of this distinction on cognitive grounds (see note 23.)

30. See Gentile, *Sommario di pedagogia come scienza filosofica*, Vol. II, *Didattica* (Bari: Laterza, 1914), chap. i.

31. In a more recent article, Casotti discusses the meaning of education in the light of metaphysics, and clarifies the relation between philosophy and education. See "Pedagogia e metafisica," *Rivista di filosofia neoscolastica*, XLI (1949), 137–52. This article also discusses moral habits, which are handled in an aprioristic fashion.

32. G. Busnelli, S.J., "Filosofia e pedagogia," *Civiltà Cattolica*, LXXXII (1931), III, 413–22; IV, 30–40, 229–38, 309–25. Apparently published as a book under same title (2d ed.; Roma: Civiltà Cattol., 1932).

33. Casotti remarks that first principles or "categories" are not innate in the Cartesian sense of the word, as though the mind possessed them prior to sense experience. But they are a priori, like dispositions present in the intellect, passing suddenly into act when the first sensible experience stimulates them. See *Maestro e scolaro*, p. 260.

This is a misleading *reification* of first principles, which are "dispositions" in the intellect only in the sense that man has a natural habit by which he knows being as intelligible in some way, in every instance of intellectual knowledge. In virtue of this habit he is able to formulate first principles; but first logical principles need never be formally and explicitly known, nor do they impose themselves upon sense experience, like Kantian categories. Busnelli does not state the problem clearly; he also misses the fact that the "a priori category" interpretation leads Casotti to let a *logical* analysis stand for a *psychological* explanation of the relationship between first principles and subsequent knowledge. *Sense experience* as a first principle of cognition and learning is very rarely discussed by writers on Thomistic learning theory.

The problem of first principles in learning will receive more detailed discussion in chapter 6.

34. Brescia: La Scuola, 1931.
35. In "La neoscolastica e la pedagogia," *Rivista di filosofia neoscolastica, suppl. spec.* XXVI (1934), 241–47.
36. The most recent Italian works on educational theory are the following (neither having been located):

    M. Casotti, *Pedagogia generale* (2 vols.; Brescia: La Scuola, 1947–48).

    Giuseppe A. Mangieri, "Presupposti di un' educazione nel pensiero di s. Tommaso," *Sapienza,* IV (1951), 309–24.
37. Milwaukee: Bruce Publishing Co., 1929.
38. Hyacinth Woroniecki, "St. Thomas and Modern Pedagogy," *Catholic Educational Review,* XXVIII (1930), 170–80.
39. *L'ami du clergé,* LII (1935), 593–601.
40. L. Keller, "Lehren und Lernen bei Thomas von Aquin," *Angelicum,* XIII (1936), 210–27.
41. Robert J. Slavin, O.P., *Proceedings of the American Catholic Philosophical Association,* XIII (1937), 22–38.
42. *Ibid.,* p. 30.
43. R. J. Slavin, O.P., "The Thomistic Concept of Education," *Essays in Thomism,* ed. R. E. Brennan, O.P. (New York: Sheed & Ward, 1942), pp. 311–31.
44. "Terry Lectures" (New Haven: Yale University Press, 1943).
45. The same notions are used extensively in *Creative Intuition in Art and Poetry* ("Mellon Lectures," National Gallery of Art, 1952; New York: Pantheon, Inc., 1953), especially chaps. iii and iv.

46. Thomas Corbishley, S.J., "St. Thomas and Educational Theory," *Dublin Review,* No. 424 (1943), 1–13.
47. G. J. Shannon, C.M., "Aquinas on the Teacher's Art," *Clergy Review,* XXXI (1949), 375–85.
48. Francis C. Wade, S.J., "Causality in the Classroom," *Modern Schoolman,* XXVIII (1951), 138–46.
49. Wade, "St. Thomas Aquinas and Teaching," *Some Philosophers on Education,* ed. Donald A. Gallagher (Milwaukee: Marquette Univ. Press, 1956), pp. 67–85.
50. E. Gilson, "The Eminence of Teaching," *Truth and the Philosophy of Teaching* ("McAuley Lectures," 1953; West Hartford, Conn.: St. Joseph's College, 1954), pp. 5–15. Reprinted in *A Gilson Reader,* ed. Anton C. Pegis (New York: Hanover House, 1957), pp. 298–311; also as the second selection in *Disputed Questions in Education* (New York: Doubleday & Co., 1954).
51. Though they have not been published, two Master's theses done at St. Louis University may be noted here: J. Quentin Lauer, S.J., in "The Art of Teaching according to the Principles of St. Thomas" (Dept. of Philosophy, 1943), gives a precise location to teaching among the arts; the discussion of teaching itself is relatively brief, since most of the study is devoted to a consideration of the genesis, types, definition, end, and function of art according to Thomistic and Aristotelian principles.

John W. Donohue, S.J., in "The Teaching-Learning Process according to St. Thomas and Henry C. Morrison" (Dept. of Education, 1944), handles well a number of the significant elements involved in learning through teaching; his study, unlike many which treat similar questions, is based on a broad selection of texts from Aquinas' works.
52. See note 23.
53. James Collins has elaborated this point in a recent paper, "Toward a Philosophically Ordered Thomism," *New Scholasticism,* XXXII (1958), 301–26.
54. *In the citation of texts* from Thomas' works, standard abbreviations are used. Roman numerals signify the main divisions of the *Summa,* "q." signifies "question," and "a." designates "article." Answers to the objections following each article in the *Summa* are symbolized by "ad." Thus, the reference *S. T.* I–II, q. 17, a. 4, ad 2 means: first division of the second Part of the *Summa Theologiae,* question 17, article 4, in answer to the 2nd objection.

When only part of an article from the *Summa* is pertinent to the matter at hand, references are made to the Piana edition (Rome, 1570–71) as re-edited by the Dominican Fathers of Ottawa (Vols. I–IV; Ottawa: Impensis Studii Generalis O. Pr., 1941–44). Though the Ottawa-Piana is not a critical edition, it contains in footnotes the textual emendations of the critical Leonine version. It has been used primarily because references can be given to column and line as well as to page. Thus, "ed. Ottawa II, 805a35–37" means: vol. II of the Ottawa edition, page 805, column *a*, lines 35 to 37. *When a whole article* is being referred to as pertinent, this additional reference is not given.

In quoting other writings of Aquinas, critical editions are used, when they exist. The author takes the responsibility for all translations that appear in this study. Lengthier Latin texts translated in the body of the work appear in the Appendix.

55. Although Aquinas states the methodological principles proper to a philosophical analysis in his earliest writings, his personal *use* of the method undergoes a gradual development. See T. W. Guzie, S.J., "Evolution of Philosophical Method in the Writings of St. Thomas," *Modern Schoolman*, XXXVII (January, 1960), 95–120.

1

THE PHILOSOPHICAL
APPROACH TO LEARNING
THEORY

A PRESENTATION of learning theory, taking this notion in its broadest sense, may be made from the point of view either of pure science or of applied science. The former approach will be concerned with the exposition, systematic development, and verification of theoretical propositions. Applied science, on the other hand, presupposes the theoretical and is concerned with the practical application of such principles as an aid in the solution of concrete and specific problems; thus, part of educational psychology is devoted to applied learning theory. The present study, however, prescinds from application to specific classroom problems; it is rather an exposition of theoretical principles upon which applied psychology may be based.

Without becoming involved in an analysis of the nature of science qua science,[1] we may define pure science in general as any systematic intellectual knowledge of an object by means of reasoning processes employed within a definite and disciplined methodology. However, within the area of pure science a further distinction must be made between philosophical and experimental science—or, for our purposes, between philosophical psychology and experimental or scientific psychology. Although learning theory is our primary concern, it cannot be treated apart from the larger context of psychology as a whole, since it is that aspect or branch of a psychology which concentrates explicitly on man's learning activities. Letting this tautological description of learning theory suffice for the moment, we may add that its methodology will be the same as that of the type of psychology in which it finds its place. The various types of contemporary experimental psychology can for our purposes be grouped together since, in spite of differences in *theory,* they all employ the scientific *method.*

The general theme of this chapter, however, must be carefully qualified. No attempt is made here to discuss the inter-disciplinary problems and conflicts that have arisen in the course of history, owing to distortion of method on the side of both scientist and philosopher; this would constitute any number of separate projects.[2] Secondly, only the most salient features of experimental methodology are discussed, and the analysis is oriented solely toward showing its relationship to philosophical reasoning. While special emphasis is laid on the *independent status* of each of these knowledges, it would be impossible to explore the intricacies of either—and especially the complexities of specific experimental approaches—within the compass of a dozen or so pages. The following analysis, then, is intended to be sufficient only for the purposes of the present study.[3] Finally, inasmuch as the philosophical method will be illustrated concretely throughout the remainder of the work, the discussion of it here is somewhat proleptic.

Both philosophical and scientific psychology study, speaking in a very general way, the activities of man. Science treats these activities insofar as they are subject to observation and measurement, philosophy insofar as they reveal man's ontological nature. This gross distinction of the two forms of knowledge by material and formal object[4] needs much refinement. It will be seen that the formal object implies the entire philosophical or scientific methodology and that, since there are differences even at the level of material object, really the only thing the two sciences have completely in common is their general subject, man. The inductive stages of the two sciences will be considered first, and aims and methods compared. Analysis of the judgmentally organized stage will then involve a comparison of forms of conceptual knowledge and some considerations on various relationships between the two knowledges.

PHILOSOPHICAL PSYCHOLOGY:
AIM AND METHOD

Although the philosophical psychologist must be as carefully precise and accurate as any scientist, the method that he employs is relatively incomplex as compared with that of the experimental scientist. His starting point is the evidence that is immediately revealed upon direct contact with reality; such evidence, which can be obtained by introspection as well as by external observation, we may call *experiential*. It differs from *experimental* or scientific evidence in two ways. It is not obtained through specialized techniques or instruments which mediate the experimental scientist's contact with concrete reality, nor is it selected on the basis of a statistical sample. Hence—and this is the second difference—experiential evidence covers the entire scope of human experience.[5] Since this evidence is of such broad scope and is not statistically *selected,* it must be very accurately *limited* to what is pertinent to the philosophical quest through careful analysis of the meaning of each fact. Experimental evidence as such is not pertinent to the philosophical method; the extent to which this type of evidence may be relevant and useful will be noted later.

Confronted with the facts of existent things, the philosopher subjects them to reflective analysis; his aim is to discover through these evidences what man is, the nature of his cognitive powers, the ontological structure man must have in order to act as he does. To gain this sort of knowledge, the philosopher accepts, as a primitive datum of experience, the existent world of objects around him. These objects, the things that men perceive and undergo, are the philosopher's given, just as living things or moving bodies are the data for the biologist or mechanical physicist.[6]

But even though the philosopher is intent on abstracting from the particularities of singular material existents, he must maintain contact with his data throughout the course of his analysis, continually checking his reasonings and conclusions against the concrete facts with which he began. If he were to abandon his data and retreat into the world of concepts, he would simply be abandoning the philosophical method, since he would be isolating himself from his only means of verification. The selective construction of ideas is perfectly legitimate for the scientist, who is able to confirm or reject a hypothetical statement experimentally because it is restricted to phenomena. But propositions about a thing's intrinsic nature, which is non-phenomenal and not immediately experienced, cannot be verified except by recourse to the direct intelligibility which the object reveals through its operations and characteristics. Hence, a philosopher's retreat from things constitutes a false use both of the scientific and of the philosophical method, as well as a sacrifice of the truth-value to be attributed to his statements. For, such a procedure terminates necessarily in the formation of a conceptual scheme into which reality must be fitted as upon a Procrustean bed. But while contact with primitive evidence must be maintained, it is significant to note that use of the imagination in the philosophical method must be carefully restricted to illustrative analogies alone, since actual reification of some kind of sensible example or "model" would reduce philosophy to a naive physics. The primary difficulty of philosophy, as Stace succinctly puts it, "lies almost wholly in the struggle to think non-sensuously."[7]

The rational movement of philosophical psychology, consequently, proceeds from observable human properties and activities to their inferentially intelligible implications, namely, the essential principles or causes of being and of activity which make it possible for the activity itself to be and to be experienceable. If introspective evidence becomes involved in this analysis, the distinctive method of philosophy makes of this subjective experience an object that is capable of disciplined study.[8] The analysis of knowledge as a total experience will be one of the most fundamental evidences, especially in the context of learning theory.

At this point it should be clear that, although the basic *approach* of philosophical psychology entails a kind of phenomenological description, the rational movement does not terminate in a phenomenalism that leaves the reality of man unaccounted for and the human knower imprisoned in subjectivity. The distinctive feature of philosophical reasoning is that the process leads gradually to an insight into the necessity of the connection between the terms of the conclusion formulated. And the necessity of the proposition is an expression within the mind of a real ontological necessity.

When it is stated, for instance, that "the intellect is an immaterial power," the entire validity of the judgment rests upon the insight obtained into its necessity through the coerciveness of experiential evidence. "Intellect" arbitrarily denominates a real power, the principle or source of thought activity. And it is denominated "immaterial" or "non-sensory" because its activities reveal that it cannot be the form of a sense organ. Note that, in order to reach a conclusion of this sort, the philosopher must consider all of the experiential evidence pertinent to his study. In terms of our example, this means that those things common to all thought activity must be very carefully analyzed. Without such analysis, the conclusion would be meaningless, and the inductive process could not result in a personal grasp of the necessity of the fact. Hence, purely a priori propositions are either useless or misleading in this type of reasoning, which we may for the sake of a term call *experiential induction.*[9]

The meaning of the phrase "direct insight into the necessity of a proposition" may now be clarified. As has been noted, experiential induction terminates in a judgmental expression of some extramental necessity. Concrete reality determines philosophical knowledge. Hence, the necessary judgment is not a form imposed upon unintelligible matter, nor on the other hand is it a pure intuition.[10] What is directly grasped is a necessary aspect of a real being as known *through* judgment (a point which will be developed further in later chapters). Finally, direct insight does not necessarily imply *temporal* immediacy of insight, for experiential induction may and generally does involve lengthy reflection and analysis—reasoning from fact to cause, resolution to fundamental principles, and the like. The analytic process itself is flexible and always subject to the data under consideration.

"Direct insight," consequently, implies essentially two things: first, that the understanding attained is a result of direct contact with reality, unmediated by any artificial technique; and secondly, that when the understanding is attained whether by an immediate grasp of meaning or through analytic reasoning, it is attained once and for all. No further philosophical verification is needed and the truth-value of the conclusion is constant, since the insight if it is to be at all valid is founded upon a consideration of all the pertinent existential evidence. The insight, indeed, may be only partial, in the sense that only one aspect of the nature of man is understood; intelligible grasp of the total ontological nature of man entails many such insights. We shall return to this point at the end of this chapter.

SCIENTIFIC PSYCHOLOGY:
AIM AND METHOD

Turning now to the experimental or scientific psychologist, we find him meeting the philosopher at the level of experience and studying the subject common to both, namely, man. The experimentalist's quest, however, is not for knowledge of the *ontological* nature of man and the essential causes of his activity. Having discovered and accumulated facts about man, the scientist becomes interested in formal relationships *between* human acts, the conditions under which they occur, temporal sequences of acts, ways in which the acts might be more efficiently performed.[11] Moreover, he desires to be able to extend his experimental generalizations to new situations, in order that behavior may be predicted and controlled. To achieve these functional goals, the scientific psychologist restricts himself to a study only of what is observable and, ideally, measurable in man—the level of modifiable activity or behavior.

Corresponding to these aims are the major procedures of the experimental psychologist, which may be somewhat arbitrarily schematized as follows: (1) *symbolization,* which may be verbal or mathematical—the assignment of names to objectively observed, sometimes subjective, or conceptual events; (2) *description*—symbolic systematization of directly revealed relationships among phenomena (classification, seriating or simple ordering, correlation); (3) *explanation and theorizing*—abstraction from descriptive data to conceptual meanings and finally to a higher-order conceptual framework or theory.[12] Psychology thus utilizes the general procedure of any experimental science concerned with phenomena; the final specification of psychological method (particularly in the third stage just mentioned) arises from the factors studied rather than from the methodology itself.

As the scientific procedure suggests, *experiential* evidence is not pertinent until it has been set into the symbolic framework proper to an experimental inquiry. Direct existential facts are therefore selected on the basis of the hypothesis that the psychologist formulates in order to arrive at his behavior laws. The *experimental* evidence is generally obtained by various specialized tests or instruments which mediate the scientist's contact with his object, and the selective process is subject to statistical laws of sampling and the like for determining its validity. The relation between selection of evidence and theorizing in this hypothetico-deductive method is essentially circular. A new selection may involve a differently phrased hypothesis, just as the hypothesis itself will determine the choice of evidence. Thus, the hypothesis is always reformable; and evidence is "deduced from the hypothesis," that is, abstractively selected in accord with the hypothesis.

This procedure may be contrasted with that of the philosopher who, if he is to remain inductive within the proper limits of his own method, may not let an arbitrary hypothesis determine his selection of evidence. Neither the scientist nor the philosopher, however, is cast in a bad light by the procedure of the other. The aim of the philosopher is a knowledge of natures, of what activities reveal upon abstraction as directly intelligible. Consequently, an hypothesis for the philosophical psychologist is an assumption that is either useless or misleading, since in itself it tells him nothing about the nature of man. The experimentalist's aim, on the other hand, is the formulation of a substitute- or *surrogate-sign of essence*[13] in the form of a symbolic concept or theory by which behavior can be explained and possibly predicted and controlled. Knowledge of the ontological nature or essence of an object may in fact be quite useless for achieving this goal. Consequently, scientific propositions are operational or *functional* rather than essential; and such functional laws necessarily involve the hypothetical method, if they are to be experimentally revealed as the best laws. If an explanation of the ontological essence of man is attempted through the use of the hypothetico-deductive method, the scientist suffers consequences similar to those of the philosopher who has isolated himself from experience. For it is impossible to verify experimentally propositions concerning an area of reality that is non-phenomenal and hence not in itself subject to experimentation.

At this point the distinctive character of the experimental methodology can be seen. All scientific description, explanation, and theorizing revolves around the type of induction employed by the scientist, which differs from that of the philosopher. The difference has its roots in the material object of experimental psychology, which studies *behavior*—that is, selectively abstracted activity—and not human *operations* in themselves. Since the scientific goal is surrogate-signs of essence—optimum behavioral laws, symbolically expressed in as precise a fashion as possible, the scientist does not attain (nor, precisely as scientist, is he interested in attaining) what we have called "direct insight" into the necessity of a relationship. Let us say, for instance, that there has been verified some theory expressing a formal relationship between anxiety and learning inefficiency: the only necessity that can be assigned to the proposition is that which the selective and partially arbitrary experimental evidence reveals. Since the experiment remains a part of the conclusion inferred, which in its turn cannot be interpreted without reference to specific experimental data, science asserts only that under such-and-such conditions this particular relationship will be found. An hypothesis, and a fortiori any functional law deduced from it, is subject to further experimental data, which can either verify or fail to confirm the theory. Continued verification generally leads to a more precise symbolic expression of a law, which may in some cases be subsumed eventually into a higher-order theory—as, for example, classical mechanics gave way to and can itself be deduced from relativity theory.

In order to distinguish the highly complex and *indirect* mode of discovery proper to science from philosophy's experiential induction (which, though at times complex, always involves direct intelligibility), we may simply call it *experimental induction.*[14]

The differences in aim and methodology of philosophical and scientific psychology may be summarized as follows. The philosopher moves from the level of operations to the level of essence and essential determination-to-act; he is thus primarily concerned with relationships on the level of activity (thought processes, for instance) only insofar as operations reveal to him the directly intelligible ontological principles that make activity possible (the intellect and its formal determination-to-act). These ontological sources of operation are not themselves experienceable even though their existence is reasoned to through experience. Hence, they are not *in themselves* subject to scientific observation.

The scientist, on the other hand, is concerned with relationships on the level of activity itself.[15] Hence, activities are abstractively selected in accord with the relationships being explored. As to the level of essence or nature, the scientist may begin by assuming a power which is specified to act (the power of memory or of intellect, for example); or he may realize in the course of or at the conclusion of his investigations that there is such a power. However, since the power is not subject to observation in itself but only through its operations, the postulation of its existence is irrelevant to *science.* This does not exclude its significance for the *scientist,* who may become interested in the directly as well as indirectly intelligible implications of the activities that he is studying. This interest, however, would require a switch into the philosophical form of reasoning.[16]

PHILOSOPHICAL AND SCIENTIFIC FORMS
OF CONCEPTUAL KNOWLEDGE

The inductive moment of scientific and of philosophical psychology gives way in both approaches to a judgmentally organized stage, the way of demonstrative exposition, in which propositions are precisely formulated in accord with what the inductive process has revealed. This stage complements and in a disciplined fashion completes the rational movement. A scientific demonstration is formulated, generally in mathematical or symbolic terms, in such a way that empirical laws other than the hypothesis itself are deduced from the hypothesis. A philosophical demonstration is generally lined up in a syllogistic form, so that the argument may *appear* to be a deduction; in this way, conclusions are tied in with the first principles of being and knowledge and are examined in the light of these principles. However, the various premises leading to the conclusion contain and have their ultimate validity in the inductive evidence. The interplay between the inductive and judgmentally organized moments of any form of knowledge will be elaborated from a psychological point of view in subsequent chapters.

A comparison of the forms of organized conceptual knowledge proper to philosophical and to scientific psychology is in order at this point. Corresponding to the philosophical aim of reasoning to the ontological causes of activity are propositions consisting of *ontological* knowledge—knowledge, that is, in which the object is revealed through experiential induction in such a way that sensory evidences and observable behavioral patterns are subservient to the direct intelligibility implied by the being's activity. Definitions and judgments are thus made in terms of the principles of being and its various analogous classifications.[17] Individual concepts are also ontological in form, in that they express aspects of the object as it is in reality.

Corresponding to the experimental goal of achieving symbolic behavioral laws are propositions that are *empiriological* in form;[18] that is, direct intelligibility is subordinated to the phenomenal or measurable, and knowledge of essence—*what* the object really is—is replaced by observation, measurement, and hypothesis. Ontological elements may be found in scientific knowledge; but the point is that such elements are not sought for their own sake and are formally present only to the extent that they serve as a basis for scientific definition and construction. Hence, definitions are formulated in terms of the experiment itself, which is retained as part of the conclusion. Some definitions (the IQ, for instance) are interpreted in terms of a scale of measurement. But all scientific propositions must be read strictly in the light of the selectively abstracted data involved.

Since science employs surrogates for essence, its individual concepts are constructural rather than ontological in form. That is, they are created for functional purposes in order to replace the proper intelligibility of an object, while obliquely corresponding to that intelligibility, to a greater or lesser degree. As was noted above, direct knowledge of a nature may be wholly useless for these functional purposes; the scientist is simply interested in a different type of intelligibility. Constructural concepts (which, needless to say, often reveal brilliant ingenuity on the part of their creators) may be proper to learning psychology itself or borrowed from other experimental sciences.[19] Such borrowing is quite legitimate plagiarism since the criteria for the validity of a given construct are merely its pertinence to the data and its value for a theory and for prediction and control. By reason of the prominence given to these special concepts, judgmental knowledge in science is also called *constructural* in form.[20]

RELATIONSHIPS BETWEEN SCIENTIFIC AND PHILOSOPHICAL EVIDENCES AND CONCLUSIONS

The foregoing discussion sufficiently reveals the primary point that motivated the analysis—namely, that neither philosophical nor scientific psychology is formally dependent upon the other.

Certain *evidences,* however, are shared in common, most obviously those which involve immediate experiential contact with reality. Such ontological evidences may be found within a constructural framework; for example, the intellectual process of abstraction, which can be known directly from a careful analysis of experience, becomes a symbolically designated factor in Spearman's ability theory.[21] Hence, scientific or experimental evidence may aid the philosophical psychologist to the extent to which it can be detached from its symbolic or constructural framework. For instance, an intelligence test as such (constructed specifically for determining an IQ) would be relatively useless for determining the nature of the intellect; while experiments on the unity of perceptual experience, involving much direct data, would be helpful to the philosopher for integrating what he has learned about the distinct powers of man. The philosophical psychologist, however, must exercise care in using experimental evidence, even that which can be non-constructural. Such evidence is of its nature selective and hence must be employed by the philosopher in the light of his total experience of human activity and with an emphasis that is proportionate to his proper quest.[22]

Conversely, ontological or experiential evidence may aid the scientific psychologist to the extent to which it is subject to observation and, ideally, measurement. Actually, any two consistently related activities, which thus form a behavioral pattern, can be studied in terms of the scientific method. Hence, analysis of an act of remembering, an existential evidence from which the philosopher can learn something about the nature of the memory, would be practically useless to the scientific thinker for determining memory efficiency; no behavioral relationships are involved in such an analysis. On the other hand, an evidence like the experiential unity of sensory and intellective activities in man would be helpful for defining the place and value of conditioning in the learning process.

What has been said thus far concerns interrelationships of evidences on the *inductive* levels of scientific and philosophical reasoning. Relationships of *conceptually elaborated* knowledge propose another problem. The philosophical psychologist can use a higher-order scientific construct only as an indirect witness to his object, since any construct is a functional substitute for a concept expressing a real nature as it actually exists. An IQ, for instance, testifies from the philosophical point of view only to the common experiential fact that intellectual capacities differ and that various influences on a sensory and emotional level affect the accuracy and efficiency of thought processes. It is difficult to say how high-order empirical laws in branches of psychology other than testing may be of use to philosophy, since no such well-established, highly elaborated laws comparable to those of the physical sciences as yet exist. Present laboratory hypotheses indicate little more to the philosopher than that sensory drives exist and that the object desired (say, by a rat) must first be known, either by its actual presence or by memory through a conditioned stimulus (if indeed the conditioned response is really the same as the original response).

Conversely, the scientific psychologist can make use of judgmentally organized philosophical knowledge, and he can personally accept the certainty of conclusions yielded from an experimental induction. But as a *scientist* performing an experimental induction, he will have to hold these conclusions in an hypothetical mood. For, the philosophical form of reasoning together with the conclusions that emerge from it does not belong to the constructural method. Thus, as a man, I know that man is rational. As a scientist, I will use an "if-then" form of proposition. Employed as hypotheses to be confirmed experimentally, the pertinent propositions of philosophical psychology can have a positive function in pointing out to the experimental theorist certain things to look for in man. In this way, philosophical statements could serve a *heuristic function* without interfering in any way with scientific aims or methods and consequently without instituting a formal dependence of science upon philosophy.

It may be observed in a given instance that science and philosophy have reached *similar* conclusions. Both may conclude, for example, that thought is not explained by organic complexity alone. However, as has already been indicated, the concluding proposition will be formulated by each in different terms and on the basis of different types of evidence. The philosopher formulates his conclusion in ontological terms and on the basis of an induction that employs experiential evidence. The scientist expresses his laws in terms of the technical experiment and on the basis of experimental induction, which employs scientific—mediate, technical, selectively abstracted —evidence. Hence, although scientific and philosophical conclusions may definitely complement each other, it must be kept in mind that each is answering a different sort of question. The two conclusions are not saying exactly the same thing and consequently cannot be set parallel with each other.

Scientific conclusions may form the basis for further deductions, which are then set up as new hypotheses for further experimental investigation; as the theory is expanded and made more precise by the addition of further confirming evidence, experimental certitude is increased. But, as has been noted, an inference is always subject to revision or possibly to replacement by another more complete construction.[23] Similarly, if a philosophical conclusion is used for further deductions, the conclusions remain subject to the critique of existential fact.

Considering the disagreement continually existing between philosophers, it may seem most peculiar to state that philosophical reasoning is blessed with more certitude than experimental science, an area in which more consistent agreement is generally found. To elaborate the differences between the truth-values possessed in a distinctive way by each of these forms of knowledge would take us far beyond the limits of the present study. However, the basis for resolving this paradox may be seen in the unique character of scientific and philosophical evidences. Hawkins' comparison summarizes the matter pointedly and will provide a final comprehensive glance at the scientific and philosophical schemata.

Experimental evidence is public and detailed. It rests on a multiplicity of determinate observations which can be controlled by a number of investigators at the same time. Consequently, in any one period there may be general agreement about the conclusions which it yields. But these conclusions are deficient in logical precision, and new evidence may necessitate their modification. Hence the contours of scientific theory vary from age to age.

Metaphysical evidence is comparatively private and elusive. It depends on the power of appropriate abstraction possessed by the individual thinker, and so it is much easier in philosophy than it is in experimental science for different solutions to be put forward by different individuals in the same period. But a metaphysical truth, once adequately apprehended, is precise and rigorous. Consequently the same solutions recur from age to age and the ways of thinking and the conclusions of the great philosophers are still alive. To read them has a value quite different from the historical interest which attaches to the study of the scientists of former ages. The state of philosophy at any period depends to a great extent on the capacity of the contemporary individual to recapture the refinement of mental vision possessed by the greatest of his predecessors.[24]

Thus, as long as the inexhaustible truth of things is to be further unfolded and rigorously established, philosophy can never become a closed system. Philosophical psychology or any branch of philosophy is not a study of concepts; it does not terminate in Cartesian clear and distinct ideas that entertain the fond hope of exhausting reality, leaving nothing more to be said. For concepts are referred to the existential order in the very judgments which express the nature of man and of his powers. Hence, though direct insight and certitude may have been attained with regard to the basic aspects of human nature, the appearance of new scientific and behavioral disciplines, all expressing in their own way fresh aspects of existence, brings to light a further question: what does this insight *mean*?[25] It is in partial answer to this question that every philosophical study, including the present one, is written.

NOTES

1. For a brief analysis of the nature of speculative science in general (whether philosophical or experimental, i.e., scientific in the modern sense), together with the mental acts involved in scientific

knowledge, see F. D. Wilhelmsen, *Man's Knowledge of Reality* (Englewood Cliffs, N.J.: Prentice-Hall, 1956), pp. 185–204.

2. For some historical reasons and some formal sources of the conflicts especially in the area of psychology, see Mortimer J. Adler, *What Man Has Made of Man* (New York: Longmans, Green & Co., 1938), pp. 139–42. The historical clashes between religion and science are discussed and well evaluated throughout Mary B. Hesse, *Science and the Human Imagination* (New York: Philosophical Library, 1955).

3. Countless analyses of scientific methodology can be found, some explicitly on the method of psychology; the philosophical method has also been treated in various contexts. However, competent *comparative* studies are few in number. Most helpful for my purposes have been Jacques Maritain's excellent and detailed analysis of different forms of knowledge in *The Degrees of Knowledge,* tr. Bernard Wall (New York: Chas. Scribner's Sons, 1938); and the brief but precise comparative study explicitly on philosophical and experimental psychology by George P. Klubertanz, S.J., in *The Philosophy of Human Nature* (New York: Appleton-Century-Crofts, 1953), pp. 393–96; also pp. 4–6. Although it is not concerned explicitly with psychology, E. F. Caldin's *The Power and Limits of Science* (New York: Harper, 1949) has been helpful and most suggestive. Other references will be given in the course of the chapter.

4. On the distinction of sciences by material and formal object, see G. P. Klubertanz, S.J., "The Doctrine of St. Thomas and Modern Science," *Sapientia Aquinatis* (Rome: Catholic Book Agency, 1955), pp. 89–104. This paper (originally presented at the Fourth International Thomistic Congress, Rome, Sept. 13–17, 1955) is an important critical analysis of the precise relationships existing between philosophy and science; copious references to contemporary philosophers of science as well as to Thomistic texts are included; the theory advanced by some Thomists who would deny the independent status of science and attempt to subsume science into philosophy is also criticized.

5. On these terms, see Robert J. Henle, S.J., *Method in Metaphysics* ("Aquinas Lecture"; Milwaukee: Marquette University Press, 1951), pp. 5, 59.

6. The givenness of a world of objects that are intelligible to man lies at the heart of the Thomistic analysis of being. Since material reality is given in sensible experience and grasped by man in a composite act

of intellect and sense, the givenness is an immediate evidence rather than something to be inferred, demonstrated, or postulated. The problem of a starting point in knowledge, considered from the "metaphysical realist's" point of view, is brilliantly explored in Etienne Gilson, *Réalisme thomiste et critique de la connaissance* (Paris: J. Vrin, 1939), espec. pp. 184–212. A good *summary* of the problem of a Thomistic realism since Descartes may be found in Wilhelmsen, *Man's Knowledge of Reality,* pp. 8–42. If one should wish to see the development of the "epistemological problem" from ancient to modern times, together with stimulating considerations on the *psychological* genesis of and reactions to the problem throughout the history of thought, there is no more original study than that of Louis-Marie Régis, O.P., *Epistemology,* tr. Imelda Choquette Byrne (New York: Macmillan Co., 1959), pp. 3–147. Neoscholastic attempts to establish a critique of knowledge in the tradition of Descartes and Kant are evaluated in *ibid.,* pp. 93–104; cf. also Régis, *St. Thomas and Epistemology* ("Aquinas Lecture"; Milwaukee: Marquette University Press, 1946).

7. W. T. Stace, *A Critical History of Greek Philosophy* (London: Macmillan & Co., 1928), p. 12.

8. Cf. André Marc, S.J., *Psychologie réflexive,* Vol. I, *La connaissance* (Paris: Desclée de Brouwer, 1948), p. 57. Behaviorism's criticism and rejection of the introspective method employed so extensively in earlier scientific psychology does not extend to philosophical psychology, because of its difference from the former in both aim and method.

9. It is worthwhile to note that this type of reasoning avoids the category of meaninglessness into which logical empiricists relegate some "metaphysical" propositions. "The two senses in which the term 'metaphysics' covers enterprises that seem objectionable to the logical empiricist are of course (1) transcendent, i.e., in principle untestable, assertions, and (2) the belief in factual truths that could be validated a priori, i.e., in complete independence of the data of observation" (Herbert Feigl, "Some Major Issues and Developments in the Philosophy of Science of Logical Empiricism," *The Foundations of Science and the Concepts of Psychology and Psychoanalysis,* ed. H. Feigl and M. Scriven, Vol. I of *Minnesota Studies in the Philosophy of Science* [Minneapolis: Univ. of Minnesota Press, 1956], p. 22). The propositions formulated from experiential induction are reducible to the data of observation, i.e., to factual experience; hence, they are testable by the experiential evidence from which they were

obtained. Feigl has made room for the validity of this type of knowledge, which he would call "inductive metaphysics" (*ibid.*).

10. However completely one may understand a thing's nature, a real
existent cannot be "intuited" and totally grasped in its existential
uniqueness; as will be developed in chap. 2, this type of intuition
would involve physical union between knower and known. Thus,
existence cannot be conceptualized, but only assented to, which assent (made in the judgment itself) is not an intuition. Hence, the
concept expressed by the term *existence* is intelligible only if understood as the act of the existent. On the concept of existence, see
James F. Anderson, "Some Disputed Questions on Our Knowledge
of Being," *Review of Metaphysics,* XI (1958), 553–58. On the judgment and apprehension of existence, see Gilson, *Réalisme thomiste
et critique de la connaissance,* pp. 204–27.

    The intellect's contact with existence in the act of judging will be
discussed from a phychological point of view in chap. 4, where
further references will also be given.

11. Cf. Clarence W. Brown and Edwin E. Ghiselli, *Scientific Method in
Psychology* (New York: McGraw-Hill, 1955), p. 36.

12. Cf. *ibid.,* pp. 43–54. See also H. Feigl, "Some Remarks on the Meaning of Scientific Explanation," *Readings in Philosophical Analysis,*
ed. H. Feigl & Wilfred Sellars (New York: Appleton-Century-Crofts,
1949), pp. 510–14.

13. Maritain, *Degrees of Knowledge,* p. 249.

14. For further discussion of scientific theory-construction, considered
especially in its historical evolution, see Hesse, *Science and the
Human Imagination,* pp. 47–160.

15. The scientist is interested in the interaction of variables which, if
causally classified, would be in the line of efficient causality. Thus, if
we wish to speak in philosophical terms, we can say that the scientist
is concerned with the efficient causes of (selected) activity on the
level of activity itself. As the boundaries of a particular experiment
become limited and the hypothesis to be verified is more precisely
formulated, these causes are reduced to formal causes; in this way,
the conclusions can be symbolically expressed in terms of formal
relationships. This philosophical description of scientific causation,
of course, prescinds from the many different forms of interaction
that can occur between variables. E.g., see Philipp Frank, *Philosophy
of Science* (Englewood Cliffs, N.J.: Prentice-Hall, 1957), pp.
260–96.

16. Two terms that Maritain uses (*Degrees of Knowledge,* pp. 248–49)

have an etymological significance that suggests a spatial analogy of this relationship between philosophy and science. If we symbolize man by a circle, the philosopher's reasoning may be described as *dianoetic;* he reasons "through" to the inner constitution of the being. The scientist's reasoning is *perinoetic,* since he is concerned with the "circumference," the observable behavior of man. (Maritain employs the terms used with a much broader and less picturesque meaning than is given them here. Moreover, such spatializations, though helpful summaries, involve an oversimplification and are not to be understood as explanatory of the scientist's or philosopher's entire method.)

17. Though the philosophical psychologist uses various metaphysical concepts, he cannot use them aprioristically, but only as his subject, man, reveals them. The nature of man, in other words, cannot be deduced from metaphysical principles, as the "rational psychology" of rationalist systems would do. Metaphysics and philosophical psychology, then, are not the same science; the latter studies human nature, which is but one part of existent being; hence, while more particular than metaphysics, it is less complete. See Klubertanz, *Philosophy of Human Nature,* pp. 397–99.

18. On the terms *ontological* (which here refers to all philosophical knowledge, not just metaphysics) and *empiriological,* see Maritain, *Degrees of Knowledge,* pp. 178–88.

19. Some original constructs (from psychological testing): the "IQ"; or the "cognitive-*g* factor" in Spearman's theory of ability, a functional concept that includes noegenesis and abstraction. See C. Spearman and L. W. Jones, *Human Ability* (London: Macmillan & Co., 1950), p. 69.

It is difficult to isolate individual constructs that have had their entire origin within the framework of psychology alone, since psychology has borrowed so heavily from other scientific disciplines. E.g., from mathematics: "probability," "function"; from electromagnetics: "excitatory potential," "oscillatory inhibition"; from mechanics: "drive," "tension"; and innumerable biological concepts. On this historical introduction of biology and physiology into scientific psychology, see George Sidney Brett, *Brett's History of Psychology,* ed. R. S. Peters (London: Geo. Allen & Unwin, Ltd., 1953), pp. 586–641; 701–709. On immediate relationships between psychology and biology, see Adler, *What Man Has Made of Man,* pp. 47–51.

20. Four basic types of theoretical constructs may be listed: (1) *me-*

chanical model concepts, largely proper to physics; (2) *operational definitions,* which define an object in terms of the acts which may reveal it; (3) *mathematico-real* or *schematico-real* concepts, which involve purely mental components and are intended to explain, organize, and (when possible) predict; (4) *taxonomic* concepts and their relatives, which are proper particularly to the sciences in which description and classification hold a major position. See G. P. Klubertanz, S.J., "A Program for Progress in the Philosophy of Science," *Actes du deuxième congrès international de l'Union Internationale de Philosophie des Sciences* (Zurich, 1954), Vol. I, *Exposés généraux: Plenary Sessions* (Neuchatel, Suisse: Editions du Griffon, 1955), pp. 78–84.

The different scientific psychologies make use in various ways of all but (it seems) the strict mechanical model. E.g., operational definitions are used particularly in those areas of psychology where the phenomena under investigation have not yet been strictly isolated; most experimental definitions of learning are of this type. Mathematico-real and schematico-real constructs are employed in most laboratory experiments and in psychological tests. Variations of taxonomic concepts are used in the form of reifications which treat a behavioral trait that is not in reality isolated (e.g., an explicit drive in a white rat) as a subsistent event. Many and perhaps most psychological constructs are complex combinations of these basic types of theoretical concepts.

21. Spearman and Jones, *Human Ability,* p. 69.
22. For some scientific evidences that are particularly significant for the philosophical psychologist, see G. P. Klubertanz, S.J. "The Psychologists and the Nature of Man," *Proceedings of the American Catholic Philosophical Association,* XXV (1951), 66–88.
23. Cf. T. G. Andrews, "An Introduction to Psychological Methodology," *Methods of Psychology,* ed. Andrews (New York: Wiley & Sons, 1948), p. 4. An almost melancholy statement of the radical reformability of science can be seen in Vannevar Bush, "Science and Progress?" *Science in Progress,* ed. Hugh Taylor (New Haven: Yale University Press, 1957), pp. 1–23. We may note in this context that scientific certitude, though it involves a unique type of relative truth, does possess a genuine ontological basis. In a philosophical perspective, scientific certitude is founded *ultimately* upon the necessity of essence—that necessity by which a given existing nature consistently exhibits all the characteristics and relations consequent upon its real essence. It is these properties and relations which con-

tribute to the relative uniformity of nature presupposed by the scientist and which are involved in scientific surrogates of essence, to a greater or lesser degree depending upon the particular construct. The basis of the degree of accuracy to which a given theory corresponds to the real essence of an object, of course, may be extremely difficult to ascertain, since the scientist is attempting to get at a different sort of intelligibility from that which immediately interests the philosopher. Hence, although scientific constructs are by their very nature reformable, experimental science, viewed as founded upon this ontological basis, is not merely a set of additive or probable generalizations.

24. D. J. B. Hawkins, *Causality and Implication* (New York: Sheed & Ward, 1937), pp. 121–22. For an interesting discussion of the place of "dialogue" in philosophy, see Aimé Forest, "The Meaning of Dialogue," *Philosophy Today,* II (Summer, 1958), 116–18.

25. Cf. Henle, *Method in Metaphysics,* pp. 53–54. F. D. Wilhelmsen remarks that "many men in many civilizations can see the same truth, but they will see it in their own way" ("The Philosopher and the Myth," *Modern Schoolman,* XXXII [1954], 49). His thesis is that a plural incarnation of the same true philosophy is not only possible, but a cultural necessity.

2

THE STRUCTURE OF
KNOWLEDGE AND
THE KNOWER

IT IS UNIVERSALLY AGREED that all learning involves cognition. Thinking is clearly a cognitive process, and even simple conditioning in animals depends upon sensation for the initiation of the response. Cognition or knowledge in general—the two terms and their derivatives may be taken as synonyms in the analysis at hand—may thus be understood to include anything from gross sensory awareness to the higher reaches of deliberate thought and reasoning. Learning also embraces emotional and motivational elements; but, as will be noted shortly, these elements can be analytically distinguished from the cognitive aspects of human learning, to which the present study is confined.

In the previous chapter, it was noted that in scientific knowledge a constructural idea mediates one's contact with an external object; the idea is used as an instrument in exploring the object, so that whatever is known is understood in terms of the concept involved. It could be misleading to approach an analysis of cognition as such in terms of this unique and highly sophisticated form of knowledge, since the scientific way of knowing is not the way of all knowledge.

Hence, it might be well to begin a philosophical inquiry into the nature of knowledge by taking an arbitrary example of simple perceptual experience. What is learned here about the nature of cognition in general through an examination of simpler forms of knowledge may then be refined in subsequent chapters in terms of higher types of knowing and learning.

"I know my desk." This statement, expressive of a fact of perceptual experience, will be seen to have its psychological nuances and implications. But, fundamentally and apart from any further analysis, it describes an experience *of* something *by* someone who is capable of such an experience.

THE IDENTIFICATION OF THINGS

In order to map the direction of our subsequent explorations, we may remark that there are several ways that this experience might be philosophically approached. Prescinding from the cognitive experience itself, the following statements could be made. Whatever my nature is, I am what I am; whatever be the nature of the desk, it is what it is. From this or a similar point of judgmental assent, one could become directly involved in a metaphysical analysis of what it means to be, what it means for me and the desk each to have a proper act of being. Secondly, the actual essential natures of the man and the desk might be the objects of inquiry. However, it is a third metaphysical act or perfection belonging to different beings which is of interest here. Cognitive *activity* is the focal point of the present inquiry, and the nature of man will become involved in the discussion to the extent that cognition necessitates speaking of the human structure. This chapter, then, is intended to present neither a complete metaphysics nor an exhaustive philosophy of human nature.

The question then becomes: how does the phenomenon of cognitive experience reveal anything other than the experience itself? This question involves the principle of reasoning underlying the method of philosophical psychology and deserves an answer at this point.

That a man perceives a desk is but one aspect of a condition that is found throughout nature. If the world of being were static, consisting only of empty forms with an act of being, a man could not be distinguished from a rock except by some difference in superficial qualities. But in reality, an object once constituted in being reveals a pattern of activities consonant with its nature, so that an animate being exhibits dynamic tendencies, inclinations, a kind of "reaching out" to attain as full a perfection as its nature will allow. Whatever name is given to this inner dynamism will be quite arbitrary, since we are here met with the primitive facts of nature. Trees tend to grow from a barren sprig to luxuriant stature; animals, guided by sense and instinct, seek to protect themselves; men, desiring to know about things, entertain a natural curiosity about the world. Even inanimate things reveal tendencies like that of iron to unite with oxygen and rust, as well as gravitational and magnetic attractions.

Underlying the actual observable operations of living things, then, are the tendencies which incline them to act. Just as the tendencies of a being are made manifest through its activities, these same operations lead to a knowledge of what kind of being it is that is acting. Thus, in the normal process of nature, a tree grows; and by observing this phenomenon of growth, I know that the thing must have an essential structure which is capable of growth. More precisely, the kind of activity exhibited by a being is proportioned to the real or ontological structure of the being; and, conversely, a being endowed with a specific nature will reveal itself through the operations that flow from that nature. Thus, we do not expect a tree to talk, precisely because the nature of a tree is not such that it *can* talk. A man, on the other hand, must be ontologically equipped or structured in such a way that he can communicate his thoughts. Accordingly, given a recognition of the varied dynamism of things and the procedural principle based on it, an explicit analysis of cognition, one of the manifestations of being, can be undertaken.[1]

THE COGNITIVE UNION

Perhaps the most evident fact in my experience of my desk is that I know the desk—not my act of understanding, or an idea of the desk, but this object having an existence distinct from myself. Unlike scientific knowledge of a higher order, this cognitive act possesses an immediacy, for it directly embraces the object itself. The existent object, consequently, is the fundamental cause of what is known about it; apart from any previous experience that I might want to contribute to my present knowledge of the desk, the object itself is the ultimate reason why anything is known about *it,* here and now.[2]

Two facts concerning knowledge thus present themselves at this point. While the cognitive act grasps the object, so that there seems to be formed some sort of union between knower and known, the thing itself whose existence causes my knowledge is not affected by the act of knowledge. To see these facts in a proper light, it will be necessary to step back from this cognitive experience for a moment and consider the relationships that can exist between me and the desk.

I can like or dislike the color and shape of the desk when I see it. I might dislike the desk as it is so much, in fact, that I decide to saw off a portion of it and paint the whole thing a different color. But these reactions to the desk do not in themselves constitute my knowledge of it. Although my emotional reactions may take place in the precise instant when I know the desk and be experientially indistinguishable from the cognitive act, they actually presuppose, from an analytic point of view, an act of cognition. Thus, affective response to the object and practical decisions that would actually affect the object involve, metaphorically speaking, a kind of movement from me to the object, a movement connoted in the word "response" itself. On the other hand, when I simply know the desk causally prior to responding to it or perhaps without responding to it emotionally at all, it is I who am in some way "moved" by the object; for now I am knowing it, while before I was not. Hence, the movement here is from the object to me, which may or may not involve a causally subsequent movement from me to the object.[3] What, then, is the nature of the activity by which I know the desk?

Of all the activities known by man, external movement would seem to be primitive in his experience and most easily understood, since it is sensibly perceived.[4] It is evident, however, that cognition is not simple movement from one place to another; I can know the desk without either me or the desk moving locally. Nor is it the sort of activity that has its effect in an object outside the agent, as would be the case if I painted the desk. Though we are inclined to speak of knowledge as "touching" an object or of a student as "grasping" something, this kind of language can indicate any sort of relationship or union between knower and known. And yet a union there must be; for without a union of some sort there is no knowledge. The union, moreover, leaves the object as it was, while the one who knows it is perfected in some way. For, one who knows an object and learns about things has broadened his experience, transcended in a way the limitations of his own existence.[5] Again, the acquisition of perfection in knowledge does not require the loss of another perfection in the same order. My desk would lose its original shape when, upon being cut, it took on a new shape. But the person who learns and the teacher who imparts knowledge do not lose their previous knowledge, even though they become physically tired and lose a perfection in a different order from that of knowledge.

As a perfective activity, then, cognition has two characteristics. Since the knower alone is perfected while the object remains unaffected by the cognitive act, knowledge is an immanent activity, that is, it remains in the knower and is the knower's own act, not that of the object. Secondly, the knower is perfected by means of the union achieved between himself and the object.[6] But cognition is not total immanence. As retaining its own existentiality, the object known retains a character of existential relation to the knower. The problem thus becomes one of resolving the two facts of *immanence* and *existentiality*. This resolution calls first for a further analysis of what is meant by the union between knower and known.

The notions of "union" or "identity," relatively simple descriptive terms in themselves, lose their simplicity when one reflects on the union of knowledge. It is evident that my desk is not absorbed into me when I know it, like salt dissolved in water; this kind of union would not respect the desk's independent status. Nor do I "become the desk" in the way that a log, when set on fire, becomes a fiery thing. For, the perfection acquired in knowledge does not require the loss of another perfection in the same order—unlike the log, which loses at least the qualities directly connected with coolness in acquiring the quality of intense heat. Nor, again, do my desk and I unite to form a third thing, as hydrogen and oxygen form water; for, although somehow united, both knower and known retain their existentiality.

A purely physical union, then, not only does not explain knowledge, but rather in every case would destroy the relational character of object to knower. Moreover, as Aquinas suggests, if knowledge were a purely material union, if the thing known were present in the knower in a material way alone, there would be no reason why one inanimate object could not know another.[7] One blazing fire would know the log it is consuming, and my desk would know a blob of ink that soaked into its top. Consequently the facts of cognitive experience indicate that *some degree of nonmateriality* is a necessary condition for any cognitive union.[8]

Denial of purely physical union in knowledge is only one side of the cognitive coin; immateriality also has positive connotations that expand the description of knowledge. First, if the object-as-known has a certain immaterial presence in the knower, the thing actually known and the knower share a single act, the act of knowledge itself. Secondly, because of this non-material union, the knower must be *in some sense* immaterial. And finally, the object as actually known exercises a unique mode of existence in the knower. A detailed consideration of the immateriality of the knower will be left to the analysis of cognitive powers. For the present, a discussion of the kind of being that knowledge is will lead to an analysis of how the cognitive union is causally achieved.

There is no ready-made category in which cognition can be classified, since in experience there is found no other activity quite like knowledge. One term that has come to be used to describe the status of knowledge is *intentionality*.[9] Etymologically, the word (which in this usage has nothing to do with "intention" or "purpose" in a volitional sense) has the advantage of emphasizing the dynamic relation between knower and object. For in the act of knowing the knower "reaches toward" or "extends himself to" the object (*in + tendere*). However, apart from descriptive connotations, which do not sufficiently distinguish cognition from tendency in general, what does intentionality mean?

The knower possesses the object. But the object is not subjectively possessed, as the glass of water possesses the salt, for the object retains its own natural state of being. Rather, the knower grasps the object objectively, grasps the other as distinctively other. Intentional being, therefore, is that peculiar immaterial mode of being in which an object, while remaining other, is nonetheless presented to and objectively united with a knower in a single immanent act. This is but another way of saying that cognition is a state of being involving a union or identity which nevertheless respects the object's existential relation to the knower. Needless to say, all these attempts at definition of knowledge become almost tautological, since every approach to knowledge reveals it to be a unique kind of experience. It thus defies strictly logical definition by genus and species.

Now the thing known must be presented to the knower in such a way that the two may be intentionally united; some causal principle, in other words, must consummate the union between knower and known. Moreover, the knower must be formally determined to *this* act of knowledge rather than to that; when I know my desk, it is my desk that I know and not my ceiling, though I *could* know either. Hence, in every act of knowledge there is required a causal determination, by which the object known is united to the knower in such a way that the object may be actually known.[10]

This definition implies the precise functions of the causal principle involved (or, in Aquinas' terminology, the cognitive *species*): the determination of the knower, who is capable of knowing an infinite

number of objects, to a particular act of knowledge; the formal presentation of the object known to the knower; and the intentional
union thereby achieved between knower and object. This may be said
in another way. Experientially, an act of knowledge is specified
by the thing known. "I know my desk." In the order of formal causality which is not directly experienced, the knower is determined to
knowing this object which is intentionally united to him. Thus, (by
a formal determination-to-act) "I know my desk."

Language offers a special difficulty here, since speaking of a
causal principle as a *thing* can mislead us to identify it as the thing
actually known, in the way various thinkers have made ideas the sole
objects of knowledge. Such an inference would contradict a fact of
experience. If we knew only formal determinations (or, for that
matter, ideas) there could be no knowledge of objects and ultimately
no way to bridge the gap between mind and reality or to judge the
truth of knowledge-content.[11] If, however, the precise causal functions described above are kept in mind, this philosophical and causal
explanation of the cognitive union will not be confused with a rationalist or a representational theory of knowledge.

An analogy (and merely an analogy) might be drawn between
causal determination in knowledge and the sound track on a recording tape. The tape does not look or feel any different to the naked
eye or hand after a recording has been made; but unless the tape has
been "formally determined," it would be impossible to hear any sound
when it is played back. Similarly, though cognitive determination-to-
act is not experienced in knowledge activity but only reasoned to, no
actual knowledge is possible without it. But what is known is the
object itself, not the causal principle that formally presents the object
to the knower—much as the original sounds are heard, as carried or
presented to the recorder and speakers by the electronic sound track
on the tape.[12]

The facts revealed in the preceding analysis cannot alter the primitive fact of experience with which the analysis began—namely, that
when I know my desk I know it as it is in itself and not as something
in my mind. Hence, the notion of *union* must at this point be inte-

grated with the existential *relation* that the object has to the knower. This analysis will also draw together the various elements in the above description of cognition in general.

It is because the object has its own proper being that the cognitive union is made at all possible. No object, living or non-living, is metaphysically inert and inactive. Essentially constituted of onto-logical acts analogous to those of the knower (its proper act of being, its essential and accidental perfections), any object in nature can offer itself metaphysically to the activity of the knower and become intentionally united to him.[13] And thus, through the formal deter-mination of the knower, the act of the object as actually being known *is* the act of the knower.[14] Now because of this unique intentional identity, the object cannot be known in a purely material way (though one can know *that* the object is material). Hence, when it is stated that the desk is known as it is in itself, what is meant is that *what* is known is the desk, as it exists in outer reality. But the *way* in which the desk is known is necessarily different from the way in which the desk exists outside the mind; for the desk is known immaterially, while in itself it exists materially.

This may be stated in terms of relation and identity. That which is known constitutes the immanent intentional *union* of cognition, for what is known is the same in both knower and object. But the mode of being of the object in itself and the mode of being of the object-as-known differ. For, the object-as-known shares the being of the knower, which is different and distinct from the natural being of the object. It is this difference in being that allows an exis-tential *relation* between knower and object, a relation which is not subsumed into the immanence of cognition.[15]

THE UNITY OF COGNITIVE EXPERIENCE:
SYMBOLS

In the performance of his various activities, man is able to have direct knowledge of the operational unity of such acts. Awareness of one's bodily states, and self-consciousness or awareness of the self as the real source and term of one's own activities are several types of direct knowledge enabling one to arrive at this unity through careful and deliberate reflection.[16] Volitional acts that terminate in some specific activity give a further indication of unity of operation. When he has determined to do something—say, to paint a picture—a person's whole being cooperates in the activity. The artist's hand, moved with the aid of neural and cerebral processes, executes the painting; complex knowledge guides the physical activity; and the volitional act expressive of the artist's motivation keeps the whole creative process moving toward the goal that has been set. Thus, the innumerable parts that make up the human composite are, in a complex act like this, brought into a goal-directed operational oneness.[17]

Cognitive experience, considered in itself and apart from the larger scope of goal-directed activity, also exhibits a unity. Contemporary thinkers have employed the analysis of signs in elucidating human modes of discursive and artistic communication. The same type of analysis is helpful in the present context, for it can illustrate the unity of cognition and the differences between animal and human knowledge.[18]

Speaking in a very general way, a sign is a sensible presentation of some sort that leads to knowledge of something other than its own material reality.[19] Especially pertinent in a psychological context are two basic types of sign—signals and symbols.

Smoke indicates that there is fire, lightning that there will be thunder, a wet landscape that there was rain. Bells announce dinner, class, someone at the door; sirens indicate that someone has been hurt, that a house is on fire, that crime has been done. Whether the relation between sign and signified be natural or artificial, definite or vague, all *signals* of the sort just mentioned have this in common: they *merely indicate* or point to or announce something as existing in the past or present or as likely to exist in the future. Interpretation of and response to signals is common to men and animals alike, for this is the area of instinctive and conditioned responses—the cry of pain, the response to a call, the sheep fleeing the wolf. In this sense, even language can be a signal; both a

dog and a man can answer to the name "Sandy." Animals, moreover, can be taught to use artificial as well as natural signals; a dog,
for instance, can be taught to "beg" in a certain fashion.

But man, unlike an animal, can know that a signal *is* a sign; he can
rise above mere response to a signal, for he can invent them and
think about their meaning. Moreover, he can create signs that are
no longer mere signals, but instruments of thought, of non-sensuous
meaning. Here we reach the level of *symbols,* which no longer merely
announce the existence of an event or an object or a condition. To
the user, a symbol is a vehicle of communication; to the perceiver, it
is an instrument leading to conscious knowledge, to meaningful conception of the thing signified. An animal can be taught to respond
to the name "Abe Lincoln," which functions in this case as no more
than a particular collocation of sounds; a man can think about the
historical figure signified by the name, which then functions as a
symbol. An animal's significant movements are an expression of a
physical need or biological condition; a human gesture, on the other
hand, may be an expression of meaning quite detached from a utili-
tarian need.[20]

Thus, a spontaneous cry or jerk of the head is a signal; the cry
of an actor and a deliberate nod are symbols. Signals generally call
for a response, for action; a symbol calls for thought, for grasp of
meaning, or for aesthetic contemplation. Helen Keller's description
of her first real experience of meaning points out well the radical
difference between signals and symbols. Deaf and blind from in-
fancy, Miss Keller relates the joy and new hope she experienced when
she realized that the use of a simple sign like "water" was not just a
means for getting more easily what she *wanted,* but also an instrument for thinking about and *expressing the meaning* of this "wonderful cool something" which she could touch.[21]

Human language is one type of symbol, an artificial and conventional instrument for the expression of personal thought. A symbol
might be simple or more complex; a single word like "desk," for
instance, expresses one meaning, while a sentence like "I see my desk"
expresses another. From a psychological point of view, the articula-

tion of both the word and the sentence flow from *single* acts of knowledge. When I say that I see my desk, I am not saying that I first see a conglomeration of grays, then infer that this batch of colors must inhere in something, conclude that that something is material, and finally reason that this particular arrangement of colors-in-a-material-something is a desk. Again, I can make perceptual judgments about the desk, like "there is a green book on the desk." This does not mean that I mentally put green-in-a-thing together with gray-in-a-thing. Rather, I have in a single judgmental act assented to the precise fact that there is actually a green book on the gray desk. This assent is then communicated, in this particular case, in a verbal symbol.[22]

The sentence may be broken down *logically* into its numerous component grammatical elements; but *psychologically* it remains an expression of a single meaning. A parallel situation can be found in the arts. The parts of a work of art have an intelligibility as parts. In the lower left-hand corner of a painting, say, is the figure of a man; but the meaning of this figure in *this* particular painting is not fully intelligible apart from the whole art work, which is one whole symbol. Similarly, the logical meaning of "desk" remains fundamentally the same in any sentence; but the logical signification of the word is merely one part of the mental utterance, expressive of only part of the total meaning. The figure in the painting and the word in the sentence are thus psychologically subordinate to the whole meaning of the sentence or the art symbol.

The subordination of part to whole in communicative symbolism will be further elaborated when we discuss the structure of judgment; the distinction between signal and symbol will also receive further treatment. The salient point to be noted here is that a human cognitive act can be a single act embracing in psychological unity several logically distinct intelligibilities. Knowledge, in other words, is not necessarily atomistic. In terms of cognitive intentionality, the knower is united to an object *as he knows it*. The cognitive content of this union might be able to be expressed verbally not in a simple noun but only in a complex sentence. This unity of cognitive experience will keep recurring throughout our study and must be kept in mind in the course of the subsequent analysis, which will be oriented toward a closer look at the elements that contribute to the unity of an act of knowledge.

DISTINCTION OF POWERS WITHIN
THE UNITY OF COGNITION

Distinct factors become apparent in the psychological oneness of a cognitive act. The eye sees colors, the light coming from an object; it sees the object as extended, but only as this concrete extendedness is revealed by light. Other external senses can also grasp extension in this concrete fashion. The sense of touch feels, the sense of taste savors some extended thing, so that extendedness is sensed under the aspects of pressure and flavor as well as of light. Hence, while light is sensed only by the eye, concrete extendedness is known by several senses. Again, when I know my desk or make a series of judgments about the desk, I know that the object is a "desk" from previous experience; a person who has never seen an object of this sort being used would not have such a functional notion. And yet, in the actual occurrence of the perceptual experience, I *see* the *desk*. This judgment can be made without the least reflection upon the fact that the notion of "desk" comes from past experience.

Thus, while a perceptual experience of this type is an "all at once" sort of knowledge, the contents of the experience reveal that there is more than one *source* of cognition, more than one cognitive power by which the total object is known here and now. Within the perceptual unity, there are aspects of an object—like light, flavor, sound—that are *proper* to a single sense power and are immediately and of themselves known by one power only. An aspect like concrete extendedness, however, is *common* to several sense powers, though it is known immediately under the aspect of some proper sensible object. Perceptual experience finally reveals *incidental* sensible objects, like "desk"; this cognitive object, while known together *with* proper and common sensibles, is immediately grasped *through* some other source of knowledge that can embrace more than what is revealed by the concomitant external sensory stimulus.[23] The unified cognitive experience with its distinct elements is thus somewhat analogous to a sentence which, while expressive of a single meaning, has distinct grammatical parts contributing to the total expression.

The inductive progression from *objects* known to *acts* of knowledge has thus naturally led to a consideration of the *sources* of these acts. As we have already considered in some detail, the knower is ultimately determined to a particular act of knowledge by the object known, the object which is intentionally presented to him. Similarly, the powers by which he knows will ultimately have to be specified by and distinguished on the basis of the object known. However, since the same real object can be simultaneously known under different aspects, a gross consideration of the object in its total reality is not enough to discover the sources of cognition within the knower. The *different aspects* under which the object is known must provide the basis for analytically distinguishing the power of knowledge.

But *simple* differences are not adequate either; on this basis, one would need a different power of sight for seeing different colors, which is an evident contradiction of experience. The desk is the object of sight, not because it is a desk or even because it is gray or blue or green, but rather because it is colored. Similarly, the sense of touch is affected, not ultimately because the object is soft or hard or warm or cold, but fundamentally because it is tangible. These evidences can be summarized by saying that the *proper object* of any power is the thing in its total reality considered precisely as object of this power; it is the object of cognition as ordered or proportioned to a particular source of cognition. If we wish to speak of the precise aspect or formality of the proper object which makes it just that—namely, proper to a particular power—this aspect may be called the formal object. Thus, the proper object of the power of sight is a "colored thing"; the formal object, or that aspect in virtue of which the power of sight knows the object, is simply "color." The meaning of this analysis will become clearer in its application.[24]

It may be noted that the formal-object analysis is circular. To speak of a proper object implies speaking of a power; to speak of powers necessitates speaking of proper objects. This, however, is the nature of our approach, for neither objects in themselves nor powers in themselves are here being subjected to analysis. Rather, we discover man knowing different aspects of things, and it is this total experience that offers itself to analytic consideration. The analysis in turn is oriented toward discovering the real sources of activity within the human knower. For, as was noted at the opening of this chapter, the ontological structure of a being, known only through a consideration of its activities, must be such that the being be capable of exhibiting the activity.

The most fundamental distinction between cognitive acts and the powers from which they proceed can be approached by way of a further consideration of language as symbolic.

INTELLECTION

The enunciation of a symbol expressive of a meaning takes place in space and time, since the external expression involves some sort of matter—the movement of a pencil, the gesture of a hand, the sound emitted from the vocal cords. This holds true for any symbol, whether it be discursive, like our everyday linguistic communication; or artistic, like a poem, a painting, a piece of music. Since a symbol has a material reality of its own, its articulation depends upon matter and the conditions of matter.

But, as has been noted, a symbol as sign is not the same as a symbol as actually significant. As expressive of a meaning, the parts of a verbal sentence, like the parts of a single work of art, are ordered to and receive their total intelligibility from the meaning or total thought expressed. Now articulation of the sentence with its successive linguistic parts is enveloped in and dominated by an act of understanding that is *without* succession. For, the unity and communicative value of a symbol of discourse depend ultimately upon such an act which is not *in itself* dependent upon the conditions of matter, namely, the space and time involved in a material expression of the act. Analysis of the linguistic parts which contribute successively to the expression of a single thought actually presumes the pervading simultaneity of thought that gives a sentence its meaning, the single unextended matrix of meaning lying beyond the words.[25]

One of the best experiential indications of these facts can be seen in a person's attempt to understand a difficult piece of writing. When the author's meaning is finally conceived after several readings of the sentence or paragraph which expresses this meaning, the barrier of words and grammatical structure fall away and the thought of the writer is grasped in an act that lacks verbal parts. The reader might then go on to re-express the same idea in his own words, a re-expression which in its turn is meaningless unless the succession of material signs involved itself has a pervading meaning.

This analysis reveals only that thought is *distinct* from the material expression of it, not that the act of thought can be had *without* the presence of some sensible image or without being joined to space and time.[26] However, the presence of an image, whether concrete or general, does not mean that thought is to be equated with an image. For, while any symbol can be imaginatively represented or recalled, its mental representation in the form of a verbal or pictorial or auditory image remains particularized and involves matter. Thus, an image has a relation to thought analogous to that of an external symbol, for an image embraces the conditions of matter. However, because the act of thought in itself lacks extension, the essential characteristic of matter, thought is strictly immaterial. Consequently, the operative power from which thought proceeds—the intellect— must also be strictly immaterial, possessing in itself no sense organ; for the nature of the activity reveals the nature of the operative power from which it proceeds.[27]

The absence of matter and a sensory organ in the intellect can be established from another point of view, by a comparison of the objects of sense and intellect. Any sense power has as its object some aspect of an object in its particularity. For the thing is known according to the individualized disposition that it has outside the knower, and this particularity is presented to the sense power in its causal determination-to-act. Thus, a man is sensorily known as a particular figure of a certain shape, extendedness, color, and so on.

In intellection, on the other hand, a thing like "man" or "extension" is grasped apart from the particularities of this man, this extended thing. This type of knowledge is more than a composite or highly abstractive image. An image always retains some particularity, some location in space of that which is imagined. Although images can succeed one another with great rapidity, no single image can simultaneously represent a man with two arms and a man with one or both arms missing. And yet, in either case, a person can understand what a man is, at least vaguely, apart from physical perfections which some particular man may or may not possess.[28]

The intellect thus prescinds from individual existence in knowing an object. To say this is only to refine the above description of an idea's lack of successive parts and extension, for these are the conditions of individuality. The intellect's determination-to-act does not carry material particularity in the formal presentation of the object so known to the power of intellect. And since the act of intellection does not in itself include matter, the power of intellection is strictly immaterial.[29]

Besides prescinding from particularities, the intellect can also consider one intelligible aspect[30] of an object apart from another. For example, I can understand that the object I see is colored or has extension and the like without giving explicit consideration, here and now, to the fact that the object is a desk. In fact, I might see an object and know nothing else about it than that it is "something"; but even this very imperfect and confused knowledge is still knowledge, which thinking can perfect. The intellect is able to direct its attention to different meaningful aspects of things in such a way, moreover, that knowledge retains its objectivity. This is possible because, although the object is one in reality, its various perfections admit of independent and objective consideration in the order of knowledge. Considering one aspect of a thing apart from another admits of many nuances in different types of knowledge; but this considering is all that is fundamentally meant by *abstraction*.[31]

In an act of simple perceptual knowledge, then, the proper object of the human intellect, the object naturally proportioned to it, is an intelligible aspect of sensible things. *Things,* in other words, reveal themselves meaningfully to the intellect. And yet, human knowledge is clearly not confined to perception and consideration of real objects. Employing the basic knowledge supplied by sense experience, man proceeds to further knowledge of reality and is able to form entirely new notions—functional and logical concepts, scientific constructs, mathematical sets, and so on. Hence, the object of the intellect, considered as an operative power and apart from any particular intellective act or knowledge-content, is anything which in some way *is*.[32]

When the intellect knows an object, whether it be something in outer reality or a notion of its own construction, the fruit of its act of understanding is found in a "mental word" which it produces.[33] The mental word is thus the psychological locus of the intelligible content, whether it be a simple idea or a complex judgment. In highly *abstract* knowledge, the mental word is itself the object of understanding, and it is in such cases that the word can be experientially discovered in consciousness. When I understand, for instance, that force is the product of mass and acceleration, I know that I am understanding something that is meaningful, though the object of understanding is not a concrete thing. In direct *perceptual* knowledge, on the other hand, the mental word is not the object of immediate awareness.[34] In this case, it serves only as a type of instrument by which the intellect has intelligible content in its knowledge of real objects outside the mind. In the case of perceptual knowledge, then, the function of the mental word is analogous to that of the formal causal principle that determines the intellect to act; it is a principle and not an object of knowledge. It may be observed from these remarks that the mental word is the locus of the most perfect intentional union between knower and known, a union in the order of meaning. For the mental word *is* the object-as-intelligibly-known.

Although more can and will be said about the intellect, its acts, and the mental word, these considerations are sufficient for the present and provide us with a general framework within which to work in subsequent discussions. The point to be emphasized here is the essential difference between intellectual understanding and sense cognition; the consequences of this distinction for learning theory will be exploited in the following chapters.[35]

SENSATION

Although in approaching the nature of intellection various remarks have already been made concerning sense cognition in general, some further considerations on the nature of sensation and the powers of sense are in order. Scientific psychology has contributed a great deal to our knowledge in this area; however, no attempt will be made to summarize this plethora of data here. Only those aspects of sensation that are pertinent to a philosophical inquiry and especially to a philosophical discussion of learning will be treated in the following pages.

As has already been suggested, sensation is the immediate knowledge of an object as that object directly affects a sensory receptor.[36] However, as our general analysis of the cognitive union revealed, all knowledge precisely as intentional is in some way immaterial. A simple example may serve to illustrate the extent to which sensation is immaterial. Light impinging upon the sensitized plate of a photoelectric exposure meter creates a proportionate electrical impulse in terms of which the intensity of the light is measured. Similarly, light striking the retina of the eye causes a stimulus to be sent to the brain via waves of depolarization (according to the present theory) in the optic nerve. But the exposure meter, unlike the eye, does not have sensory knowledge of the light striking it. The greater complexity of the structure of the eye explains its extreme sensitivity to color variations and its ability to focus instantly; but visual *knowledge* as yet remains unexplained. The point to be noted, then, is that the change effected by an object in a sensory organ is not the same as the sensory knowledge of that object. A cognitive sense *power,* in other words, is not to be equated with a sensory *organ.*

Thus, when a sensible object affects a sense power, two types of change take place. The sensory *organ* is physically modified by the external stimulus. But since knowledge results from this change, the stimulus also causes a formal determination-to-act of the sense *power* which, prior to the stimulus, was not actually knowing the object in question. Accordingly, the determining principle of the sense power formally presents to the power that aspect of the object known in its particularity and precisely as it affects the power.[37]

A sense power is thus not distinct from the sensory organ in the way that the intellect is in itself independent of an organ, since in sensation the object is known *in* its particularity. Each power of sense is but *one* power with a two-fold aspect—physical, inasmuch as the organ stimulated undergoes a physiological modification; and intentional, insofar as an immanent act of knowledge takes place on the occurrence of an external stimulus. A complete sense power, consequently, is a living informed organ; within the total power the organ is related to the sense itself somewhat in the way that matter is related to form.[38]

To arrive at a knowledge of the proper objects of the different sense powers requires a careful analysis, one that may be aided by the findings of scientific psychology. This detailed analysis will be prescinded from in the following remarks, which will be dependent upon what has been more critically established elsewhere. Since the image and its function in learning will be especially important in the chapters to follow, the discussion here may be centered around the way in which the various powers of sense contribute to the building of the image.

The primitive gathering of the distinct sensations of the individual external senses[39] occurs in an internal *unifying sense,* which has as its proper object the whole sensible thing as it is apprehended by the

combined external powers.[40] Experientially, the unifying sense—
which is the seat of sensory awareness—has its effect in and with the
imagination. The content of an immediate perception is relatively
small, the total perceptual image being built up and contributed to
by images from past as well as present experience. Three-dimensional
space, for example, is not immediately perceived by the eyes alone;[41]
nor does a person know from only one experience that the sound he
hears is, for instance, that of an automobile horn. Repeated experience forms such associations. This blending of past and present perceptions thus gives rise to the possibility of perceptual error.

Since a perception can rarely and only with difficulty be isolated
from concomitant images of past sensations—images which, in the
case of spatial relations, have become quite abstractive and detached
from specific sense qualities—it is scientifically convenient to treat
the unifying sense and the power of imagination as a single sense in
perceptual experiments.[42] Analytically, however, they are distinct;
for the *imagination,* the power that retains the presentations of past
sensations, does not in itself account for the unification of immediate
external sensations.[43]

Apprehension of concrete relations, of things as sensibly good or
harmful to oneself, involves another type of sense knowledge. Concrete estimations of this kind are illustrated by various unlearned
activities that are characteristic of different animals. Thus, birds
build their nests without being taught how to do it, and the sheep
instinctively flees the wolf. Another sense power, the *estimative sense,*
fulfills the cognitive function and is the seat of what is often called
"animal instinct." This internal sense thus explains an animal's apprehension of signals,[44] for any signal is something sensorily apprehended as beneficial or harmful to the animal. The knowledge of the
concrete relation may be guided by some natural predetermination
in the animal's cognitive structure, as in the case of the sheep's natural fear of a wolf. Or the relation may be learned, so that automatic
responses are gradually developed. But in any case the signal is
cognitively apprehended and involves a sensory judgment of the
estimative sense.[45]

The activity of the estimative power in *man* is difficult to isolate, since it is ordered to and intimately connected with reason. For, man's activities, unlike those of an animal, are not confined to fixed and uniform patterns. Thus, a man at least initially learns his responses to a signal—say, a dinner bell or a fire alarm—by a process embracing *some* intellectual realization of the meaning of the signal rather than by a pure sensory apprehension of a concrete good or evil. A few clear-cut instances of cognitive apprehension followed by emotional response will illustrate the function of the estimative sense in man. When an object that is immediately pleasing or displeasing is perceived—a choice steak, for example, or an ugly picture—the estimative power is not directly operative. Rather, the immediate pleasure emotions work directly through the imagination, since a pleasing or unpleasant image is sufficient to excite them. On the other hand, a reaction like that of fear involves an apprehension of some particular thing as concretely related to the perceiver, as concretely harmful to him. The situation is not immediately pleasing, and because it is *known* as such the typical emotional response comes into play. Hence, the aggressive emotions (in both animals and man) operate through the estimative sense rather than directly through the imagination.

We have done little more than to indicate the existence of the type of data that demonstrates the estimative power. A much more careful analysis of experience is here called for, but again we shall appeal to other critical studies on this question. Prescinding then from the complexities of the evidence in this area, we may go on to see how the formation of the image is affected by the human estimative power. Because of its close connection with reason, the human estimative is called the *discursive sense*. The proper object of this internal power, however, is the same as that of the animal estimative—something concretely beneficial or harmful.

The discursive power's function in cooperation with reason is illustrated by concrete situations that call for *practical judgments*. Precisely in its apprehension of sensory good or evil, the discursive sense prepares images for the practical consideration of reason; or, in more formal language, it functions in the organization of the experiential matter for the particularized premise of the practical syllogism. Thus, through the composite operation of intellect and discursive sense + imagination, a man cognitively evaluates a concrete situation which presents itself as sensibly beneficial or harmful, acts upon it in accord with his apprehension, takes specific precautions, and so on. To choose a simple example: a person comes upon a steep narrow stairway with no railing; there is a reaction of fear, causally preceded by a sensory judgment of the discursive sense which tells him that the situation is a concrete danger for him. He descends the stairway cautiously, taking means to prevent his falling or slipping off the side of the steps. The discursive sense thus presents and organizes for rational consideration the images that psychologically represent the particular situation at hand.

Besides preparing images for practical reasoning, the discursive power may function in focusing *attention* upon what an image represents to consciousness. There is nothing particularly appealing, for example, about a geometrical diagram and hence no reason for the immediate pleasure emotions working through the imagination to come to the aid of the intellect when a man is learning geometry. But through the discursive power, guided by reason, the diagram may be *sensorily* judged as beneficial for speculative knowledge. In this way, *interest* may be reinforced, on a sensory as well as intellectual level, upon an object that offers nothing to the desiderative emotions. Thus, when a person sets himself to a task which is not immediately pleasing to him but still must be done, the discursive sense may come to his aid.

The function of the discursive power will become more meaningful when, in the chapters to follow, we consider the role of the image in judgment and in learning activity.[46]

MEMORY

The importance of memory in learning is evident, and scientific psychology has contributed much to our knowledge of mnemonic activities and patterns. The broad area of operations included under the general notion of "memory" is scientifically divided according to various memory functions into behavioral sets that are convenient for experimental purposes. Philosophically, however, memory involves several operative *powers*. The power of *imagination* embraces the activities that we usually speak of in terms of "memory," since it is through this power that images are retained and recalled.[47]

However, it is also evident from experience that we retain our *understanding* of things once they have been learned. This aspect of memory thus brings the intellect, the power of thought, into play. Since what was understood is more or less readily recalled, the intellect cannot have been completely unaware of the object of understanding prior to actual recall; nor, on the other hand, was the intellect *actually* understanding prior to recall. Hence, in the case of intellectual memory, the causal principle that formally determines the intellect to actual understanding of an intelligible object must be retained by the intellect in a state which is neither strictly potential nor actual—an intermediate state of simple possession. The intellect, however, does not retain past experiences as such, since apprehension of the past always involves particulars; this is a function of the imagination and the internal senses.[48]

In this as in all other cases, the intellect works closely with the imagination. Remembrance of something previously understood might be occasioned by the recall of some image from past perceptual or learning experience; but, as will be noted in greater detail further on, intellectual recall is always necessarily connected with sense memory. It is because sensory memory includes a physical organ that laws of memory can be formulated in terms of such factors as fatigue, time lapses, retroactive inhibition, reminiscence, and the like. In themselves, such laws pertain only to the sensory memory-imagination and its retention and/or recall of images, whether the image be simple or complex and highly abstractive. However, the activity of the intellect can enter into sense memory, for understanding of a thing as represented psychologically in the image will affect the vividness of the image and thus the readiness of recall in many cases.[49]

STRUCTURAL UNITY

The philosophical analysis of sensory and intellectual memory points once again to the close cooperation discovered among the powers of man. Our discussion of distinct cognitive powers began with an affirmation of experiential unity, and the distinction of powers must be understood within the context of this unity. For, though analytically distinct, the powers are not operationally separated. Although in a formal analysis we tend to hypostatize the cognitive powers by saying that "the intellect knows this" and "the senses know that," it is not the powers which know; they are causal sources of cognition, operative principles *by which* man knows. Or, to say this in another way, it is *man* who knows, through the proper activity of each of his powers. If these statements are kept in mind, there will arise no contradiction between the experiential assertion that man knows real things directly and the psychological statements which explain from a structural point of view the operative principles that enter into this knowledge.[50]

The unity of cognitive experience has been emphasized in calling the object of the *intellect* in perceptual knowledge an incidental *sensible* object—"desk," in the example we used above. In the light of the fuller analysis just completed, this means that the intellect grasps the intelligible reality of an object in perception, whether it be some aspect of the real nature or an intelligible function (such as "desk") based on the real nature of the object.[51] Thus, attentive *perception,* philosophically considered, is a single *composite act* of sensation and intellection by which an object present to the senses is immediately known.[52]

Given, then, the operational unity which has been emphasized from a cognitive standpoint in this chapter, but which we have also seen to be discoverable in other human acts; and proceeding on our initial principle that activities reveal their ontological sources, we are naturally led to the ultimate structural principle of human activity. For, that by which all the operations of man—biological, sensory, rational—are brought into an operational unity is the human soul, the single substantial form of the body. To speak of the essential union of body and soul is, therefore, only to speak of the real structure of man that ultimately makes it possible for him to exhibit unified activity. For it is through the proper existence given the whole human being by the soul that a human person is both human and one person.[53]

Our discussion of cognitive powers may at this point be synthesized and the powers seen in the light of the whole human person. The powers from which human operations proceed have their existence in and through the human substantial structure. Since sensation involves bodily organs, the powers of sense have their existence in the composite of body and soul. The intellect, however, which is in itself strictly immaterial and not the act of any organ, has its being in the soul alone, which is not in itself material. Hence the soul, while it is the act of the whole living body in the structural order, is the subject of operative powers either in itself or together with the body in the operational order.[54]

Looking at the human structure as a unified whole, we may note that the powers of man are structurally ordered one to another. In the process of growth toward full manhood, the lower biological powers with their nutritive and augmentative functions prepare the body for the operations of sense, which become more perfect as the organism grows. When the internal senses are sufficiently developed, the intellect is able to perform its distinctively human operations. Structural order can also be seen in the mature human, for the more imperfect powers naturally assist the more perfect. Correct functioning of the biological organism prevents physical conditions that can impede cerebral processes. Unhampered by such conditions, the senses can in turn aid the operations of reason with maximum efficiency. The order of powers is further illustrated by the influence of the higher powers upon the lower. The rational powers exercise control over the operations of the internal senses. Thus, reason guides association of images in a disciplined thought process, and it governs the operations of the discursive sense when practical judgments come into play. Human cognitive powers can in turn influence the lower physiological operations. This is best illustrated by the adverse somatic effects that sometimes result from psychic conditions.

This context also suggests the ontological roots of the scientific study of *individual differences* and abilities. Relative perfection of the powers of sense, particularly the internal senses, directly affects the degree to which the intellect understands what is sensorily presented to it. In terms of the total human structure, the perfection of the intellective soul is proportioned to the perfection of the body of which the soul is the formal act.[55]

Just as a formal analysis tends to hypostatize powers that are in themselves only operative principles of activity, so does it tend to render static what in reality is dynamic. The dynamism of existing things was spoken of at the opening of this chapter, and it may now be seen in the light of human existence. Sense cognition brings the sensory emotions into play when a sensible thing is apprehended as a concrete good or evil; some indication of this was given in our analysis of the internal estimative sense. Similarly, an intelligible good known by the intellect leads causally to an act of will. Consideration of these aspects of human nature together with the problems of motivation would embrace a whole new analysis which, while necessary for a more complete view of the structure of man, lies beyond the scope of this book.

Yet *tendency* is found, not only in the instance of goods actually apprehended, but also in the cognitive powers themselves. For, every knowing power has this relation to the object which is naturally proper to it, "that when it does not possess it, it tends toward it, and when it does possess it, it is at rest with it."[56] This is Aquinas' way of describing, with reference to the structure of man, the basic fact of human experience that underlies all learning—"all men by nature desire to know."[57]

THE ANALOGY OF COGNITION

The present chapter opened with an exploratory description of cognition, and the analysis of knowledge was conducted in terms of simple perceptual knowledge. Leaving to subsequent chapters any discussion of higher forms of knowing and learning, we can at this point refine the meaning of *cognition* or *knowledge,* in a judgmentally organized fashion.

Our discussion of knowledge as a total experience and of the cognitive union revealed that there are certain features common to all knowing. There is the union of knower and known in a single immanent act, a union perfective of the knower and causally achieved by means of a dynamic and formal determination-to-act. This aspect of immanence is balanced by the existential or relational character of knowledge; for, the object known, while intentionally immanent, is existentially other than the knower.

But owing to the differences between cognitive powers, the term *cognition* cannot have a univocal meaning. This fact can be summarized in terms of an example. Extension, a single effect of quantity in a material object and thus in itself materially one thing, is formally known in different ways by different cognitive powers. Thus, the sense of sight attains concrete extendedness as colored, the sense of touch attains it under the aspect of temperature or pressure, the internal estimative sense reaches it as something concretely beneficial or harmful, and so on. Now the fact that all of the senses, including the unifying sense and the memory-imagination, can attain a common sensible object like concrete extendedness indicates that, though formally different, the senses do share a generic community.

On the other hand, extension as known by the intellect—apart from the particularities of this extended thing—is known in a way that is *essentially* different from the knowledge gained by the senses.

The reason for this difference is that the intellect is not the act of an organ and is therefore strictly immaterial. The sense powers, on the other hand, are immaterial only in the sense that their physiological organs are informed by a power of the human structure that enables them to have life and actual knowledge. From the point of view of their operations, the senses are immaterial only because, though their acts are extended in space and time, the qualitative changes in their organs are not the knowledge itself. But the operation of the intellect is in itself neither extended in space and time; nor, since it lacks a physical organ, is it directly involved in a quantitative change.[58]

Since the term *knowledge* or *cognition* covers all of these operations, which share both different and common elements, it has an analogous meaning. And the analogy is an existential one; for each type of actual cognitive operation differs from another in the very act of being similar to it, just as each cognitive power is at once both similar to and different from every other power. This fundamental analogy of knowledge will be developed in various perspectives in the following chapters, where we shall center our attention upon the role of the image in understanding and learning.

NOTES

1. The different kinds of tendency in nature and in man are summarized in *S. T.* I, q. 19, a. 1; I–II, q. 8, a. 1.

   On the principle of identifying natures by an analysis of their activities, see *S. T.* I, q. 14, a. 6 (ed. Ottawa I, 97b12–17); Aquinas' use of this principle will be found exemplified in many of the texts cited throughout this study.

   One of the classic texts analyzing the degrees of living things is *S. T.* I, q. 18, a. 3. The levels of being are considered from the point of view of tendency in I, q. 59, a. 1.

2. Cf. *S. T.* I, q. 16, a. 1, ad 3. For a more complete discussion of external reality as the cause of knowledge, see Louis-Marie Régis, O.P., *Epistemology*, tr. Imelda Choquette Byrne (New York: Macmillan Co., 1959), pp. 193–221.

3. On this double relationship of object and person, see *S. T.* I, q. 78, a. 1 (ed. Ottawa I, 473a12–36). See also below, note 6.

4. St. Thomas suggests that external movement is the primary analogate in our knowledge of "act"; thus, the meaningfulness of any use of this analogous term is ultimately derived from the fundamental experience of movement. See *Commentary on Aristotle's Metaphysics*, Bk. IX, lect. 3 (ed. Cathala [2d ed. rev.; Taurini: Marietti, 1926], p. 523, nos. 1806–07).

5. On the expansion of nature involved in immanent activity, cognitive and appetitive, see *S. T.* I, q. 54, a. 2.

6. The texts in which St. Thomas contrasts transient and immanent activity are legion; a few of the more significant texts, pertinent directly to knowledge, are *S. T.* I, q. 14, a. 2 (ed. Ottawa I, 92b48–93a16); q. 18, a. 3, ad 1; q. 54, a. 2 (334a 5–20); q. 56, a. 1 (341a24–42); q. 85, a. 2 (527a25–41). These texts also discuss the causal principle by which the union of knowledge takes place.

 Although the biological operations of growth, nutrition, and reproduction, as well as appetitive operations are also immanent activities, none of these operations involve the additional characteristic of a union achieved within the knower and the distinctive relationship of object to knower. On appetition as opposed to cognition, see above, pp. 51–52. Two key texts distinguishing appetition and knowledge are *S. T.* I, q. 16, a. 1; I–II, q. 22. a. 2.

7. *S. T.* I, q. 84, a. 2 (ed. Ottawa I, 513b 29–36). In this context Thomas is answering the Greek Naturalists who posited that man knows fire by an internal fire, water by a watery principle, etc.

8. See *S. T.* I, q. 14, a. 1 (ed. Ottawa I, 91b41–92a14); q. 84, a. 2 (513b37–14a18). These texts argue directly from matter as principle of limitation. A more detailed argument from the perfection of knowledge may be found in *De Veritate*, q. 2, a. 2.

9. Aquinas does not often use the term "intentional being." However, in *S. T.* I, q. 56, a. 2, ad 3, for instance, he must use some term to distinguish the natural being of an angel (which, though natural, is nonetheless immaterial) from its knowledge, which he calls "intentional being." The term is thus more exclusive than words like "immaterial" which he uses elsewhere.

10. Definition gathered from *S. T.* I, q. 56, a. 1; cf. q. 14, a. 5, ad 3 (ed. Ottawa I, 96a30–42). See also the texts cited above, in note 6. The term "impressed species" was devised by Scholastics following Aquinas as a general term to cover the formal determining principle of both sensory and intellectual powers; Thomas himself does not use this term, but rather speaks of the *species obiecti, species sensibilis* or *intelligibilis*, depending on the context.

The term *species* is generally avoided in this study since, being applicable also to logical and biological concepts, it is equivocal; when it is used, it will be italicized. In general, any hypostatization will be avoided here as much as possible, owing to the many misinterpretations concerning the object of knowledge that have arisen since Aquinas' day. Unless one is well acquainted with Thomas' terminology, a word like *species* can be most misleading.

11. This problem is discussed in an historical context in *S. T.* I, q. 85, a. 2. Aquinas will in one breath speak of the *species* as a *similitudo* of the object (in order to emphasize its presentational function) and in the next assert that the *species* is not the thing known. This sounds contradictory to the modern ear; but the problems and terminology connected with ideas in the traditions of rationalism and empiricism were unknown by Thomas, who thus could not have seen any semantic difficulties in this context.

12. Aquinas suggests the following analogies. There is an act-potency relationship between a power's formal determination-to-act and the cognitive power itself, analogous to the relationship between matter and form; the determining principle is thus a quasi-form or perfection of the power. And as actual existence follows metaphysically upon the form by which a thing has a specific kind of existence, so does actual knowledge follow upon the formal determination by which the knower in potency is specified to knowing a particular object. For these analogies, see *S. T.* I, q. 55, a. 1 (ed. Ottawa I, 337b31–38); q. 14, a. 5, ad 2 (96a18–24); and q. 14, a. 4 (95a13–15).

13. St. Thomas expresses this by saying that it belongs to the very nature of an object outside the knower to become united to him in knowledge—literally, "*nata est* animae coniungi et in anima esse per suam similitudinem." See *S. T.* I, q. 78, a. 1 (ed. Ottawa I, 473a12–19).

14. Cf. the dicta of Aristotle: "the sensible in act is the sense in act" and "the intelligible in act is the intellect in act." See *De Anima*, Bk. III, chap. ii, 426a16; chap. iv, 430a3. Aquinas often employs these expressions to summarize the metaphysics of knowledge; e.g., see the discussions in *S. T.* I, q. 14, a. 2, et ad 2; q. 55, a. 1, ad 2; q. 85, a. 2.

15. Thomas conducts a similar analysis, in the context of the epistemological doctrines of the Greek materialists and of Plato, in *S. T.* I, q. 84, a. 1. The double meaning involved in "knowing something as it is in the knower" is discussed in q. 14, a. 6, ad 1. A similar equivo-

cation can be involved in saying that "a man understands a thing other than it is"; see *S. T.* I, q. 13, a. 12, ad 3; cf. q. 76, a. 2, ad 4.

For further considerations on knowledge as a total experience, see Francis H. Parker's essay on "Realistic Epistemology" in *The Return to Reason,* ed. John Wild (Chicago: Regnery Co., 1953), pp. 152–76. Parker's study is particularly good on the relational features of cognition. More detailed considerations particularly on the cognitive *union* may be found in Jacques Maritain, *The Degrees of Knowledge,* tr. Bernard Wall (New York: Chas. Scribner's Sons, 1938), pp. 134–43. Elaborate discussions of the immanence of cognitive activity and the exteriority of the object, including a copious selection of texts from Aquinas, may be found in Régis, *Epistemology,* pp. 157–93; pp. 254–306 include discussions of this point with respect to both sensible and intelligible objects, which are explicitly handled in the light of the cognitive powers.

16. A detailed textual study of Aquinas' views on the various kinds of self-awareness may be found in Marcel-Marie Desmarais, O.P., "L'auto-perception de la personne psychologique," *Etudes et recherches,* Vol. I, *Philosophie* (Ottawa: Collège Dominicain, 1936), 11–47. On reflection on the self, with a contrast between Aquinas' and Descartes' views, see P. Hoenen, S.J., *Reality and Judgment according to St. Thomas,* tr. H. Tiblier, S.J. (Chicago: Regnery Co., 1952), pp. 274–86. J. Wébert, O.P., concludes a verbal study of Thomas' use of the term *reflexio* with a summary that includes two types of reflection pertinent here: *réflexion-considération,* the mind's knowledge of its nature through careful attention to its acts; and *réflexion-reploiement,* an even more direct type of self-consciousness. See " 'Reflexio': Etude sur les opérations réflexives dans la psychologie de s. Thomas d'Aquin," *Mélanges Mandonnet,* I (Bibliothèque thomiste, XIII; Paris: J. Vrin, 1930), 285–325; summary of the above types, 315–19.

17. A key text discussing the unity of the human substance, especially from the point of view of the "commanded act," is *S. T.* I–II, q. 17, a. 4; see also *S. T.* I, q. 18, a. 3 (ed. Ottawa I, 128b6–24); q. 81, a. 3; q. 76, a. 5, ad 3. *S. T.* III, q. 19, a. 2 (ed. Ottawa IV, 2553b36–54a34) gives an excellent summary of the unity of the human act.

Further considerations of Aquinas' statements concerning operational unity may be found in George P. Klubertanz, S.J., "The Unity of Human Activity," *Modern Schoolman,* XXVII (1950), 75–103. Numerous scientific evidences—biological, chemical, psychological —for the unity of man are given in Klubertanz, *The Philosophy of*

Human Nature (New York: Appleton-Century-Crofts, 1953), pp. 12–38.

18. I am using here the classification of signs (though not the entire logic) suggested by Susanne Langer and outlined in *Philosophy in a New Key* (2d ed.; Cambridge: Harvard Univ. Press, 1951), pp. 53–78. On the terminology employed (the term "signal" is borrowed from Charles Morris), see the Preface to the 2d ed., p. viii; cf. Langer, *Feeling and Form* (New York: Chas. Scribner's Sons, 1953), p. 26.

   The classic Scholastic analysis of signs is that of John of St. Thomas. Since his terminology is more useful in a logical than in a psychological context, it is not employed in this study. For his analysis, see *Cursus Philosophicus Thomisticus,* ed. B. Reiser, Vol. I, *Ars Logica* (Taurini: Marietti, 1930), Part II, qq. 21–22, pp. 646–722; summarized in his shorter work, *Outlines of Formal Logic,* tr. F. C. Wade, S.J., (Milwaukee: Marquette Univ. Press, 1955), pp. 31–32.

19. In the case of a *formal sign,* the reality of the sign is not distinct from its meaning. *Knowledge* can be viewed as this type of sign: it exists and finds its whole reality only in making the object as object present to the knower. It thus differs from other natural and artificial signs, which have a material reality of their own apart from what they signify.

20. For some differences between animal and human significant movements, see André Marc, S.J., *Psychologie réflexive,* Vol. I, *La connaissance* (Paris: Desclée de Brouwer, 1948), pp. 22–27; the sign-analyses of numerous contemporary French writers are summarized in pp. 19–32.

21. Helen Keller, *The Story of My Life* (New York: Doubleday & Co., 1955), p. 36 [1st ed., 1902.]

22. All attentive perceptual knowledge grasps the substance of the thing perceived, even if only in a vague way. A child who knows no more than that the colored thing he sees is some colored *thing* (which would seem to be the vaguest possible sort of knowledge) still has a knowledge of substance, which need not be *defined* in order to be *known.* (In perception substance is an "incidental sensible"; see below, pp. 60–61 and 72.) The necessity of "inferring substance" arises only when the critique of knowledge begins with an analysis of ideas. For the historical epistemological problem involved here, together with an analysis of the realist's position, see Henry Babcock

Veatch, *Intentional Logic* (New Haven: Yale Univ. Press, 1952), pp. 85–93.

23. On proper sensible objects, see *S. T.* I, q. 57, a. 1, ad 2; q. 18, beginning of a. 2. A rather detailed consideration of common sensibles may be found in q. 78, a. 3, ad 2. On incidental sensibles (*sensibilia per accidens*), see *S. T.* I, q. 12, a. 3, ad 2 (ed. Ottawa I, 63a32–37); q. 77, a. 1, ad 7; q. 87, a. 1, ad. 1. Aquinas will also discuss these objects in connection with the problem of truth and error in the senses; see *S.T.* I, q. 17, a. 2; q. 85, a. 6. See below, note 37.

24. What is here called "formal object"—that in the proper object which makes it proper—is called by St. Thomas the *ratio obiecti*, i.e., that precise "aspect" or "intelligibility" by reason of which a power reaches the object. Thus, the *ratio obiecti* serves to distinguish the *ratio actus* and thereby the power. One of the more comprehensive analyses of the formal object as the basis for distinction of powers is found in *S. T.* I, q. 77, a. 3. Aquinas' insistence on the insufficiency of simple differences ("material" as opposed to "formal") for this task may be seen in *S. T.* I, q. 59, a. 2, ad 2; q. 77, a. 3, ad 2; q. 79, a. 7; q. 79, a. 10, ad 3; q. 80, a. 1, ad 2.

25. For further elaboration of this point, see Marc, *Psychologie réflexive*, I, 28–30.

26. Thought is joined to space and time in judgment, as will be developed in chapter 4.

27. Attempts have been made to confirm the immateriality of thought scientifically, in the "imageless thought" type of experiment; for a discussion of these attempts, see below, chapter 3, note 14.

28. This is not an insignificant point, since the confusion of ideas with images has caused considerable difficulty in the history of modern thought. John *Locke*, whose noetic is sometimes equated with that of Aquinas, had trouble explaining how an abstract "idea" of a triangle, for instance, could simultaneously include "all and none" of the specific shapes and qualities of different particular triangles. He thus concluded that, owing to the extreme difficulty of conceiving them, all abstract ideas are pure fabrications of the mind with no existence of any sort in the real world.

Of this *Berkeley* remarked, "Whether others have this wonderful faculty of abstracting their ideas, they best can tell: for myself, I find . . . the idea of man that I frame to myself must be either of a white, or a black, or a tawny, a straight, or a crooked, a tall, or a low, or a middle-sized man. I cannot by any effort of thought conceive the abstract idea" of the sort described by Locke. Moreover, "it must be acknowledged that a man may consider a figure merely as triangular, without attending to the particular qualities, or relations of the sides."

Though Berkeley's own notion of the nature of an "idea" rejects other evidence of experience, his critique of Locke's abstraction doctrine is to the point and illustrates what abstraction is *not*. Cf. D. J. B. Hawkins' remark that in this instance Berkeley had an experiential insight which neither Locke nor Hume after him had (*Crucial Problems of Modern Philosophy* [New York: Sheed & Ward, 1957], p. 32). Locke's problem is seen in *An Essay concerning Human Understanding*, IV, vii, 9; Berkeley's statements are taken from *The Principles of Human Knowledge* (2d ed., 1734), Introduction, 10 and 16.

29. For various contrasts between the powers, acts, and objects of intellection and sensation, see *S. T.* I, q. 50, a. 2 (ed. Ottawa I, 316b18–31); q. 75, a. 5 (444a2–24); q. 14, a. 12 (103b39–4a8); q. 54, a. 5 (336b4–14); q. 76, a. 1, ad 2; a. 2, ad 4. Another proof for the immateriality of the intellect is given in *S. T.* I, q. 75, a. 2.

30. "Some intelligible aspect" is used throughout this study as a *general* English equivalent for the various Latin terms used by Aquinas to designate the object of knowledge, e.g., *quidditas* and *forma* or *natura universalis*. Two remarks should be made concerning Thomas' use of these terms in many of the texts cited or quoted throughout this study:

(1) Whatever is known about an object is known in virtue of its acts or ontological perfections, and the substantial and accidental perfections of things are in *analogous* senses called "forms"; "quiddity" and "nature" generally refer to the substantial nature of a thing. Hence, these various terms designate the actual intelligibility of the object known, i.e., that particular "intelligible aspect" of the object which is actually being known.

(2) In a psychological or metaphysical context, the Latin term *universalis* is always opposed to the object as *particular* and does not necessarily connote univocity. Thus, a notion like "life," which is *analogous* and not univocal, can be called a "universal nature" (cf. *S. T.* I, q. 18, a. 2). In English, we would be more inclined to speak of "abstract natures"; in Aquinas' Latin, however, *abstrahere* and its derivatives are employed to describe the act of the intellect by which the idea is known, and not the idea itself. E. g., in *S. T.* I, q. 85, a. 2, ad 2, Thomas uses the adjective *abstractum* explicitly to refer to the *logical* universal, which includes both the universal nature of the thing and the intention of universality itself.

Concrete illustrations of these points can be seen, e.g., in *S. T.* I, q. 40, a. 3; q. 76, a. 2, ad 3; q. 86, a. 1, ad 4.

31. For a summary of Aquinas' teaching on abstraction, see *S. T.* I, q. 85, a. 1. The problem of the different kinds of abstraction has been greatly complicated by the Renaissance commentators on Thomas. A good critique of the commentators' misinterpretations along with a textual study of Aquinas' teaching on this matter is: Francis A. Cunningham, S.J., "A Theory on Abstraction in St. Thomas," *Modern Schoolman,* XXXV (1958), 249–70.

One of the most important texts on this subject, especially with regard to the *judgmental* abstraction involved in metaphysical knowledge, is in Thomas' *Commentary on Boethius' De Trinitate,* q. 5, a. 3. On this matter, see also L.-B. Geiger, "Abstraction et séparation d'après s. Thomas," *Revue des sciences philosophiques et théologique,* XXXI (1937), 3–40.

32. The texts in which Aquinas speaks of the *proper* object of the human intellect, which he usually designates "quiddity" or "nature" (see note 30), are innumerable. See especially *S. T.* I, q. 84, a. 7 (quoted below, pp. 119–21); cf. q. 85, a. 1 (ed. Ottawa I, 524b21–25), a. 5 (531b14–19), a. 8 (534b5–14); q. 86, a. 2 (536b23–27); q. 87, a. 3 (543a26–37). All of these texts give explicit statements, from various points of view, of what the proper object entails.

The *general* object of the intellect may be called "being," but must not be equated with the "being" treated in metaphysics. The object of the intellect might be an hypothetical being, e.g., a mathematical construct; or it might be an error; or the intellect might intelligibly understand that a non-circular circle is *un*intelligible. But in any case the *formal* consideration under which the intellect attains its object is the *intelligibility* of what is understood. This is another way of saying that the intellect can understand anything (though this will be conditioned by its dependence on the senses).

Aquinas will speak of the general object of the intellect as *ens universale* and similar expressions; the formal object is most frequently designated as *ratio entis*. See *S. T.* I, q. 78, a. 1 (ed. Ottawa I, 473a5–8, 22–24); q. 79, a. 7 (487b35–88a15); necessary qualifications are made in q. 79, a. 2, and a. 9, ad 3. As will be noted at some length in chap. 3, whatever higher understanding the intellect has, it has only in virtue of some primitive experience of concrete reality, which experience can be refined in many ways.

33. The act of understanding is not that which the intellect in act understands; the mental word is thus analytically (not operationally)

distinct from both the act of understanding and the formal principle that determines the intellect to act.

A recent, well-handled textual study which includes most of the significant elements of Aquinas' teaching on the mental word in human cognition is that of William W. Meissner, S.J., "Some Aspects of the *Verbum* in the Texts of St. Thomas," *Modern Schoolman,* XXXVI (1958), 1–30. Another study, directed more immediately toward Thomas' doctrine on the *verbum divinum,* is the series of articles by Bernard J. Lonergan, S.J., "The Concept of *Verbum* in the Writings of St. Thomas Aquinas," *Theological Studies,* VII (1946), 349–92; VIII (1947), 35–79, 404–44; X (1949), 3–40, 359–93. As a careful study of Aquinas' own ideas on this matter, Meissner's article is preferable.

34. E.g., see *S. T.* I, q. 85, a. 2 (ed. Ottawa I, 527a41–47); *De Veritate,* q. 4, a. 2, ad 3. Many authors in the Scholastic tradition have interpreted Thomas' references to the mental word as a *medium in quo* to mean that the intellect knows external reality in the mental word as in a mirror. This doctrine, which amounts to transferring psychological or causal analysis to the level of direct experience, has no real foundation in Aquinas' works. See Meissner's study of this point, "Some Aspects of the *Verbum,*" pp. 21–25.

35. For further considerations on the immateriality of thought and some contrasts between thought and animal instinct, see Jaime Castiello, S.J., *A Humane Psychology of Education* (New York: Sheed & Ward, 1936), pp. 17–33. The author's discussion of human thought and learning throughout the book are generally excellent; his presentation, however, almost totally presumes the philosophy of knowledge upon which its meaningfulness rests.

36. Scientific psychology employs fundamentally the same definition of sensation, except that the notion of "consciousness" might replace what we have called "immediate knowledge." The experimentalist, however, does not deal with consciousness *as such,* and many psychologists would prefer not to include this element in their functional definitions. E.g., see the remarks of C. H. Graham, "Visual Perception," *Handbook of Experimental Psychology,* ed. S. S. Stevens (New York: Wiley & Sons, 1951), p. 870. The manifestations of consciousness are the primitive data for the scientist (cf. chap. 1), who is interested in behavioral relationships *within* consciousness; he need not account for consciousness itself any more than the mechanical physicist need explain the ontological nature of material bodies.

For a different opinion on this matter, see T. V. Moore, *Cognitive Psychology* (Philadelphia: J. B. Lippincott, 1939), p. 88; Moore states that "biology and psychology must deal with the concept of living substance." T. J. Gannon (*Psychology: The Unity of Human Behavior* [Boston: Ginn & Co., 1954], p. 61, asserts that the notion of consciousness ought to be included in functional definitions. Statements like those of Moore and Gannon are probably reactions against extreme forms of behaviorism that go to the extent of *denying* consciousness. Numerous psychologists, however, now agree that the phenomenon of consciousness is a reasonable scientific postulate, even though it cannot be isolated experimentally. E.g., see O. H. Mowrer, "Ego Psychology, Cybernetics, and Learning Theory," *Learning Theory, Personality Theory, and Clinical Research: Kentucky Symposium* (New York: Wiley & Sons, 1954), p. 84.

37. Since the senses have knowledge only insofar as they are affected, it is not quite accurate to speak of *error* in the senses as affected by their proper objects. The source of error may lie in internal sensation, and it is formally found in the mistaken judgment made concerning the sense data presented. See *S. T.* I, q. 17, a. 2; q. 85, a. 6. A discussion of this matter may be found in Klubertanz, *Philosophy of Human Nature* (henceforth referred to as *PHN*), pp. 428–31.

38. On the two-fold change involved in sensation, see *S. T.* I, q. 78, a. 3. (ed. Ottawa I, 475b26–40); I–II, q. 22, a. 2, ad 3. On the passivity of sense knowledge, see *S. T.* I, q. 79, a. 3, ad 1; I–II, q. 22, aa. 1 & 2.

On the analogous use of matter and form in explaining the composition of things other than complete substantial beings, see below, chapter 3, note 22.

39. On the external senses, see Klubertanz, *PHN*, pp. 104–11. Aquinas' principal analysis of the external senses in the *Summa* is in I, q. 78, a. 3; for a compact analysis of the internal senses, see *ibid.*, a. 4. Though Thomas' remarks concerning the *organs* of sense lack the precision made possible in our own age by the large amount of scientific data at hand, his analysis is directed primarily toward the philosophical question of the *powers* of sense. For further development of the philosophical aspects of external sensation, see J. P. Ledvina, *A Psychology and Philosophy of Sensation according to St. Thomas Aquinas* (Washington, D.C.: Catholic Univ. Press, 1941).

40. The concrete unification of sensations is illustrated by our linguistic cross-comparisons of sense experiences—"loud color," "bright tone,"

etc. See Klubertanz, *PHN*, pp. 124–28. This unification cannot be achieved by the intellect itself, since the particularities of matter are directly involved. A detailed textual study of Aquinas' teaching on this sense is: Edmund J. Ryan, C.PP.S., *The Role of the "Sensus Communis" in the Psychology of St. Thomas Aquinas* (Carthagena, Ohio: Messenger Press, 1951), esp. pp. 74–148; for a summary of *scientific* data, see *ibid.*, pp. 153–85.

41. As has been confirmed frequently in scientific experiments on vision, the *stereoscopic effect* achieved by the position of the two eyes does not account for the perception of three-dimensional space. For example, persons with congenital cataract removed in adult life have felt that the objects seen for the first time were actually touching their eyes: see Moore, *Cognitive Psychology*, pp. 313–21. A summary of experimental data with copious references to specific studies may be found in Graham, "Visual Perception," *Handbook of Exper. Psych.*, pp. 868–920.

42. T. V. Moore's "synthetic sense," for instance, embraces aspects of both of these internal sense powers; see *Cognitive Psychology*, pp. 237–71.

43. The imagination and the image, its product, will keep recurring in discussions through this study. On the imagination as an operative power, see Klubertanz, *PHN*, pp. 128–34.

Probably owing to the immensity of the task, no complete textual study has yet been done on St. Thomas' teaching on the imagination as such. Arthur D. Fearon chooses especially those texts which point out the importance of the imagination in perceptual experience ("The Imagination," *New Scholasticism*, XIV [1940], 181–95); he calls attention to various Scholastic authors' neglect of this fact in their restriction of the imagination to the functions of retaining and recalling past experience. Robert E. Brennan, O.P., did a follow-up study ("The Thomistic Concept of Imagination," *ibid.*, XV [1941], 149–61) oriented not so much toward elucidating Aquinas' thought as toward showing that the imagination's important contribution to perception has always been recognized in the Scholastic tradition.

One might add to all this that naming the *formal object* of the imagination as past sensations does not deny its function in present perceptions, since such a statement implies that the imagination can retain and recall sensations as well as create new images from the wealth of its data (cf. *S. T.* I, q. 12, a. 9, ad 2; q. 85, a. 2, ad 3). Hence, one must take care in any textual study to distinguish between the places where Aquinas is speaking about the proper *object* of the imagination qua operative power and those that treat of the *opera-tions* and/or *product* (image) of the power.

44. For the meaning of "signal" as it is used here, see above, pp. 57–58.

45. Further considerations on animal instinct and the relationships between the animal estimative and physiology may be found in Klu-bertanz, *PHN*, pp. 134–42, 151–55; see also the following note. De-tailed and multiple examples of animal "instinctive" activity have been gathered and are considered in relation to human behavior in Mark A. Gaffney, S.J., *The Psychology of the Interior Senses* (St. Louis: B. Herder, 1942), pp. 155–248.

46. For a summary of the activity and functions of the discursive sense, see Klubertanz, *PHN*, pp. 142–46. Throughout his writings Aquinas has analyzed an amazing amount of experiential data (gathered from both animal and human activity) tangent upon the estimative-dis-cursive power. A detailed and definitive study of Thomas' teaching on this matter may be found in G. P. Klubertanz, S.J., *The Dis-cursive Power* (St. Louis: Modern Schoolman, 1952), pp. 149–264; for a synthesis of the study, see pp. 265–95. The preparation of images for practical reasoning is closely related to the habit of pru-dence and is generally discussed by Thomas in this context; see *ibid.*, pp. 214–19, 248–54, 286–88; on the preparation of images for speculative knowledge, see pp. 288–93; on the sensory judgment in-volved in the operation of this internal sense, see pp. 233–37; on the relation between sensory emotions and the estimative sense, see pp. 227–30.

Attention should again be called to our very sketchy treatment of the internal senses; though the discussions here will serve the pur-poses of the present study adequately enough, they are hardly suffi-cient for a critical philosophical study of internal sensation. Typical instances of "conditioned" behavior—where the intellect's opera-tions become minimal and the role of the internal senses more pre-dominant—have been for the most part deliberately passed over, since a discussion of this matter is more significant in the context of an analysis of *habit,* which lies beyond the scope of the present study.

47. In the writings of Aquinas, the imagination or sensory memory in the ordinary sense of "memory" is to be distinguished from what he calls the *vis memorativa* (or sometimes simply *memoria*), which has as its proper object past *estimations* and not simply images. I may be led by circumstances and series of images, for instance, to recall my childhood dislike for baths; in this example there is an appre-hension of a past estimation, of a past situation precisely *as past.*

Following the lead of the Arabian philosophers, Aquinas teaches that a distinct internal sense, the *memorativa,* is needed for retaining and recalling past estimations of the discursive estimative, much as the imagination retains the sensations presented it by the unifying sense. See *S. T.* I, q. 78, a. 4 (ed. Ottawa I, 478a28–38); cf. q. 79, a. 6, & ad 2. See Klubertanz, *Discursive Power,* pp. 260–62, for a discussion of the different terms used by Aquinas to express the various kinds of memory; *memoria* is an equivocal term in medieval Latin, a fact which is overlooked by most of the Scholastic commentators on Aquinas' works.

Knowledge of past estimations is an evident experiential fact, and the importance of the discursive sense's activity on an image for subsequent retention and recall has been experimentally confirmed. (E.g., see Sister Mary Constance Barrett, R.S.M., "An Experimental Study of the Thomistic Concept of the Faculty of Imagination," *Studies in Psychology and Psychiatry, Catholic Univ. of America,* Vol. V [1941], no. 3.) However, the proof for the memorative function's constituting a *distinct power* is not strong; it can be argued that the past precisely as past does not constitute a formal object and thus that the imagination suffices for this activity. (For a brief indication of this, see Klubertanz, *PHN,* pp. 139–40.) Whether there is a distinct power here or not, the indubitable memorative *function* is of more interest to us in this study; hence, we shall refer to sensory memory as a whole, often by using the term *memory-imagination.*

48. On intellectual memory and various comparisons of this activity with sense memory, see *S. T.* I, q. 79, a. 6, & ad 1, ad 2; q. 79, a. 7 & ad 2, ad 3.

The formal determining principle or intelligible *species* is retained in *habitu,* in Aquinas' terms. This does not mean "habit" in the modern sense of the word; a person might be able to recall intelligible objects and still have a very poor habit of memory.

49. Experimental studies on various aspects of memory may be found summarized in Carl I. Hovland, "Human Learning and Retention," *Handbook of Exper. Psych.,* espec. pp. 645–65; pp. 679–89 include a copious bibliography. On the cerebral functions in memory and on memory traces, see Clifford T. Morgan, "The Psychophysiology of Learning," *ibid.,* pp. 780–84.

For experimental data on the intellectual memory and its connections with sensory memory, see Moore, *Cognitive Psychology,* pp. 462–72.

50. Aquinas is very conscious of this unity and will often begin and

conclude his formal analyses with a restatement of the powers as *principles* of operation and not *things* or beings in themselves. For an explicit consideration of this question, see *S. T.* I, q. 77, a. 1, ad 3; q. 75, a. 2, ad 2.

51. See *S. T.* I–II, q. 31, a. 5 (ed. Ottawa II, 883b20–28); cf. I, q. 75, a. 6, (I, 445b31–34); q. 57, a. 1, ad 2.

52. This philosophical definition of perception must be distinguished from the *functional* notion of perception employed by scientists. Some view it as an aggregate of sensations (e.g., Graham, "Visual Perception," *Handbook of Exper. Psych.*, p. 870). Others understand perception to mean a complex psychological process involving present and past experience and resulting in recognition (e.g., Gannon, *Psychology*, p. 158). If by "recognition" is meant a meaningful grasp of the object as well as sensory synthesis, the latter definition is a close experimental surrogate of the philosophical one given above.

53. For more detailed discussions on the human soul, which need not delay us here, see Klubertanz, *PHN*, pp. 298–321, and *S. T.* I, the whole of q. 76.

54. On the proper subjects of operative powers, see *S. T.* I, q. 77, a. 5; cf. q. 54, a. 5; q. 76, a. 8, ad 4. On the powers as accidents caused by the soul, with the type of causality involved, see q. 77, aa. 6 & 7. On the immateriality of the soul, see q. 75, aa. 2 & 6.

The operative powers are not the substance itself. Since potencies are known only through their proper acts, each irreducibly different kind of act (distinguished by the formal-object analysis) indicates a different potency. Now substance is in potency to the act of being, which is different from operations. Hence, there must be within the substance (having their existence through the act of being of the substance) different and distinct powers, which are in potency to distinct kinds of operations. See *S. T.* I, q. 54, a. 3; cf. q. 77, a. 1; q. 54, a. 1.

55. On the order of powers (a notion which St. Thomas seems to have taken up only in his later writings), see *S. T.* I, q. 77, a. 4; on "individual differences," see q. 85, a. 7.

56. Quaelibet autem res ad suam formam naturalem hanc habet habitudinem, ut quando non habet ipsam, tendat in eam, et quando habet ipsam, quiescat in ea." *S. T.* I, q. 19, a. 1 (ed. Ottawa I, 131a 10–13).

57. The opening statement of Aristotle's *Metaphysics* (ed. McKeon, *Basic Works of Aristotle* [New York: Random House, 1941], p. 689).

58. Although the immateriality of sensation is significant in a philosophical analysis, this aspect of sensation does not affect the *scientist's* treatment of sense knowledge. About all it means in an experimental context is that one cannot point to a "piece of knowledge" in
the organ of sense; thus, an image on the retina of the eye is not
the knowledge of the image. The immateriality of intellection has
slightly different scientific consequences, the most significant of
which is that one cannot discover any *organ of thought* as such.
However, this statement must be carefully qualified. Although there
is no organ of thought—and we are here taking this statement in its
strict analytic meaning, namely, that the intellective power is not the
form of an organ—all of the internal senses might be conveniently
considered as "organs of thought" in a *scientific* context. Thus, one
might look upon thought, from an experimental point of view,
as a "function of the brain" without contradicting any philosophical conclusions. In fact, owing to the dependence of the intellect
upon imagery in all of its operations (a fact which will be developed
in the next chapter), thought is by no means an independent variable
in the thought-imagery frame of reference. The intellect, in other
words, is in no way an isolated Cartesian-like "mind."

In this context, reference might be made to T. V. Moore's survey
of pathological data concerning severe organic damages and their
consequent hindrance of thought activity (*Cognitive Psychology*,
pp. 3–73). Having found different instances of damage to every
single part of the nervous system, and noting that some other neurological center takes over at least to some extent the function of the
damaged part, thus permitting at least some distinctively intellectual
activity, Moore concludes that "there is no place in the nervous system where we can hope to find a point center of mental life to which
all perceptions must be referred and from which all control of conduct must proceed" (p. 73). This statement confirms experimentally
(but does not prove philosophically) that there is no single organ of
thought.

3

THE IMAGINATION AND
THE INTELLECT

FROM AN ANALYTIC POINT OF VIEW, the image is the product of the
power of imagination or sense memory and represents past sensations. Functionally, however, the complexity of images and the
physiological aspects of the power from which they proceed give rise
to new questions concerning human behavior. Seen in this perspective, the image has a plethora of effects.

THE IMAGE AND BEHAVIOR

Association of images, a broad term which may here be used to
designate the formation of image groups and their actual recall,
affords one framework for examining the function of the image in
consciousness. Complex images become established through the
similarity or dissimilarity of one image to another in some respect;
or through contiguity, their proximity in time or place.[1] Deliberate
recall, aroused emotions, and present perceptions are the chief
causes operative in the recall of such images in ordinary experience.
Images can normally be controlled, and disciplined thinking depends

to no small extent upon such control. But even the normal person whose cognitive processes are well adjusted to reality lets his thoughts wander, thus allowing free association of images, caused largely by present perceptions. Literature has exploited this facet of human behavior in the stream-of-consciousness technique, and the analysis of associated patterns as revealed in dreams is a well-known method of studying behavioral problems. Instances of more or less complete loss of rational control over association bring us into the area of behavior where varying degrees of autistic thinking manifest themselves, sometimes culminating in total loss of control over reality. Although images are not thoughts, sensory association of images can evidently result in a more or less parallel succession of thoughts, whether in normal or psychotic behavior.

Perceptual experience suggests another group of problems that can be centered around the function of the image. We have already noted how images from past experience enter into an immediate perception. But there are wide variations in the area of perception, just as there are in the case of association. In normal conditions the contribution of past sensations to present perceptions aids in the concrete judgment of such things as depth, distance, and size. Thus, one person can become a better judge in this area than another, owing perhaps ultimately to individual differences especially in sensory equipment and emotional balance. Although the possibility of perceptual error is already introduced at this level of normal behavior, natural or artificial collocations of perceptual conditions can lead to consistent illusion on the part of a large group of persons. Such *illusion* can still be called normal, as long as the conditions are considered. From this point on, the function of imagery in perception can be looked upon as shading off into various degrees of abnormality, in which imagery of the past or perhaps images of one's own creation are grossly confused with the actual data of sense. Such *hallucinations* can involve images of any of the general types of data presented through the different external senses.

Again, we might look at the ways in which imagery can function in the twilight zones of consciousness, in a *subconscious* or *unconscious* fashion. The gradual building of an image or of image patterns results in the formation of highly connotative imagery that has a definite influence on behavior. Automatic fear or anxiety in a given situation, or habitual emotional reactions toward a certain person or object spring from such images ingrained in consciousness. Behavior of this sort can be traced, in terms of the human structure, to the complexus of internal sensation and to such factors as the contribution of the sensory emotions to the image's formation, through the agency of the discursive sense and the imagination.[2] Often such image patterns can be consciously attended to by a shift of attention, even though they might influence ordinary behavior at the *subconscious* level. One can generally discover upon deliberate reflection, for instance, why he is nervous before an important test or why he reacts unfavorably to a certain person.

But once again we are met with varied degrees of subliminal imagery, for in some instances a certain image pattern might become totally *unconscious,* so that a person cannot by any effort of attention call the image to consciousness and subject it to rational control. Analytically speaking, the image is in a state of act in the power of imagination; but the individual is not actually *aware* of the image because the internal unifying sense, the seat of sensory awareness, is not operating concomitantly with the cognitive power of imagination.[3]

A few examples will illustrate the effects of unconscious image patterns. The "three faces of Eve" type of abnormality affords a popular instance of an extreme psychosis in which distinct image-sets function in separate behavioral patterns, thus producing the phenomenon of multiple personality. The distinct patterns of imagery in this particular case could apparently come into contact from only one direction; Eve White was for quite some time unaware of the existence of Eve Black, while the latter personality had some control over the former.[4] Unconscious imagery, however, need not result in radical psychoses but might be restricted to only one very limited area of behavior. Impotency and frigidity are often conditions of this type; in spite of the individual's efforts to overcome the condition rationally, sensory images that cannot be consciously reached exert their emotional and physiological effects. Cure of the wide variety of mental conditions rooted in unconscious imagery entails among other things bringing the subliminal images to the person's conscious attention by various therapeutic means, thus helping him to reorganize and gain rational control over them.[5]

Behavioral disorders centered around imagery of various types are by no means always psychogenic, since actual *organic damage* is the primary factor in many cases. Damage to the organ of the memory-imagination, for instance, can result in partial or total loss of the ability to retain or to recall past experience (the functions of the operative power of imagination). Thus, in certain types of aphasia, a person is unable to *recall* some areas of past experience, while experiences occurring since the appearance of the condition (which might be psychic as well as organic in origin) are retained and readily recalled. In other cases the pathological disorder affects the *retentive* ability while the other mnemonic function remains. This condition may come in a more mild form simply with the deterioration of the organism through age, as is illustrated by old people who readily recall experiences from the distant past but fail to retain the most recent of experiences. Severe concussion can, of course, impair both mnemonic functions.[6]

The foregoing discussion of the effects of the image on behavior together with its gathering of psychopathological data has been introduced for several reasons. It is important to note, first, the number of directions from which the function of imagery in consciousness can be approached; and almost any approach suggests the complexity of the problems that are inevitably met. It is clear, too, that psychological abnormalities affecting perception, association, and one's control over reality can seriously hamper learning.

But the above discussions of various phenomena of consciousness do not *solve* any behavioral problems. The reason for this is that the philosophical method of analysis is simply not oriented to this end.

Data can be gathered which will throw some light on the real nature of man, especially with respect to the complexity of the structure of human consciousness. This data can then be organized and interpreted in terms of the operative powers that contribute to the behavioral pattern as it is actually observed. In some cases, a philosophical analysis of this sort may suggest a means of approaching behavioral data experimentally; this is the possible heuristic function that the philosophical method can serve.[7] A complete study of the image's role in behavior, however, cannot be undertaken without the aid of the scientific method. For behavior entails patterns of activity, and the study of behavioral patterns in its turn involves the technique of selective abstraction along with all of its methodological consequences. Functional relationships *between* activities or series of activities are the immediate object of an experimental inquiry, and not the nature of *an* activity.

Hence, the type of approach taken in the preceding pages serves in a somewhat negative way to focus attention upon the kind of question that will be dealt with in the present chapter. Far from ignoring the behavioral aspect of image patterns, we must grant its importance and its complexity. But we shall also prescind from it, for it is not directly relevant to the matter at hand. We are still concerned with the structure of knowledge, or more explicitly with one aspect of that structure: how does the image function in an act of understanding? This general statement of the question indicates that relationships between *distinct* activities are not of concern here. Rather, there is question of the nature of a cognitive operation and of the operative powers—analytically but not experientially distinct— that contribute to a single unified act of knowledge.

Since every act of understanding is properly an act of intellect, the causal relationship in question is that which exists between image and intellect. The task of the present chapter, accordingly, will be to examine this relationship in the light of different types of knowing. The image, considered in its special relationship to the operative power of intellect, will be designated by the term *phantasm*.

THE PHANTASM AND THE INTELLECT

In the perspective of knowledge considered as a total experience, man understands things about reality. Elaborating this primitive fact from a psychological point of view, we observed in Chapter Two how the intellect in some way gets its conceptual or abstract knowledge through the agency of the external and internal senses, especially through the product of the power of imagination—the image or phantasm. Thus, at least in *perceptual* knowledge there is a dependence of the intellect upon the phantasm. Before examining the nature of this relationship, it will be necessary to see how far this dependence extends. At first sight, it would seem that once the intellect had some working data supplied it by the senses, it could pull away from the particularities of sensory phantasms in its exercise of *abstract* reasoning. In fact, detachment from the purely sensible would seem to be a requisite for any sort of intellectual generalization.

In the course of his writings, Thomas Aquinas frequently turned his attention to this problem, which was quite pertinent in his day owing to the prevalence of Platonic teaching with its emphasis on purely intelligible objects of knowledge. In an article in the *Summa Theologiae*,[8] Aquinas presents the problem whittled down to its essential shape, and his discussion will provide a good framework for our subsequent considerations. The question having been proposed whether the intellect can understand without phantasms, Thomas answers that

it is impossible for the intellect in its present state of union with a corruptible body to have actual understanding of a thing unless it turn to phantasms. Two evidences illustrate this fact.

First of all, since the intellect is a power that does not in itself employ a bodily organ, it would in no way be hindered in its activity by damage done to an organ if its act did not require the act of some power that does make use of a bodily organ. Now such organs are employed by the senses, the imagination, and the other powers belonging to the sensitive order. Hence, it is evident that for the intellect actually to understand—not only when it attains new knowledge, but also when it uses knowledge already acquired—there is need for an act of the imagination and the other sense powers. For when the activity of the imagination is obstructed by a damaged bodily organ (as in mentally diseased persons) or, again, when the activity of the memory is hindered (as in the case of drowsiness), we observe that a person is prevented from actually understanding even those things that he already knows.

Secondly, as anyone can observe from personal experience, when he is trying to understand something, he forms phantasms of some sort to serve as examples; and in these he as it were sees what he wants to understand. Thus it is that, when we wish to help a person understand something, we present examples to him, in order that from these he can form phantasms for the purpose of understanding.

Modern scientific data such as that cited at the opening of this chapter has provided a more rigorous confirmation of the first experiential evidence adduced to indicate the dependence of the intellect upon phantasms. Thus, we can add the innumerable varieties of psychogenic disorder in the internal senses to the physiological hindrances suggested by Aquinas. His second evidence directly implies one function of the teacher in learning, a notion that will be developed further on in our study. In the remainder of the same article, Thomas moves from the *experiential* to the *causal* level, sketching the reasons for this dependence in terms of the natural structure of man.

The reason for this fact is that a knowing power is proportioned to the thing known. Hence, the proper object of an angelic intellect, which is completely separate from a body, is an intelligible substance separate from a body; and through intelligible objects of this sort the angel knows material things. The human intellect, on the other hand, which is united to a body, has as its proper object a quiddity[9] or nature existing in corporeal matter; and through such natures of visible things the human intellect rises to some knowledge of things that are not visible.

Now it is characteristic of such a nature to exist in an individual thing that has no existence apart from corporeal matter. For instance, it belongs to the nature of a stone to be in this particular stone, and to the nature of a horse to be in this particular horse, and so on. Hence, the nature of a stone or of any other material thing cannot be known completely and truly unless it be known as existing in the particular. And we apprehend the particular through sense and imagination.

Thus, for the intellect actually to understand its proper object, it must necessarily turn to phantasms in order to perceive a universal nature existing in the particular. If however the proper object of our intellect were a separated form, or if, as the Platonists assert, the forms of sensible things subsisted apart from particulars, our intellect would not always have to turn to phantasms in an act of understanding.[10]

It is worthwhile to recall the various facts of experience that come into play in the present context. Intellectual knowledge considered in itself is in no way material or reducible to any type of sense cognition. While this fact as elaborated in Chapter Two must stand intact, it must also be integrated with the experiential and scientific evidences indicating that there is never any instance in which sensory disorder does not impede the activity of thought.

Now, a further examination of the kind of knowledge we are able to have reveals that all human cognition, including abstract knowledge in the sciences, depends in some way upon experience of material reality. Aquinas suggests this in his remark that whatever knowledge man has of things that are not immediately present to the senses he has because of his experience of sensible reality. Thus, without experience of bodies in motion, man could not conceive the development of a mechanical physics; or if behavior were never experienced, a science of behavior would be inconceivable. Again, if man did not have some basic grasp of series of things, a science of number could not be constructed; nor could the mathematician postulate the hypothetical existence of any mathematical object unless he at some time had experience of actual existence. The single point at issue in all of these examples is that, when our fundamental experience of reality is abstractively refined or even directly denied for some scientific purpose, the refinement or denial would be basically unintelligible without the prior experience of that which is abstractively refined or denied.

If these facts are read in the light of what has already been established concerning the composite nature of man, they can be summarized in terms of the object *proper* or *proportioned* to the human intellect by reason of its natural constitution. For, to state that the proper object of the intellect of man is an intelligible aspect of some sensible thing is only to state, in terms of that intellect's nature, that whatever man knows he knows ultimately because of his direct, meaningful experience of concrete reality. To draw further attention to this fact, Aquinas contrasts the object of the human intellect with what we are able to ascertain concerning the kind of knowledge had by the angelic intellect, which as pure form is not united to a body. The essential point of the comparison is that any conceptual knowledge having its radical origins apart from experience of reality is knowledge foreign to the nature of man. Such knowledge is in fact not found in human experience and, considering the composite nature of man, the reason that it is not found becomes apparent.[11]

In this broader light of the natural structure of human understanding, the experientially discovered dependence of thought activity upon phantasms also becomes clear. If the intellect is to understand its proper object, which is some intelligible aspect of a particular existent (the prepositional phrase is especially operative here), it must see its abstract conception in the phantasms that psychologically represent the object in its individuality. The nature known by the intellect does not subsist in itself, but only in the real object. Hence, the intellect's knowledge of its proper object in that object's reality necessitates a turning to the phantasms which represent the particularized reality of the object.[12]

The consistent dependence of the intellect upon phantasms is not too difficult to establish where *direct knowledge* of concrete reality —the proper object of the human intellect, in other words—is in question. But does the same thing remain true in the case of more *abstract and scientific knowledge,* which is often far removed from the particularities of sense data? In approaching an answer to this question, we might recall Aquinas' second evidence in the above text, where he calls attention to the way in which we create concrete examples in attempting to understand something. In a similar vein, contemporary theorists have advanced and developed the point that "original thought *always* depends, both for its form and for its content, on past perceptions, and quite often on past perceptions of a very concrete kind."[13] We shall consider this matter in more detail later on; for the present, a few evidences from immediate experience will illustrate the point.

It is difficult deliberately to call up an abstractive visual or audial phantasm, in which some indefinable shape or symbol or sound represents a broad area of associations, without concretizing the phantasm in the very act of deliberately calling it forth. Moreover, when we are engaged in abstract thinking, we are directly aware of what we are thinking about, and not of phantasms. But at certain points more definite phantasms do present themselves. In reading and writing, for instance, the intellect works with verbal phantasms that are always on the fringe of awareness. Or when we are engaged in conversation over some issue, we find that at certain points we become aware of some external object which might be involved in the conversation; or of complex series of images that represent the subject of the conversation; or of certain key words in our statements or particular gestures that keep attention focused upon what we are attempting to express. "Losing the train of thought," in fact, is nothing more than allowing irrelevant phantasms to interrupt the chain of thought. Hence, though we are not always immediately aware of phantasms, experience does not reveal any instances of thinking in which phantasms are *absent;* and, far from being a detriment, they prove themselves to be a positive aid to understanding and creativity.[14]

The reason for this can once again be seen if, moving to the causal level, we integrate these various evidences with the nature of human understanding. It is a direct corollary of the human intellect's dependence upon sense experience for the origins of all its knowledge that the intellect of man can understand only those things the intelligibility of which is made manifest through sense data. For concrete reality is the only storehouse of meaning from which man can ultimately draw. Now the scientific refinement and meaningful development of the intelligibility primitively grasped by the human intellect in its proper object does not negate this dependence upon matter. The intellect can operate only according to its determined nature, and the nature of its operation is determined by its essential union with a material body. As dependent in its operations upon matter, consequently, the intellect can grasp actual meaning only through the use of phantasms. Hence, *one idea cannot give rise to another* without phantasms; and the linking of meanings in processes of thought, however abstract, depends every step of the way upon phantasms.[15]

Now, the gradual and variegated symbolification of sense data that is requisite for more abstract and scientific thinking does not alter the sensory nature of the phantasm, which always remains in some way particularized. But neither does this sensory and abstractive or symbolic refinement of concrete data represented in phantasms destroy the meaning that the intellect is able to know through phantasms, for symbolic phantasms are often most pregnant with potential meaning. There is, consequently, neither *experiential* nor *theoretical* contradiction involved in asserting that the human intellect must make use of phantasms in every act of understanding, and that the blocking of the sensory processes which build the phantasm will impede both the conception and the use of intellectual knowledge. Thus, far from serving an ephemeral function in the mere conception of an idea, phantasms endure as a foundation for all of the processes of thought.[16]

The intellect's dependence upon phantasms has been elaborated in some detail, since the *fact* of such dependence is evidently the groundwork for any further discussion.[17] Before we look at the role played by the image in different acts of understanding, it will be necessary to give a more precise statement of the relationship that exists between image and intellect.

THE CAUSAL RELATIONSHIP

Retracing our steps for a moment, we might take another glance at the cognitive situation. Knowledge, as we saw in Chapter Two, is an intentional union between knower and object; and the union is achieved by a formal and dynamic determination that specifies the knower to an actual knowledge of the particular thing known. Now, how is this causal determination-to-act produced in the knower?

On the *sensory* level there is no difficulty. The material things that we know act directly on the organs of sense. The occurrence of the stimulus, as we have seen, produces a two-fold effect—the physical modification of the sense organ itself *and* the causal determination of the power to particularized knowledge of the thing affecting the sense.[18] Although internal sense knowledge is much more complex than that had by the external senses, the dynamic determination is produced in the same way; for the internal sense organs are also affected by neurophysiological stimuli.

The *intellect,* on the other hand, is strictly immaterial; in itself, it possesses no sensory organ, even though it needs the imagination in order to operate. Hence, the phantasm, which carries the particularities of concrete objects and presents the knowable object to the intellect, cannot itself act on the intellect and cause the intellect to be determined-to-act in the same way that material things impress themselves on sense powers. For there is nothing material upon which the phantasm can impress itself. The problem thus becomes a metaphysical one of efficient causality between two distinct ontological orders—the material and the strictly immaterial.

It would be well to recall what the content of intellectual knowledge is. Through his intellective power, man knows things as meaningful, as intelligible. Now meaning, as we saw in Chapter Two, is not extended in space and time; its real character depends upon its being *non*-physical, in contrast to the material particularity of sense cognition. Concrete reality is nonetheless *potentially* meaningful— that is, it *can* be known in an intelligible, non-particularized way. But the *actual* intelligibility of sensible things depends upon the disengagement of that meaning from the particularities of matter. Once again, though meanings are drawn from experience of matter and occur in consciousness along with a sensory image, a meaning does not include knowledge of matter in its sensory particularities; thus, I am thinking about man, but what any particular man looks like has nothing to do with my thoughts. Now, the concrete object is the cause of intellectual knowledge in the sense that the intellect here and now conceives the meaning of *this* object and not another. But, since it is material, a sensible object cannot cause *itself* to be meaningfully, immaterially, intelligibly known.

These facts, then, call for an efficient cause of knowledge that may render potentially meaningful things actually intelligible. Or, to say this in another way, there must exist a causal agent in virtue of which the presence of the phantasm can result in the intellect's being formally determined to an actual understanding of what the phantasm represents. Now a material phantasm, as was indicated above, cannot itself produce immaterial knowledge, any more than a desk in itself can generate a flower; once again, there is question of two different ontological orders. Consequently, since the determining principle produced in the intellect by this agent as well as the intellect itself and the resultant intellectual knowledge are all strictly immaterial, the efficient cause or agent in question must be strictly immaterial. Finally, the immaterial *agent* belongs to the *intellective* soul of man, for it is this individual man who has intellectual knowledge. On the basis of these facts, the immaterial efficient cause of intellectual knowledge may be denominated the *agent intellect*.[19]

It is important to call attention to a number of facts concerning this analysis. First, the agent intellect is not what we normally refer to in talking about "intellect," nor does it bring to the phantasm any knowledge-content. In short, it is not a *knowing* power. The various facts drawn from experience that lead us to recognize the existence of an agent intellect enable us to establish only that it is the immaterial efficient cause of the immaterial knowledge had by the cognitive intellect (often called the "possible intellect").

Secondly, the agent intellect does not affect or "do anything to" the phantasm. In freer language borrowed from our experience of motion, we are inclined to speak of the agent intellect as a thing which "draws meaning" or "disengages intelligibility" or "abstracts intelligible *species* from" phantasms. However, as Aquinas remarks, the real effect of the agent intellect is the production of the formal principle or intelligible *species* by which the cognitive intellect actually understands what the phantasm represents, "not that one and the same form previously in phantasms is subsequently in the possible intellect, like a body taken from one place and transferred to another."[20]

Thirdly, the distinction between agent and possible intellect is made only on the analytic basis of differences in *function* and in formal object. The object of the agent intellect, in this frame of reference, is that which is potentially intelligible, while the object of the cognitive intellect is that which is actually intelligible.[21] The two powers do not operate *separately,* any more than do the other cognitive powers that contribute to the experienced unity of knowledge activity.

At this point, one may see *how* the causal relationship between intellect and phantasm is made possible. Any time the intellect actually understands something, it must be brought to consider that particular meaning through the causality of the agent intellect which either brings from the state of memory[22] or produces the causal principle that determines the intellect to understand the meaning. Thus, the activity of the agent intellect is necessary for the intellect to understand, somewhat in the way that light is necessary for the eye to see colors.[23]

But the *phantasm* is also an *efficient cause* of intellectual knowledge. We have seen that it must be present in every act of understanding. Now, if we integrate this fact with the analysis just completed, it becomes clear that phantasms play the part of representing in some way the potential meaning that the intellect actually understands. Hence, if *both* the agent intellect and the phantasm are necessary efficient causes of knowledge, our problem becomes: *what* is the causal relationship between the two?

In attempting to answer this question, we shall have to proceed by way of analogy and settle ultimately for a useful description, since we simply have no other direct experience of an immaterial and a material or sensory cause concurring in a single activity. An analogy from transient activity, which is more immediate to our experience, suggests itself.

Take a carpenter making a table. The carpenter has the knowledge requisite for designing the table, determining its width, height, and so on. The tools he uses can do the cutting, the trimming, the fastening. But the tools cannot make the table by themselves any more than the carpenter can realize his conception of the table without the tools. Now when the carpenter is, say, cutting a design into the table-top, both the carpenter and his chisel are producing the design. Within this single activity of carving, the meaningful design is properly the result of the carpenter's intelligence, while the carvings in the wood are properly the effect of the chisel. In one and the same operation of producing the design, consequently, there is a lower agent subordinated to the activity of a higher, though both agents are necessary for the resultant effect. The chisel can thus be denominated the *instrumental* cause of the design, while the carpenter as the higher agent is the *principal* cause.

The relationship between agent intellect and phantasm can be described in similar terms. Since the phantasm is not sufficient in itself to cause understanding even though it represents the potentially intelligible object, it is the *instrumental* cause of intellectual knowledge. Its proper effect within this single cognitive activity is the determined *content* of what is known. And since the agent intellect has the higher power of rendering the content represented in the phantasm actually intelligible while in itself it lacks any determined cognitive content, the agent intellect is the *principal* cause of intellectual knowledge. Its proper effect is the *actual meaningfulness* of what is known.[24]

Although speaking of the phantasm as an *instrument* of understanding is only an analogy, it is a useful one, for it calls attention to a significant characteristic of the phantasm's function in intellectual knowledge. The phantasm is never the thing that is *understood*, either in abstract thinking or in direct knowledge of concrete reality. The meaningful content or fruit of an act of understanding, as we have noted, is produced in a mental word;[25] and in abstract thinking, when an idea of one's own construction is being understood, the mental word is the immediate object of awareness. Thus, though we can rather easily *become* aware of the phantasm in such thought processes, it remains merely a tool for determining the intelligible content of the mental word. In direct perceptual knowledge of concrete things, it is difficult experientially to become aware of either the mental word or the phantasm, since the immediate focus of both sensory and intellectual attention is the thing itself. In such knowledge, to use a metaphor, the phantasm is quite like a transparency.

Hence, amid all the emphasis we shall be giving to the phantasm and its role in knowledge and learning, it is important to keep in mind that it remains a mental tool for understanding, just as all the powers and causal principles of cognition are only *means* by which man knows. For only the person has knowledge. A complete *psychological* statement of the structure of knowledge would, at this point of our analysis, have to embrace all of these principles of cognitive activity. But our primitive statement of knowledge considered as a *total experience* stands intact: "I know my desk."

NOTES

1. On the ways in which images are combined and the causes of their recall (combination and actual recall are not the same thing), see G. P. Klubertanz, S.J., *The Philosophy of Human Nature* (New York: Appleton-Century-Crofts, 1953), pp. 130–31, 141–42, 145.
2. See above, pp. 69–70.
3. On the unifying sense, see above, pp. 67–68.
4. For the history of this case, see Corbett H. Thigpen and Hervey M. Cleckley, *The Three Faces of Eve* (New York: McGraw-Hill, 1957).
5. Copious examples of different types of imagery and their effects on thinking and behavior are discussed throughout Peter McKellar,

Imagination and Thinking: A Psychological Analysis (New York: Basic Books, 1957). See also David Rapaport (ed.), *Organization and Pathology of Thought* (New York: Columbia University Press, 1951).

6. On abnormalities of perception and pathological disorders of memory, see T. V. Moore, *Cognitive Psychology* (Philadelphia: J. B. Lippincott, 1939), pp. 275–312, 412–28.

7. See chap. 1, esp. p. 39. E.g., European psychologists have found the continental Existentialists' analyses of experience fruitful for scientific and clinical purposes; the movement seems to be gaining in popularity in this country. For a recent statement of the tenets and procedural principles of existential psychoanalysis, see Rollo May (ed.), *Existence: A New Dimension in Psychiatry and Psychology* (New York: Basic Books, 1958).

8. The text quoted here is *S. T.* I, q. 84, a. 7; Latin text in Appendix, no. 1.

The whole of q. 84 is devoted to the problem of how man knows material reality, and among Thomas' discussions are to be found some of his most mature doctrinal syntheses and historical criticisms. The most prominent figures in this question are the materialist Democritus and the exaggerated realist Plato; against these especially, Aquinas sets his own teachings, often in the name of Aristotle, who "took a middle path." The argument proceeds cumulatively throughout the question. Having established the fact of intellectual knowledge which, though obtained from sensible things, is universal and necessary (involving the distinction between what is known and the way it is known; see p. 56), Thomas goes on to discuss the need for knowledge to be immaterial (a. 2) and the impossibility of innate knowledge in man (a. 3). This latter point, developed in the light of the intellect's essential union with a sensing body (a. 4), leads to a consideration of how the immaterial intellect receives genuine knowledge through the senses (aa. 5–6). It is in this context that the article quoted above appears: even though it is immaterial the intellect must not only *obtain* all knowledge through sense experience but must also employ sensory phantasms in every subsequent use of knowledge previously obtained.

9. For the meaning of "quiddity," "nature," and "universal" (further on in the text), see above, chapter 2, note 30.

10. This seems to be the earliest text among Aquinas' writings in which he states so explicitly that *any* time a universal is known it must be seen in phantasms. See G. P. Klubertanz, S.J., "St. Thomas and the

Knowledge of the Singular," *New Scholasticism,* XXVI (1952), 157; other texts that give slight indications of this teaching are given in *ibid.,* note 82.

Thomas' statements here do not imply that complete intellection is always judgmental, i.e., that the intellect consciously knows the relation of its proper object *to* a particular thing, a relationship that is actually part of the meaning as it is understood here and now (see below, pp. 119–23). The difference between conceptual and judgmental knowledge is not in question in this text, where Aquinas is interested in showing only that the human intellect, precisely as human, can understand only by turning to phantasms for its abstract knowledge. The terminology he uses here is quite general, and neither type of understanding is either excluded or explicitly included in the present context; on the type of terminology used to differentiate conceptual and judgmental knowledge, see below, chapter 4, note 15.

11. It is in a context similar to this that St. Thomas gives his final answers to doctrines of *innatism.* Knowledge had independently of sense experience could not be squared with the essential union of the human intellect with a material body. See *S. T.* I, q. 55, a. 2 (ed. Ottawa I, 339a7–14); q. 84, a. 3; q. 89, a. 1 (551a11–37).

Whether the existence of angels can be proved from reason alone may be disputed. But *if* pure intellective forms like angels do exist, then we can reason on the basis of what human knowledge is to the kind of knowledge they must have. Thomas' comparison, even if looked upon as a hypothetical illustration, is still meaningful (though it is not essential to the argument).

12. Although physical union with the physical particularity of the object is not possible in cognition, the object is nevertheless known as it is in itself, owing to the nature of the intentional union achieved. On this matter and on the equivocation that can be involved in speaking of knowledge of a thing "as it is in itself," see above, chapter 2, note 15.

13. McKellar, *Imagination and Thinking,* p. 74.

14. The experiential fact that thinking does not take place without phantasms receives some negative confirmation from experimental studies on what is usually called *imageless thought.* Though these studies have generally been oriented toward proving that images are not thoughts or meanings, the difficulties that arise in attempting to establish this point scientifically serve to confirm the facts established above.

T. V. Moore, for example, conducted a series of experiments on this question, proceeding on the hypothesis that, if meaning and image are identical, the meaning must always arise in consciousness *with* the image and not *before* or *after* it. Trained subjects were told to indicate their consciousness of the meaning of the word or picture flashed before them, and in other instances to indicate the appearance of a visual or kinesthetic or verbal image. Comparison of reaction-times revealed that meaning was generally reported more quickly and thus that it appeared *prior* to the type of imagery involved. An equation of meaning with imagery was thus denied. (For a summary of these experiments, together with references to the psychological reviews in which the studies were originally reported, see Moore, *Cognitive Psychology*, pp. 334–49.)

However, the *hypothesis itself* may be weak. If an act of thought is dependent in every instance on a phantasm, it is possible that meaning *does* come with the image, which would then be psychologically identical with the word or picture on the printed card flashed before the subject. The subject would not be able, in a reaction-time study, to distinguish this perceptual phantasm from the intelligibility conceived—or, if it would be possible to observe anything at all, the meaning would be seen to appear *after the phantasm* that presented the potential meaning. More time would naturally be involved in calling up a more concrete image, or in converting a verbal into a visual image. On this basis, one might suggest that a study like Moore's proves the following: whatever appears in consciousness more quickly is not to be equated with what appears less quickly. From a scientific point of view, the former might be a less complex image than the latter, and not a meaning at all.

The "imageless thought" controversy has for the most part faded from the scientific scene, owing largely to the behaviorists' rejection of introspective evidence. For a survey of other experiments on this matter, most of which were done in the earlier part of this century, see Robert Leeper, "Cognitive Processes," *Handbook of Experimental Psychology*, ed. S. S. Stevens (New York: Wiley & Sons, 1951), pp. 732–33.

15. "A *sensible* effect is such that it can *by itself* lead to knowledge of something else; for it is the primary and direct object of human knowledge, all our knowledge taking its origin from the senses. *Intelligible* effects, on the other hand, are of such a nature that they can lead to knowledge of something else only to the extent that they are made manifest *by another* thing, that is, by some sensible object." *S. T.* III, q. 60, a. 4, ad 1; Latin text in Appendix, no. 2.

The approach to this matter by way of the intellect's *determined nature* is correlative to the analysis by *proper object* as in the text quoted on pp. 96–98. For this approach, see *Summa contra Gentiles,* Bk. II, end of chap. 73 (text quoted below, chapter 4, note 19); this lengthy chapter contains elaborate discussions of the phantasm's role in understanding and many historical considerations. Cf. *S. T.* I, q. 89, a. 1, where Aquinas directly compares the operations of the intellect as essentially united to the body and the quite different operations of separated intellects.

16. This notion is developed in the following text, where Aquinas also mentions that in the case of "divine science" (an Aristotelian term for metaphysics or natural theology) the phantasm must be present as a tool of thought even though the materiality of what it represents is *denied* in an intellectual judgment:

"The phantasm is the principle of our knowledge, as that from which the intellect's operation begins; it is not a fleeting thing, but rather remains as a kind of foundation of intellectual activity, just as principles of demonstration must remain in every procedure of science. For phantasms are related to the intellect as objects in which the intellect sees whatever it does see, whether through a perfect representation or through a negation. And hence, when knowledge of phantasms is obstructed, the intellect's knowledge must be totally obstructed even in divine science. For it is evident that we cannot know that God is the cause of bodies or transcends all bodies or is not a body, unless we could imagine bodies. But a judgment about things that are divine is not formed according to the way we imagine these things." *Commentary on Boethius' De Trinitate,* q. 6, a. 2, ad 5; Latin text in Appendix, no. 3.

17. The fact of the intellect's dependence on phantasms appears in Aquinas' earliest writings. However, as his use of the philosophical method gradually matures, Thomas bases the notion more and more directly on experience and thus draws out the fuller implications of this dependence. For a study of the development of Aquinas' thought on this matter, see T. W. Guzie, S.J., "Evolution of Philosophical Method in the Writings of St. Thomas," *Modern Schoolman,* XXXVII (Jan., 1960), 103–118.

18. On the double change in sensation, see above, pp. 66–67.

19. The metaphysical reasons for recognizing the existence of an immaterial cause of knowledge are non-existent in a reductionist frame of reference; in such a context, however, the nature of either intellectual or sense knowledge as revealed in experience is denied.

Aquinas in several places discussed the *historical aspects* of this problem. In *S. T.* I, q. 79, a. 3, he treats the agent intellect in reference to the Platonic theory of ideas, in which no efficient agent is necessary owing to the separate existence of intelligible Forms (cf. the innatism of modern Rationalism). Since, however, abstract natures exist only in particular things, such an agent is necessary to render potentially intelligible sense data actually intelligible. An even more thorough historical study is made in q. 84, a. 6. In addition to the Platonic doctrine Thomas here discusses Democritus' theory, which denies genuine intellectual knowledge and attempts to reduce all cognition to atomistic impressions of material objects on the mind (cf. Lockean and Humean empiricism). In this context, Aquinas stresses the insufficiency of the sensory phantasm to cause nonsensory knowledge in itself without the concomitant operation of an immaterial cause. These two texts complement each other in thus elucidating the necessity of an immaterial cause of intellectual knowledge, in the light of a radical *intellectualism* on the one hand and sense *empiricism* on the other.

Thomas speaks of the agent intellect in innumerable contexts, often using highly formal and sometimes mechanical descriptions to designate its functions, presupposing that his reader knows what he is talking about (an unfortunate assumption, considering what his commentators have done with this matter). The *metaphysical issue* is stated precisely and apart from all metaphors in *S. T.* I, q. 54, a. 4 (ed. Ottawa I, 335b21–39).

20. "Virtute intellectus agentis resultat quaedam similitudo in intellectu possibili ex conversione intellectus agentis supra phantasmata, quae quidem est repraesentativa eorum quorum sunt phantasmata, solum quantum ad naturam speciei. Et per hunc modum dicitur abstrahi species intelligibilis a phantasmatibus, non quod aliqua eadem numero forma, quae prius fuit in phantasmatibus, postmodum fiat in intellectu possibili, ad modum quo corpus accipitur ab uno loco et transfertur ad alterum." *S. T.* I, q. 85, a. 1, ad 3 (ed. Ottawa I, 525b52–26a12).

21. See *S. T.* I, q. 79, a. 7.

22. See *ibid.* and above, p. 71.

23. Although Aquinas uses the *light analogy* quite freely, he is precise about its meaning, in contrast again to many of his commentators. Briefly, the "light of the agent intellect" is constructural language based on *extrinsic* analogy. Thomas remarks: If one holds the theory that light does not make colors actually visible but only illuminates

the medium (one theory current in Aquinas' day), we can say no more than that the presence of the agent intellect is *necessary for understanding* as the presence of light is necessary for seeing colors. But if one holds the theory (closer to that of our own day) that light renders the colors themselves actually visible, i.e., makes them to be actual colors, then we can say that the agent intellect is the *cause of actual meaning* as light is the cause of actual color. It is important to note that this discussion (taken from *S. T.* I, q. 79, a. 3, ad 2) explicitly limits the notion of light to an analogy; and the precise extent to which the analogy can be applied to the agent intellect is expressly stated. The comparison was originally used by Aristotle (*De Anima* III, v, 430a15).

One reason for the frequent use of this analogy among medieval thinkers might be that speaking of the "light of the agent intellect" illuminating the phantasm has less connotation of transient activity than does an expression like the agent intellect "acting on" or "abstracting from" the phantasm; the latter shorthand descriptions, as noted above, have a misleading semantic character.

A second reason for this comparison might be owing to the ancient and medieval notion of light, which was looked upon as an immaterial or spiritual entity. (St. Thomas, e.g., thought that no physical change takes place in the sense of sight; see *S. T.* I, q. 78, a. 3.) Hence, light provided an apropos analogy for the immateriality of the intellect—a comparison that is not as connotative to the modern mind in our day of scientific theories of light based on more complete experimental data.

24. Aquinas frequently uses the analogy from principal and instrumental causality in transient action to describe the concurrence of a subordinate and a higher cause in a single operation; e.g., see *S. T.* III, q. 19, a. 1, where the analogy is developed at some length. Thomas employs the analogy with reference to the phantasm-agent intellect relationship in *Quaestiones Quodlibetales,* VIII, q. 2, a. 1. When he is talking simply about a composite operation of two powers, prescinding for the most part from the *effect* of the operation, St. Thomas will often compare the operation to substance and speak of the relation of one power to the other as similar to the relationship between form and matter. E.g., the act of free choice (involving both intellect and will) is developed from this point of view in *S. T.* I–II, q. 13, a. 1; cf. also the description of a sense power as form, its organ as matter (above, p. 67). A matter-form analogy in connection with the intellect-phantasm relationship is im-

plied in *S. T.* I, q. 84, a. 6 (ed. Ottawa I, 520a47–b19), where in the context of this relationship sense knowledge is described as being, not the complete and perfect cause of intellectual knowledge, but rather in a certain sense the *materia causae* (note that it is not the phantasm itself but *sensibilis cognitio* which is thus described).

In our context, the analogy of principal-instrumental cause is more useful, because the *effect* of the concurrence of agent intellect and phantasm, namely, intellectual knowledge, is directly involved, and because the phantasm in itself is not a power. The matter-form analogy is more useful, as was suggested, in describing and emphasizing the operational composition of intellectual and sensory knowledge in general. Aquinas himself will sometimes mingle the two analogies, e.g., in *S. T.* I–II, q. 17, a. 4, where the composition of the imperium and commanded act is discussed; and in *S. T.* I, q. 78, a. 1 (472b9–15), where he speaks of corporeal nature being related to the soul of man as *materia et instrumentum*.

For a more complete textual study of the principal-instrumental analogy, see James S. Albertson, S.J., "Instrumental Causality in St. Thomas," *New Scholasticism,* XXVIII (1954), 409–35.

25. On the mental word and its different functions in perceptual knowledge and abstract thinking, see above, pp. 65–66.

4

THE PHANTASM
IN JUDGMENT

MUCH AS LIVING ORGANISMS attain their perfection by a process of gradual growth, the human intellect acquires knowledge of things in a gradual fashion. Confronted with the meaningfulness of things through perception, man's primitive knowledge, confused and imperfect, is gradually perfected as he works his way from one aspect of a thing to another, reasoning to a better understanding of the world about him. This developmental procession of thought is a consequence of the human condition, of the intellect's essential union with the body. It is connoted in calling man a rational animal, for *rational* means more than a fusion of intelligence with animality; it also designates the way a man must get his knowledge.

While we are actually engaged in a process of thinking or reasoning, it is evident that an understanding of the new meaning toward which the reasoning process is directed has not yet been achieved. Even when one already knows, for example, *what* the solution to a complex mathematical problem is, he does not know *why* it is the solution until he has actually thought it out. As a type of intellectual act, consequently, reasoning is an imperfect act, ordered to the more perfect and more complete act of understanding that embraces the new meaning. It is an act of acquiring, not one of actually possessing.[1]

Reasoning is, of course, intimately associated with intellectual learning, and its psychological implications require exploration. Lying at the heart of any reasoning or thinking process, however, are acts of *judgment*. Hence, as a final preparation for launching into an analysis of the complex activity designated by the term *learning*, it will be necessary to examine the structure of judgment; and, pursuing our original course, we shall center our analysis around the role of the phantasm in this act of understanding.

THE PSYCHOLOGICAL STATUS OF JUDGMENT

In Chapter Two, the notion of *symbol* was employed to illustrate the unity of cognitive experience—how in a single but complex psychological act man can grasp many meaningful aspects of an object.[2] This analysis may now be brought to bear upon the problem of judgment.

An essential point in our original analysis of communicative symbols was that numerous elements that are logically distinct can contribute to the formation of a single symbol, thus oriented toward the conception of a single meaning. Hence, the word "desk" can be a symbol in itself, leading one to conceive the meaning of what a desk is; in this case the logical significance of the word can be equated with its psychological function. If, on the other hand, the articulation of the word "desk" is accompanied by a pointing gesture indicating some particular desk, this new symbol has quite a different meaning. Here the word + gesture (for words are not the only kind of symbol) signifies a mental judgment, which might be verbally formulated to read "that object is a desk." The logical meaning of "desk" has become subordinated to a particular psychological situation in which that meaning functions as only a part of the symbol and as part of the correspondent meaning conceived by the perceiver. This subordination becomes even more clear in such a judgment as "that desk of mine is really ancient." The logical meaning of "desk" here plays a minimal psychological role—in fact, it does little more than designate an object. What my auditor really attends to is what I have *judged* about the object (which happens to be a desk), that it is a relic.

An analysis of this sort reveals a fact of consciousness that can be looked at in several ways. It is clear that a logical scrutiny of propositions will not throw much light on the psychological status of judgment, at least initially. For when we actually understand a symbolic communication, whether it be written or spoken or articulated in some other way, we are not directly conscious of sentences with subjects and predicates or, in general, of the parts of a symbol of communicaton. What we are immediately aware of is a *meaning*, even if it be a mistaken one.

The matter of awareness of meaning can be approached from a slightly different angle, by considering the operation of the mind itself.

Just as unity of term is required for unity of movement, so unity of object is required for unity of operation.

Now it is possible that several things be taken either as several or as one, like the parts of a continuous whole. If any part is considered in itself, the parts are *many* and hence are not grasped in one operation, nor all at once through sense and intellect.

But in another way, the parts are taken as forming *one whole,* and thus they are known together in one operation, through both sense and intellect. This holds true as long as the entire continuous whole is considered, as is stated in Book Three of the *De Anima.*[3] It is in this way that our intellect understands a subject and predicate together, as being parts of one proposition; and also two things being compared, according to their agreement in one point of comparison.[4]

We have already seen, at least in germ, most of the points mentioned by Aquinas here, and his discussion will enable us to integrate various facts of consciousness. The parts of a symbol or object of knowledge are not unified in knowledge as long as they are considered precisely as parts. Thus, we can focus our attention on the subject of a proposition alone, or on a single figure in a work of art. But to be aware of the parts as forming one whole is to know them together;

the parts can no longer be known in detail as long as the whole is considered, but only in their relation to the whole.

Thus, the individual figures in a work of art are seen as forming a totality, and it is the meaning of the totality and not of the parts in themselves that is understood. Again, three pencils on my desk are known together as long as I attend solely to the fact that they are pencils. And, as we have been discussing, the subject and predicate of a proposition are known together as long as I am aware simply of the meaning of the proposition. Thus, when one object is being known—whether the object known be the whole or only a part of the thing—there is only one operation. We have already seen in Chapter Two and in analyzing the intellect's dependence upon phantasms how, in perceptual knowledge, this one operation is a composite act of sense and intellect.

St. Thomas compares the whole situation that we have been describing to external motion. As long as a body is moving to one place there is only one movement. But a further fact—or rather another aspect of the point that has been developed—comes to light. For, just as a body when it is moving to two places necessarily undergoes two distinct movements, so are there two different cognitive operations when there are two objects of knowledge. As can be seen in all of the illustrations used in the preceding paragraphs, we can be conscious of only *one meaning* at a time. This corollary of the analysis raises certain questions concerning judgment. What does it mean to say that the subject and predicate expressive of a judgment are understood "together"? That the individual meanings of the subject and of the predicate cannot be understood in a single mental operation is now sufficiently clear. What then *is* understood in a judgment?

In the example in which my desk was spoken of as being "really ancient," it was noted how my auditor would attend consciously not to the meaning of "desk" but first and foremost to the fact asserted by me that it is old. Or, looking at my own judgmental act apart from its expression, I understand a meaning and that meaning is understood *of* something, of the object before me. The object, which is a desk, is not understood in its total intelligibility as a desk; the desk here

and now is only vaguely and indeterminately apprehended as a desk
—as digitally indicated, as extended, as mine, and so on. The real
focus of intellectual attention is the meaning "really ancient," which
is judgmentally referred to the object. In terms of subject and predicate, therefore, the subject is precisely and determinately understood
in terms of the predicate; and hence, the psychological act of predication is an act in which a meaning is consciously understood *of*
something. Or, more simply, that which is understood in a unified
act of judgment is one *predicated meaning*.

The subject-predicate relationship will have to be examined further, but the preceding considerations will suffice for the present.
Enough evidence has been gathered to illustrate that only one meaning can be understood at a time and that that meaning can embrace
any number of the intelligible aspects of a thing which can be separately considered in different acts of understanding. Our reflections
on experience can now be gathered together and seen in terms of the
structure of consciousness—in terms of the *causal sources* of the
activities we have been considering. Aquinas summarizes his discussion from the article quoted above as follows:

> From this it is evident that many things, insofar as they are distinct,
> cannot be understood all at once; but insofar as they are grouped to-
> gether in an intelligible unity, they can be understood together.
> Now anything is actually intelligible insofar as its likeness[5] is in
> the intellect. Hence, all things that can be known through one in-
> telligible *species* are known as one intelligible object and thus are
> understood together. But those things that are known through dif-
> ferent intelligible *species* are apprehended as different intelligible
> objects.[6]

In an act of judging, then, the predicated meaning is formally carried in the causal principle or intelligible *species* that determines
the intellect to an actual understanding of that meaning. In one act
of judging I can understand that "this object is a desk," in another
that "the desk is really old." In each case there is a different causal
determination and a different mental word expressive of what is understood.[7] In the first judgment "desk" is formally known as the

predicated meaning. But in the second it is determinately known only in the light of the predicate, for "desk" is only the background against which its aged condition is thrown. In causal terms, "desk" is not formally known in the second judgment because the intellect is now dynamically determined by a different intelligible *species* to know precisely that the desk is a relic. In short, in a psychological perspective it is both experientially and theoretically impossible for one unified judgmental act to be a linking of two meanings or a combination of mental words.[8]

Now the single meaning understood in a judgment is not a concept. It is a predicated meaning—the intelligibility is consciously understood *of* something. Hence, any consideration of the psychological structure and process of judgment must take into account this distinctive *referential* character of an act of judging. The account can be made by integrating what we have seen about predicated meaning with the role of the phantasm in understanding. We shall first look at judgments made about concrete things and see, in the light of the phantasm's function, how judgment differs from conceptual knowledge. We can then go on to consider the somewhat more difficult problem of the judgmental process in abstract thinking, and the symbolic expression of judgment.

THE PHANTASM IN JUDGMENTAL AND CONCEPTUAL KNOWLEDGE

We may recall how, in any act of understanding, the object which can be meaningfully known must be presented for actual understanding through the instrumentality of the phantasm. In terms of judgment, then, the predicated meaning that the intellect actually understands is made possible by the phantasm, functioning as instrumental cause of the intelligible content of the judgment.

Now in direct judgmental knowledge of concrete reality, the meaning understood is predicated of some existent thing; and the object is determinately understood here and now only in the light of the predicated meaning. To express this same thing in terms of the intellect-phantasm relationship, the intellect actually understands one meaningful aspect of the object (recall that the meaning, though one, can be complex) and refers it to or predicates it of the object itself through the phantasm that instrumentally represents the potentially meaningful object. Or, to state the whole judgmental process more completely, the intellect, working in virtue of the agent intellect back through its formal determination or intelligible *species,* reflects to the phantasm, the enduring foundation of the meaning actually understood, and through the phantasm and sense powers knows that what it understands is realized concretely in a singular material existent. There is of course no question here of one power acting on another successively. Judgment, like any cognitive act, is one imma- nent operation to which many powers contribute; hence, the opera- tion cannot be broken down in immediate experience.[9]

The distinctive character of judgment can be brought to light by comparing it with purely *conceptual* knowledge. Experientially speaking, simple conceptual knowledge is not an everyday phe- nomenon. Conceptual understanding *occurs* primarily in disci- plined scientific thinking and is an aspect of what we often call "insight." It is most easily *discovered* in instances in which after considerable reflection the meaning of a thing is realized—for ex- ample, when the real meaning of "rational animal" as the definition of man is understood after all the pertinent evidence from experience has been carefully analyzed. In such knowledge (which also most clearly reveals the presence of a mental word in our thinking), the meaning is understood as it is *revealed* in phantasms; but the *relation* of the concept to any particular man or to any other meaning is not here and now understood. The intellect "abstracts from," does not actually consider this relationship, which is of the essence of judg- ment.[10]

Thus, in conceptual knowledge, the intellect is formally determined to understand some meaning without considering that meaning as related to or realized in anything else. But phantasms are necessary for the meaning actually to be conceived. This was Aquinas' point in the article quoted in Chapter Three, where we were considering the necessity for phantasms in any act of knowledge: completely human intellectual knowledge, even of a purely conceptual kind, demands that an abstract nature be seen in phantasms.[11] The phantasm, then, has the same general instrumental function in both conceptual and judgmental understanding; this point will become important when in Chapter Six the different acts of the mind are looked at in a less analytic perspective.

The *relational* character of judgment brings out further differences between judgment and purely conceptual knowledge. Because intellectual knowledge is related directly to concrete reality only in judgment, this act is the guarantor of the objectivity of all human knowledge. For it is in the act of judging that the problem of truth or the mind's conformity with reality comes into play.[12] In the case of abstract thinking dealing with higher-order philosophical judgments or with constructural knowledge, this problem takes the form of verification of meaning. But again, it is only through judgment that the reduction to sense data or to the basic principles of a science can take place.[13]

The contrast between judgment and pure conception also makes possible a clarification of the immaterial status of meaning. Meaning is not in itself extended in space and time and cannot be if it is to remain actual meaning. Although this fact was established only by a careful and refined analysis of what knowledge is, some experiential *indication* of it can be found in the sort of conceptual knowledge described above. When the meaning of a difficult concept—say, "energy" in the context of relativity theory—breaks through the long reflection on and study of this matter, the new meaning, even if it is only a partial insight, embraces the totality of what was confusedly and then more and more clearly learned in the lengthy process of thinking. The sudden insight is an instantaneous sort of thing; and, in spite of its being pregnant with many partial meanings that can be expressed at great length, the full meaning as it is understood *here and now* cannot be "measured out" in time and space. As the meaning is known in this single act of understanding, it is quite unproportioned to the time it would take to express it; and, as we saw in the analysis of symbols in Chapter Two, this meaning would be the guiding matrix in the judgmental elaboration and material expression of it.[14]

Now although an example like this points experientially to the non-material status of intellectual knowledge, it also illustrates the psychological rarity of purely conceptual knowledge, pointing rather to the primacy of judgment in human understanding. We find in cognitive experience that it is impossible to suspend or prolong such "insight" or absolute consideration in consciousness without quickly seeing the meaning precisely as related to another *meaning* or to concrete *things*. Energy, for instance, momentarily seen in pure conception, is now seen as related, say, to heat; there is a new meaning, and the intellect has been determined to act by a different causal principle through turning to phantasms which reveal the new meaning. When energy is known precisely as realized in some concrete data, the intellect must again reflect to phantasms. In either case judgment takes place.[15]

Since in purely conceptual knowledge there is no direct reference of meaning to matter as represented in phantasms, neither is there any understanding of the relation of meaning to *concrete space and time,* both conditions of matter. But when the intellect in judging reflects to phantasms that represent matter in some way, space and time can be consciously known and co-understood with the predicated meaning. A logical corollary of this is that grammatical tenses are entailed in a verbal expression of judgment, but not of concepts. Many judgments, of course, prescind from temporal elements and from many of the aspects of extension in space. But even when meanings are not consciously related to space and time in judging, it is in virtue of the intellect's reflection to the phantasm that the immateriality of meaning is "joined" to the world of matter and time without the nonsensory nature of meaning itself being destroyed.[16] Thus, the necessary process of preparing and building phantasms for understanding introduces the temporal as well as the physiological elements that so thoroughly dominate and sometimes block human thought processes.

PHANTASM PATTERNS AND THE
BUILDING OF MEANING

Although our attention has been concentrated largely on judgments made about concrete reality, the role of the phantasm does not change in the case of more abstract types of judgment not directly concerned with concrete things or events, past or present. The particular content of an abstract or constructural judgment is determined by phantasms, just as is the content of a concrete judgment involving phantasms produced in an immediate perception or drawn from the memory-imagination. This is possible because the phantasm is never the thing understood in any cognitive act, but only an instrumental cause of actual understanding. The matter of abstract judgments, however, calls special attention to the need which the intellect has for preparing specialized phantasms that may aid the processes of speculative thought.

CONTROLLED ASSOCIATION

In Chapter Three it was noted how formation of symbolic phantasms entails the abstractive refinement of the gross data supplied by any of the external sense modes. We often find ourselves deliberately constructing rather elaborate imaginative models in order to understand something. But when the meaning in question is once actually grasped, a symbolic schema[17] or abstractive reconstruction of the elaborated phantasm is often sufficient for recalling the meaning. Thus, as experience with the matter involved increases, phantasms become combined in complex ways, and the whole patterns are built up and associated in the imagination. This construction of schematic phantasms (which, of course, need not be consciously attended to) is in a way an extension of the spontaneous kind of abstraction by which the imagination provides the "composite photograph" type of image readily found in experience as well as the phantasms of quantity bereft of other qualities which contribute to our perceptions of space.[18] The only witness to the actual character of symbolic phantasms is, of course, one's own cognitive experience.

The actual recall of any pattern of phantasms, however complex it may be, depends upon some cause. For, although the memory-imagination retains and supplies the associated groups, as a passive power it is not itself the efficient cause of the *recall*. As was noted at the opening of Chapter Three, images are called up because of aroused emotions or present perceptions; these factors are the normal causes of the everyday phenomenon of "free association," entailing the random recall of images. Disciplined thinking, however, depends upon the control that reason exerts over the recall and association of phantasms, as well as upon the aid afforded by the discursive sense in focusing attention and interest on the matter at hand.

In thus controlling the *recall* from memory and the *preparation* of schematic phantasms necessary for actual understanding, the intellect is related to phantasms as an efficient cause, much as present perceptions or emotions are causes of recall in free association. But, as the necessary sensory foundations of every actual meaning, phantasms remain the efficient cause of *what* the intellect knows.[19]

PRACTICAL JUDGMENTS

More will be said about phantasms as they function in different types of thinking in the next chapter. For the present, if we integrate what has been seen about the psychological role of the phantasm in judgment with the function of the image in behavior as seen at the opening of Chapter Three, the importance of this mental instrument can be seen in a broader perspective.

Recall how phantasms representative of the objects and persons confronted in everyday experience can become impregnated with emotional associations; for the sensory emotions work through the discursive sense and imagination, the two powers especially operative in preparing the phantasms that guide concrete activity. Such image groups will necessarily affect the judgments in which they serve as instruments, especially if the emotional elements have slipped away from the direct control of reason. Conscious or subconscious suppression of emotionally undesirable aspects of the potential meaning represented in the phantasm patterns may eventually result in a psychological state in which the suppressed phantasms are no longer brought to the attention of the intellect and to actual intelligibility in a mental word. Though these phantasms continue to govern emotional and sensory behavior, the intellect does not revert to their real meaning, does not attend rationally to the meaning of the object presented in phantasms to the knowing and feeling person.

Thus, owing to a large variety of experiences and emotional factors that accumulate in the conscious and subconscious mind, people and things and tasks that were once meaningful and important in one's life receive slight attention or perfunctory treatment. The intelligible *species* that would determine the intellect to understand once again the real meaning of these things and persons remain in intellectual memory. But there is no way for the intellect to get at the meaning unless phantasms are deliberately reorganized or even reconstructed, so that potential meaning is again made available to consciousness and reason. These considerations would be important for a psychological discussion of motivation and value-judgment.

Even apart from the emotional aspects of behavior, it is evident that one's past life and experiences introduce themselves into the practical judgments of the present. As many contemporary thinkers have emphasized, every concrete situation is unique. Thus, accumulated experience with practical affairs provides new phantasms, new instruments for practical judgment, which reason must organize each time a situation presents itself. Ethical principles and the like are applied to the situation. But, owing to the uniqueness of each situation in addition to the concrete results seen in past experience and retained in phantasms, no two practical judgments are identical.

THEORETICAL JUDGMENTS

Speculative judgments, on the other hand, present a somewhat different picture. The concrete conditions of practical experience may be unique; but any number of persons can understand exactly the same thing. There is of course no doubt that a professional physicist, for instance, understands a great deal more about a concept like "energy" than does a young student. The mature scientist has through the course of much study and experimentation through the years formed complex phantasm-constructs rich in potential meaning, which readily and rapidly enter consciousness and array themselves before the intellect whenever the notion of energy presents itself. And the building of such instruments for thought and theoretical judgment never ceases as long as his scientific thinking continues to develop.

But how much of the accomplished scientist's fiber of experience is woven into a single basic judgment of physics like "energy can be understood as the ability to do work"? The novice scientist can also have an actual understanding of this fundamental principle and can know it in a single act of judgment. We would be immediately inclined to say, however, that the mature physicist realizes its meaning much more fully, in the very act of understanding it and without having to elaborate its full meaning to himself through a reasoning process.

But what does the connotative phrase "fuller realization" mean? If this expression signifies one of the results of learning more about an object of knowledge, it will be necessary to examine precisely what it means in psychological terms. Let us assume that the scientist and the student are here and now, each in a single unified judgmental act, knowing "energy" in the light of the one predicated meaning mentioned above. As was noted in the analysis Aquinas used to demonstrate the unicity of meaning, whenever part of a continuous whole is actually known, the whole itself is not being understood in any determinate fashion, owing simply to deliberate focus of attention upon the part. Comparing this matter to the situation at hand, we find that our physicist can actually understand the larger whole of energy —in the light of relativity theory, for instance—while the student cannot. But here and now he focuses intellectual attention upon only one part. Thus our question: how, psychologically speaking, can he understand the same part in one predicated meaning and yet understand more?

Let us suppose that Aquinas' "continuous whole" is a huge mural which a person of reasonably good aesthetic sense comes across. When he first sees it, he is only a few feet from it and hence perceives only a single figure in the mural, that of a man. He knows that there is much more to the whole mural, but for the moment he remains where he is, studies this single figure, sees its artistry and detail. He notes especially the pathos expressed in the countenance of this male figure. Now he moves along the mural, similarly examining the other figures he sees, and then gradually moves back a good distance from the mural and sees it as a whole, as a single work of art. Now he returns to his original spot a few feet from the mural and again examines the figure of the man he first saw. And he again judges that the man's countenance expresses pathos. The predicated meaning that our perceiver understands in this second judgment is in some way the same as that of the first judgment. And yet into the second act goes the wealth of experiencing the mural as a whole, a fuller realization of the part because of the experience of the whole. In short, once our art lover has seen the whole, the part cannot be understood in quite the same way that it was before the whole was seen.

Translating this in terms of the student and the physicist, we can for the moment use a spatial analogy and say that the *breadth* of meaning is the same. Each is knowing energy only in the light of the fact that it can be conceived as the ability to do work. Each is understanding only part of a larger whole. But the mature scientist, because he has seen energy as a much larger whole, can no longer understand that part in quite the same way that he did before he saw the larger whole. Hence, the *depth* of his predicated meaning far surpasses that of the student, though the breadth of meaning is the same.

This is ultimately nothing more than seeing from a somewhat different slant the fact that knowledge is not atomistic and, looking at the causal sources, that the intellect can embrace within its determination-to-act by a single intelligible *species* more than a single intelligible aspect of a whole. For, even when only part of a larger whole is actually being known, there is more intelligibility to the part.

Now the cause of whatever content the intellect is able to grasp in any single act of understanding is the phantasm. And thus, it is the presence of phantasms gradually built up to become rich in potential meaning that is the causal source of the depth of actual meaning known by our accomplished physicist, even when in a given judgment he actually knows only part of the total meaning represented in the complex pattern of phantasms.

The Greek thinker Heraclitus, impressed with the flux and change seen in the material world, once said that a person cannot step twice into the same river.[20] A parallel in the psychological perspective suggests itself. A true judgment remains true, for this touches what we have called breadth of meaning. But, sensory and physiological conditions being equal, a person who is continually broadening his experience in the realms of reality and knowledge and thus increasing the depth of potential meaning represented in phantasms never makes exactly the same judgment twice.[21]

SYMBOLIC EXPRESSION AND
THE ANALOGY OF PREDICATED MEANING

By returning to the subject-predicate relationship found in the judgment as it is verbally expressed, we can erect a basic framework within which to work in the next chapter in examining learning. For the moment only the personal expression of a judgmental act will be considered; to illustrate the matter, we may call once again upon our physicist and student, this time seeing them *express* the judgment about energy. The psychological factors involved in perceiving a symbol will be left to the following chapter, as will any discussion of symbols other than non-artistic, discursive language.

Recalling first the basic facts of symbolic expression, we may note that every expression of meaning is necessarily symbolic, since it entails a clothing of actual intelligibility in sensory signs that will represent the meaning potentially and enable it to be communicated. Now any sensory sign is potentially meaningful as possessing a material reality of its own; at the very least, the human intellect can understand that it is a "sensible something." Again, many such sensible tools serve only as *signals* for eliciting non-intellectual, animal responses. But, as has been noted, the whole point of a *symbol* is that it is meant by its user precisely to convey a meaning.[22]

Any symbol is woven from the material of past experience, stored in the memory-imagination; it thus directly involves a rational use of phantasms which, since they are physically contained in the neural and cerebral structure of man, serve as a kind of sensory link between intellection and external expression. Language as such, then, finds its place in verbal phantasms which with the passing years become associated in complex patterns under the guidance of reason.[23] A comparison of the different judgmental acts lying behind the proposition "energy can be understood as the ability to do work" as it is identically expressed by our two scientists will enable us to get at the *objective* symbolic status of a verbal judgment. Various subjective factors will be handled in the context of learning itself.

Recalling the psychological phenomenon described above as breadth and depth of meaning, we can observe that there exists an analogy between the judgmental acts made by the professional scientist and the novice at physics. Though each here and now actually understands energy only in the light of one predicated meaning (we are assuming that the student is not simply parroting a proposition), the intelligible *species* determining their intellects to an actual knowledge of the predicated meaning are quite dissimilar, owing as we have seen to the difference in wealth of potential meaning represented in phantasms. Now it is clearly impossible for a person to separate what has been called breadth of meaning from the depth of meaning that he actually knows; the dichotomy is an artificial one, made for the sake of discussion. Existentially, the mature scientist's judgment differs from that of the young student in the very way in which it is the same. This analogy in predicated meaning is especially significant for its consequences in the verbal expression of the judgmental act.

For the physicist himself, the verbal *subject* "energy" designates a whole area of intelligibility available to his actual understanding. Or, in psychological terms, it symbolizes the whole scope of *potential* meaning represented in the phantasm-constructs built up under the guidance of reason over a long period of study and experimentation—complex phantasms that can be called from the imagination at the intellect's command. Similarly, the verbal *predicate* signifies what he is *actually* knowing here and now about energy—the breadth and depth of intelligibility in the light of which he determinately understands energy in this single act of judgment. For though he is now understanding only part of a larger whole, sensory and physiological conditions being equal, he cannot understand the part in the same light that he did before seeing the larger whole. This is what the verbal proposition symbolizes *for him* as he formulates it. For the young student, on the other hand, the words symbolize neither as rich a potential meaning nor as deep an actual predicted meaning.

In short, there is no univocal relationship, no one-to-one correlation on the side of either the subject or the predicate, between an intellectual act of judgment and a verbal expression of that judgmental act of understanding. A single unified act of knowledge can embrace more intelligibility than can be symbolically expressed in a comparable handful of conventional symbols. Thus, objectively, words signify *conventional* meanings and nothing more. In themselves, they neither symbolize *potential* meaning, nor do they correspond directly to predicated or conceptual meanings as we *actually* know them. Words in themselves are atomic, while meaning can be large. A word in itself is impersonal. Actual meaning is personal.

NOTES

1. On the implications of "rationality," reasoning as a distinctively human act, and the incomplete character of reasoning as an act of the mind, see *S. T.* I, q. 85, a. 5; q. 58, aa. 3–4; q. 79, a. 8; q. 85, a. 3; q. 58, a. 3, ad 1.
2. See above, pp. 57–59.
3. "If in thought you think each half [of a line] separately, then by the same act you divide the time also, the half-lines becoming as it were new wholes of length. But if you think it as a whole consisting of these two possible parts, then also you think it in a time which corresponds to both parts together." Aristotle, *De Anima* III, vi, 430b-11–14 (trans. J. A. Smith; from R. McKeon [ed.], *Basic Works of Aristotle* [New York: Random House, 1941], pp. 592–93).
4. *S. T.* I, q. 58, a. 2 (text completed below).
5. On the meaning of "likeness" (*similitudo*) as the term is used here, see above, chapter 2, note 11.
6. *S. T.* I, q. 58, a. 2 as continued from above (ed. Ottawa I, 351b45–52a24); Latin text in Appendix, no. 4. Cf. q. 85, a. 4; q. 12, a. 10 (71a34–b2).
7. It is important to recall that the mental word need not be a *concept;* since the mental word is produced by an act of understanding, its intelligible content depends upon the act of understanding involved. See *S. T.* I, q. 34, a. 3 (ed. Ottawa I, 223a10–14).
8. A text like the one quoted in the preceding pages adequately states Aquinas' attitude concerning what the *psychological* nature of judgment must be. The innumerable texts in which Thomas talks of the intellect "composing and dividing" intelligibilities—as though the intellect were actuated by two intelligible *species* and judgment a combination of concepts—would seem to contradict his teaching here. However, it must be kept in mind that Aquinas treats judgment in contexts which employ a strictly *logical* breakdown of judgment much more frequently than he gives this act the type of phenomenological analysis used above. Hence, the logical texts cause no problem if they are read in context.

   George V. Kennard, S.J., carefully elucidates this point in a study that gathers all of the Thomistic texts on judgment: "The Intellect Composing and Dividing according to St. Thomas Aquinas" (unpublished Master's thesis, Dept. of Philosophy, St. Louis University, 1949), espec. pp. 158–218. Kennard attempts to reconstruct from the available texts an integral and systematic theory of judgment.

However, Patrick J. Burns, S.J., in accord with the results of his own inquiry—not as extensive as but in various respects more detailed than Kennard's—warns readers of Thomas' writings not to expect to find in his works a fully developed theory of judgment, especially with regard to the experiential type of analysis employed above. See "St. Thomas and Judgment: Selected Texts" (unpublished Master's thesis, Dept. of Philosophy, St. Louis University, 1957), espec. pp. 95–103; the author also warns that the texts be carefully distinguished according to the type of analysis actually being used by Aquinas in a given text.

Kennard's and Burns' studies have been quite helpful for the work of this chapter. A well-organized and concrete presentation of Kennard's textual conclusions may be seen in F. D. Wilhelmsen, *Man's Knowledge of Reality* (Englewood Cliffs, N.J: Prentice-Hall, 1956), pp. 101–117.

9. Judgmental knowledge of reality can be located in the larger context of *intellectual knowledge of the singular*. The intellect cannot know the singular in the same way in which the senses do, since its proper act in itself embraces no matter. Though the intellect cannot know a thing precisely *in* its individuality, however, it does know a singular object *as* material. This assent is possible because of the contact between intellect and sense, which are distinct as powers but not in any way separated in operation. Thus, in knowledge of the singular, the different powers cooperate in the unity of a composite act, in which intellection is as form, sensation as matter (cf. above, chapter 3, note 24). On *deliberate* scientific reduction of a universal principle to sense data, see below, note 13. For Aquinas' teaching on this question and the many terms he uses in talking about it, see G. P. Klubertanz, S.J., "St. Thomas and the Knowledge of the Singular," *New Scholasticism*, XXVI (1952), 135–66.

A correlative problem in this context of judgmental knowledge of concrete reality is that of the *judgment of existence*, which is especially important in establishing the science of metaphysics and has received some emphasis in recent years. See Robert J. Henle, S.J., "Existentialism and the Judgment," *Proceedings of Amer. Cath. Philos. Assoc.*, XXI (1946), 40–53; Henle, *Method in Metaphysics* ("Aquinas Lecture"; Milwaukee: Marquette Univ. Press, 1951); Leonard Eslick, "What Is the Starting Point of Metaphysics?" *Modern Schoolman*, XXXIV (1957), 247–63. For the significance of the existential judgment in the light of the Kantian critique, see James Collins, *History of Modern European Philosophy* (Milwaukee: Bruce, 1954), p. 479. This whole issue is closely related to the question of *truth* and is very frequently handled in that context; see below, note 12.

10. Abstraction, as has been noted, is essentially the considering of one thing apart from another (and hence not a question of "pulling out" an intelligible *species* from the phantasm; see above, p. 104). Abstraction also takes place in judgment, when one thing is denied of another—e.g., "the intellect is not material"; see above, pp. 64–65.

   The conceptual knowledge discussed here is what Aquinas will often call *simplex vel absoluta consideratio;* e.g., see *S. T.* I, q. 85, a. 1 & ad 1 (where abstraction is also rather thoroughly considered). Although Thomas has a large variety of terms for designating this non-judgmental consideration of meaning, he does not call it *simple apprehension,* a term that has become traditional in logic. In a psychological context, simple apprehension would be quite a different thing from simple or absolute *consideration;* for "apprehension" unlike "consideration" connotes the way such knowledge is *obtained.* The definition of man or of the nature of any being is not simply apprehended; it is a very complex apprehension.

11. See above, pp. 96–98 and chapter 3, note 10.

12. A good textbook treatment of the question of judgment and truth (which need not delay us here) may be found in Wilhelmsen, *Man's Knowledge of Reality,* pp. 134–64. For more detailed discussions, see Bernard Muller-Thym, "The 'To Be' which Signifies the Truth of Propositions," *Proceedings of Amer. Cath. Philos. Assoc.,* XVI (1940), 230–54. Many important Thomistic texts on this question are used in the discussions of Louis-Marie Régis, O.P., *Epistemology* (New York: Macmillan Co., 1959), pp. 337–64.

13. The intellect is finally determined to an object of scientific knowledge by a reduction to the fundamental principles of knowledge that give any proposition its basic intelligibility and/or by a reduction to the initial sense data (Aquinas' *resolutio ad principia et sensum*). Thus, in the case of *philosophical* knowledge, logical coherence is provided by the reduction to first principles, which are themselves an expression of the intelligibility of being; and the reduction to the data of experience provides the ultimate validity for the philosophical judgment. In the context of contemporary science, a *mathematical* proposition is reducible to the a priori postulates which are the first principles of a particular set theory. Verification of an *empirical* statement is analogous to the verification of a philosophical proposi-

tion, although, as was developed throughout chap. 1, the *kind* of sense data involved is different.

Aquinas had a highly developed "criterion of meaning" in his teaching on *resolutio,* closely related to the judgmentally organized stage of scientific knowledge (see above, pp. 36–37). For textual studies on this matter, see Burns, "St. Thomas and Judgment," pp. 66–94; and Régis, *Epistemology,* pp. 458–65. See espec. Régis' study, "Analyse et synthèse dans s. Thomas," *Studia Mediaevalia* (Bruges: De Tempel, 1948), pp. 303–330.

14. See above, pp. 62–63.

15. The notion of the intellect "turning to phantasms" (*conversio* in the Thomistic texts) indicates *any* process through which the intellect is determined to understand any meaning; the term of the process might be a mental word expressive of either conceptual or judgmental understanding (see above, chapter 3, note 10). The notion of "reflecting to the phantasm" is taken from Aquinas' use of the term *reflexio* to designate *judgmental* knowledge of the singular. E.g., see *S. T.* I, q. 86, a. 1, where Thomas states that in virtue of a kind of "reflection" in which the intellect turns to phantasms which represent singulars, the intellect forms the proposition "Socrates is a man." (*Reflexio* has five meanings in Thomas' writings, only two of which refer to knowledge of the singular; cf. above, chapter 2, note 16). This language is, of course, artificial and borrowed from transient activity; we are using it here only as a means of distinguishing judgmental and conceptual knowledge.

    It may also be noted here that the traditional division of the acts of the mind into absolute consideration (usually called simple apprehension, but see above, note 10), judgment, and reasoning is an analytic or *logical division* according to degrees of complexity. It is not an effective psychological division. St. Thomas contrasts the first and second acts principally to show how only judgments are properly true or false and involve contact with real existence (see Burns, "St. Thomas and Judgment," p. 66), while judgment and reasoning are contrasted by him generally to illustrate the incompleteness of the latter qua act of the mind (see above, pp. 114–15).

16. On space and time in judgment, see *S. T.* I, q. 85, a. 5, ad 3; II–II, q. 51, a. 3.

17. *Schema* as used here and elsewhere refers only to phantasms of a more abstract character prepared for theoretical thinking, and has no relation to the Kantian meaning of the term. Kant's "schemata of imagination" are a priori conditions for adapting the a priori cate-

gories of understanding to the concrete order of images and sense intuitions. These schematic forms are not in any way derived from sense experience and are in no sense potentially intelligible. See *Critique of Pure Reason,* A137–47: B176–87 (tr. Norman Kemp Smith [London: Macmillan & Co., 1950], pp. 180–87).

Potential meaning is not "put into" phantasms by the intellect; the intellect controls the imagination and the associative process but does not "do anything" to phantasms. The fact of experience involved here is that we can understand whatever we wish and that the recall of images can be controlled, as can the formation of abstractive image groups. This does not permit a negation of the fact already established through reasoning that *actual* intelligibility exists only in the intellect (and hence cannot be put into phantasms) and that *potential* intelligibility exists only in matter (and hence cannot be "given" to phantasms by the intellect).

18. On the imagination's spontaneous abstraction, see G. P. Klubertanz, S.J., *Philosophy of Human Nature* (New York: Appleton-Century-Crofts, 1953), pp. 131–33.

19. The following text summarizes this matter, as well as much of what we have already seen about the role of the phantasm in intellection.

"The possible intellect, like any substance, operates in accord with its own nature, and according to its nature it is the form of the body. Hence, the intellect does understand immaterial things, but it sees them in some material thing. An indication of this is that in teaching abstract matters, particular examples are proposed, and in these the intellect sees what is stated. The possible intellect, therefore, is related to the phantasms which it needs, in one way before the reception of the intelligible *species,* and in another way after it has received the *species.*

"Beforehand, it needs the phantasm in order to receive from it the intelligible *species.* Hence, the phantasm is related to the intellect as an object which puts in motion.

"After the intellect has received the *species,* however, it needs the phantasm as a sort of instrument or foundation for its *species.* Hence, the intellect is related to phantasms as an efficient cause. For, upon the intellect's command, there is formed in the imagination a phantasm that is appropriate to a particular intelligible *species,* a phantasm in which the intelligible *species* shines forth as does an ideal pattern in an object that exemplifies or reflects it. . . .

"Hence, we see that when we have once received knowledge of something, it is within our power to consider it again at will. Nor do phantasms hinder us; for it is in our power to form phantasms suited to what we wish to consider." *Summa contra Gentiles,* Bk. II, toward end of chap. 73; Latin text in Appendix, no. 5.

20. As related by Aristotle in *Metaphysics,* IV, v, 1010a14. Cratylus was even more impressed with change and critized Heraclitus for thinking he could step into the same river even once (*ibid.*).

21. The closest thing in Aquinas' writings to the type of analysis we have used here would be his analysis of the way habits can be increased. "Breadth of meaning" would correspond roughly to the perfection of a given habit considered in itself, "depth of meaning" to the intensity of the habit as possessed by a particular subject. See *S. T.* I–II, q. 52, a. 1.

   Thomas otherwise handles the question of differences in understanding in terms of the physiological and sensory factors that enable one person to understand the same thing better than another. Thus, psychologically, one person's internal senses are more perfect than those of another. Metaphysically, the perfection of the intellective form or soul must be proportioned to the capacity and disposition of the matter or body in which it is received. See *S. T.* I, q. 85, a. 7. Such factors as fatigue will of course affect the intensity with which something is understood, since preparation of phantasms is affected.

22. On signals and symbols, see above, pp. 57–59. Recall that language, inasmuch as it is a collocation of patterned sounds, can be a signal and can be known and responded to on the animal level.

23. Handling the matter of language in a psychological as opposed to logical context, Aquinas will variously speak of the *verbum mentis,* the mental word or product of intellection; the *verbum imaginis* or *vox interior,* the phantasm of the external expression; and the *verbum vocis* or *vox exterior,* the oral expression itself. E.g., see *S. T.* I, q. 34, a. 1.

5

THE PHANTASM IN
LEARNING

THE PROBLEM OF LEARNING gives rise to many questions other than those involving knowledge; for intentionality is only one figure in the total picture entitled "Learning." Motivation, adjustment, needs, habit formation, and other facets of human behavior also enter the scene. Since many of these problems go far beyond the cognitive side of human nature, we cannot in the compass of this study ask what learning is and hope to give this question a complete answer here. Hence, we must first ferret out the questions about learning that *can* be analyzed in a relatively thorough fashion within our limited perspective of a philosophical psychology of knowledge.

Any instance of learning implies an acquisition of something not possessed before the learning took place. A child learns how to eat with a fork; an adolescent learns how to drive a car. Acquisition in turn implies some kind of stability with regard to the object learned. Once a person has actually learned to use a fork or to drive a car or to solve a problem, the tasks can be performed with some ease and success. Owing to learning, then, a behavioral pattern of some sort becomes established, for we do not ordinarily say that a person has really "learned" if the results of the process are too ephemeral.

Now any modification of behavior presupposes cognition of some sort, and any exercise of a previously learned pattern is always guided by cognition. One cannot learn to use a fork unless he perceives the fork in some way; and even when he has arrived at the point where he can use the fork without attending to the "rules," he must still have perception of the external situation. In short, any response is causally preceded by some sort of perception of the stimulus.[1]

This general statement needs much refinement, but it does point to the type of problem that can be explored in our context: what are the *cognitive causes* that underlie acquisition of a skill or of some object of knowledge, thus leading in many instances to a modification of behavior? It is at the level of learning which involves understanding that a philosophical analysis will be seen to be especially fruitful. Hence, in examining the cognitive aspects of learning, we shall first trace the cognitive causes of lower forms of learning. This analysis will be used primarily to bring into focus the nature of that type of learning directly entailing disciplined intellectual knowledge.[2]

COGNITIVE CAUSES OF
BEHAVIORAL MODIFICATION

Patterns of behavior resulting simply from cumulative experience can be conceived as one type of learning. Thus, an infant can be said to learn beginning with his second act of knowledge; and when an aged person once discovers that he can no longer attempt certain tasks, he too has learned. In this context the term *learning* is evidently used in its broadest possible meaning, and the learning process here entails all of the cognitive factors discussed in the preceding three chapters. We need only call attention to some of the more significant matters that have already been discussed at some length.

LEARNING AS CUMULATIVE EXPERIENCE

Simple learning through direct experience of the world about us is largely a question of memory. Past sensations retained in the memory-imagination supply the intellect with more and more phantasms which can be prepared for practical judgments by the discursive sense operating under the control of reason. We have considered in some detail how emotional experiences can affect concrete behavior, owing to the influence of the sense emotions upon the organization of phantasms for judgment. Thus, image groups gradually become established in consciousness and sometimes guide concrete behavior at the subconscious level.

The presence of subconscious images is by no means a sign of abnormality, for such images control much of our ordinary activity. Perception of and reaction to natural or conventional signals, for instance, is often taken care of by the discursive sense and the imagination without any deliberate advertence to a situation on the part of the intellect. At the sound of an automobile horn, a driver rather automatically moves over to let a car pass him. Upon seeing that the sidewalks are icy, a person habitually walks with some caution. At some time in his life, a person must learn what horns and icy sidewalks mean. But human life would be quite inhuman if habitual behavior of this type had to be deliberately attended to at every moment. As we have seen, psychological dfficulties arise only when images that guide concrete behavior slip from rational control and cannot be attended to even by a shift of attention.

In this context it is worthwhile to recall that such things as adjustment and maladjustment, good and bad motivation, and attitudes and prejudices of any kind are learned; cognitively, they entail the formation of phantasm patterns. It has been noted how correction of adverse aspects of behavior involves, psychologically speaking, a reorganization of phantasms through conscious intellectual judgment —bringing the adverse factors to actual intelligibility in a mental word, so that the intellect can gain control over them. It is unnecessary to remark that the various agencies which contribute to learning play no small part in forming the behavioral matrices pervading an individual's entire life, and that sound guidance has much to do with establishing rational control over the phantasms governing concrete behavior.

More will be said about learning as it affects practical activity in the course of our subsequent analyses. Prescinding for the moment from any further discussion of learning as the term is taken in the broad sense of cumulative experience, we shall turn our attention to more definite types of behavioral modification. A brief consideration of the cognitive causes underlying the acquisition of skills will set the stage for an analysis of higher types of learning.

MOTOR LEARNING

Two basic facts must be accounted for in an examination of the cognitive aspects of motor activity. The exercise of a skill, first of all, never becomes independent of cognition, for perception (tactile, in most cases) always guides the activity. It is true that automatic responses of some sort are developed. But—and this is a second fact—the responses are always adapted by means of perception to the particular concrete situation at hand or to the particular instrument in question.

Thus, when a stenographer uses a typewriter different from the one to which she is accustomed, she takes a few minutes to "get the feel of it"—the slightly different spacing among and shape of the keys, the difference in touch, the distance between the keyboard and the carriage-return shift, and so on. Or take an organist. He has learned to coordinate his footwork with his manual responses and to manipulate the tabs controlling the stops quite smoothly and without having to interrupt the musical line at any point. When he plays an organ that is new to him, however, he must adapt his responses to the different instrument. The radiation of the pedal keyboard, the distance from the pedals to the organ bench, the position of the tabs controlling the stops, the distance between the different keyboard manuals themselves—all of these are factors to which he must adjust his skill.

In the light of these facts, it will be seen that learning a skill entails from a cognitive point of view the formation of accurate *kinesthetic images* which guide the bodily responses in any use of the skill. The images are retained in the power of imagination and are actually recalled through tactile perception of the instrument involved in the skill. Included in such images is a kind of tactile memory of concrete space—where the hands or feet (or whatever other part of the body may be involved) are now, and where they should go to accomplish the next step of the task. Thus, the adjustment of responses spoken of above cognitively entails slight changes in kinesthetic imagery.

There can, of course, be wide variation in the *precision* of the images necessary for mechanical activity. The techniques of a jeweler or watchmaker are clearly more difficult to learn than a simple (or relatively simple) motor activity like walking. But even in the latter instance the need for kinesthetic images can be seen, since damage to the central nervous system and thus to the organ of the imagination sometimes requires that an individual relearn even the ordinary feat of walking. It is the active presence of kinesthetic images, consequently, that differentiates the type of muscular response found in motor behavior from the pure reflex that takes place totally independent of perception.

A certain similarity can immediately be seen between the development of a motor skill and the acquisition of an intellectual habit, since in either case patterns of images are required. We have already considered how the intellect directs the imagination in the formation of phantasms suitable for supplying the potential meaning necessary for any act of understanding. Thus, the establishment of phantasm patterns in the imagination makes possible a behavioral modification at the level of understanding.

Now in experimenting with formal relationships between human acts, the scientific psychologist is able to determine functional laws related to efficiency of learning and performance. Owing to its constructural character and its procedure of selective abstraction, the experimental method can demonstrate the weakness of a method of learning and point the way toward methods that will lead more rapidly to more stable habits. Most operational laws associated with the cognitive aspects of learning are, philosophically speaking, cen-

tered around the power of memory-imagnation, since they take cog-
nizance of the physiological vicissitudes of learning. However, owing
to the complete dependence of the operations of intellect upon sense
organs, such laws also affect intellectual learning.

Consequently, questions of behavioral *efficiency* in acquiring or
using sensory or intellectual habits must be left to the scientific approach. In the perspective of a philosophical psychology of cognition,
we can say little more about the acquisition of a purely mechanical
skill than to demonstrate the necessity for images in this type of
learning.[3] For, the development of a skill is largely a question of
efficient and methodical practice and exercise. Behavioral patterns
entailing actual understanding, however, deserve a closer examination, which can be conveniently handled by comparing mechanical
skills with intellectual habits.

BEHAVIORAL MODIFICATION AT THE
LEVEL OF UNDERSTANDING

When a stenographer makes use of her typing skill, she generally
brings a good deal of practical knowledge to bear upon the exercise
of the task; she attends to such things as proper format, neatness, and
so on. The exercise of the skill itself, on the other hand, does not
require much conscious attention. Thus, we find that the proficient
typist can copy a letter while conversing over the telephone. Similarly, while a genuinely artistic performance requires that a pianist
devote his full attention to the music he is playing, it is possible for
him simply to execute the notes—in other words, to exercise his
skill and nothing more—while thinking about something entirely
different.

On the other hand, take the accomplished scientist, who has developed the habit of thinking scientifically with ease and accuracy.
However easy such thinking may have become for him through constant exercise, he must always bring deliberate intellectual attention
to bear upon any act in which he exercises his learned ability; otherwise he would not actually be understanding what he is thinking

about. He *knows* when he is thinking scientifically, and the meaning-ful character of his thinking depends upon his conscious attention to the matter at hand. A first feature of intellectual learning, then, is that no matter how highly developed an intellectual habit may have become, its exercise is never indeliberate. Ease and success and accuracy of performance, in other words, do not imply and cannot be equated with automatic and mechanical exercise.

One readily discovers in his experience with mechanical skills, on the other hand, that full rational attention exerted upon the per-formance of a well-learned activity actually *hinders* the efficiency of performance. Thus, the automobile mechanic does not ask himself in the act of tightening a bolt or aligning wheels how it is that he is able to move his wrench just so far and no further, or why it is that this particular position "feels" like the correct adjustment. And the easiest way to make mistakes in typing or in executing a memorized selection on a musical instrument is to ask oneself where the little finger, for instance, should go next. An immediate reason for this phenomenon is that the kinesthetic images involved in mechanical activity have been developed for the sake of the skill alone, to supply cognitive guidance for muscular responses. Since they have not been developed as phantasms—that is, as images directly intended to represent potential meaning to the intellect—the motor process guided by tactile perception is slowed down when the intellect at-tempts to bring these images (which in fact represent a bare mini-mum of potential meaning) to its conscious attention.

These various facts point to a second distinguishing characteristic of intellectual learning in contrast to motor learning. Since kinesthetic images are built up only for the sake of the skill, it is quite unneces-sary in learning a skill to know the *reasons* for the techniques which are learned. One need not know why a certain carburetor setting looks or feels or sounds right, or why this particular pattern of fingering provides the most efficient way of typing or executing a series of notes on a piano. This may be very useful practical knowl-edge, but it has nothing to do with the efficient exercise of the skill as such.

On the other hand, it is an absolute requisite for the formation of an intellectual habit that there be knowledge of rational procedure. A physicist must know *why* a certain reasoning process yields certain types of conclusions and *why* a particular formula is applicable to a specific concrete situation. Though he may now and then experience sudden inspirations regarding new methods or sudden insights into new aspects of his science, the scientist does not reach his conclusions accidentally. He knows *that* they are valid and *why* they are valid. But given the equation $a = \dfrac{F}{m}$, any number of persons who are not physicists could compute the acceleration of a moving vehicle. Or given a certain formula and some measuring apparatus, an individual whom we should hardly call a scientist could mix a chemical. Knowledge of techniques, therefore, does not constitute a scientific habit of thinking; and the competent technician, even though his work entails much more intellectual attention than is required by pure mechanical skills, has not necessarily learned any science.

Now in considering patterns of behavior that directly entail actual understanding—intellectual learning, in other words—we need ask no further questions concerning the cognitive causes of such learning, since explicit consideration of these problems was the work of Chapters Two and Four. However, intellectual learning is considerably more nuanced than motor learning. For it is the nature of an intellectual habit that, no matter how well it may have become established, its exercise can never dispense with the deliberate attention of the intellect or with the conscious knowledge of actual meaning that underlies fact and technique. Hence, within the context of behavioral modification at the level of understanding, we may ask a further philosophical question. In asking the question, we can prescind from experimental problems concerning the efficient acquisition and use of an intellectual habit. Apart from the physiological factors affecting cognitive behavior, what are the psychological factors *within* the human cognitive structure that especially affect the acquisition of intellectual knowledge and the habitual use of it? In answering this question, we shall be able to isolate further charteristics of intellectual learning.

TYPES AND CHARACTERISTICS OF
INTELLECTUAL LEARNING

The generalization can be made without much danger of overstatement that most of our learning takes place through verbal communication rather than exclusively through direct experience. This seems to be true at almost any level of learning. It is better that a child be told not to put his finger into a live socket than that he discover this for himself. Again, mechanical skills and ways of doing things are, generally speaking, more efficiently and more quickly learned if the learning process is at least guided by another person who already knows the technique. And especially at the level of intellectual learning, it is evident that the thoughts and scholarly contributions of past ages in any area of knowledge are learned exclusively through the spoken and written word or through communicative symbols in general.

Accordingly, one possible approach to the types and characteristics of intellectual learning would be to examine some of the things that people learn by way of verbal communication. This analysis can be made in terms of the psychological structure of judgment and the role of the phantasm in judgmental understanding (and hence the remainder of this chapter presupposes especially the work of Chapter Four). An analysis of verbal phantasms will thus provide a general schema for getting at the nature of intellectual learning.

Any symbolic communication is psychologically received through the external senses in the power of imagination, where through the cognitive contributions of the unifying sense and the discursive power the sensory datum is brought to the peak of sensation in a phantasm. Thus, a verbal symbol is presented to the intellect in phantasms and, through the concomitant causality of the agent intellect, the intellect actually understands the meaning potentially represented in the verbal phantasms. Now it is clear enough that if a person does not

know the meaning of a word the verbal phantasm cannot instrumentally cause actual understanding of the meaning symbolized by the
word. However, there are many psychological nuances connected
with the instrumentality of verbal phantasms in learning, and the
general statement just made has, as we shall see, numerous implications.

CONCRETE VERBAL PHANTASMS:
THE DESCRIPTIVE FUNCTION OF WORDS

Many if not most of the verbal symbols of everyday discourse deal
with concrete singular things and events. It is often the case that all of
the significant terms in a verbal judgment are oriented toward designating one particular fact, even though the words might in another
context serve a more universal function. For example, when Mac-
beth says that "tomorrow and tomorrow and tomorrow creeps in
this petty pace from day to day," he is not thinking about any particular day after today; whereas, "Jane will be here tomorrow"
designates one particular day and a specific fact about it. As we have
seen, words are not meanings, and there is no necessary connection
between a given word and a meaning. Perhaps this is the chief factor
contributing to the common phenomenon of experience that, when
words merely symbolize concrete singulars, we tend to "convert"
the verbal designation into a more or less vivid image of what is
designated. Thus, we would imagine Jane in some way, rather than
the words that say she is coming. Similarly, we would be more inclined to form an image associated with Caesar's crossing the Rubicon than to be directly aware of the words stating that fact.

It may be noted that we are assuming some direct consciousness
of *images* rather than of *ideas* when simple knowledge of past or
future concrete events or facts is in question. One reason why this
is a matter of general experience is that, when no general or universal
ideas are involved in an act of understanding, the intellect's role is
one of simple assent, simple commitment to the immediate intelligibility of the concrete datum in question. Thus, when one under-

stands that Caesar crossed the Rubicon or that Jane will be here tomorrow, the intellect in reflecting to phantasms understands what might be verbalized to read "it is true that" or "it is probable that" or "it is a fact that" Caesar did this and Jane will do that. The focus of attention discovered in an experience of this sort is a concern with singulars or, psychologically, with images; for the abstractive function of the intellect, here and now, is minimal. This phenomenon concerning *past* or *future* singulars is really only an extension of the fact that, when we know sensible objects immediately *present* before us, we remain directly aware of the object, even though an idea of it is conceived in the composite sensory-intellectual act of perception (usually judgmental).

This analysis reveals a significant characteristic of concrete factual knowledge. Although it is natural enough for man to communicate his knowledge of singulars verbally, it is not quite so natural for him to *think* about concrete things in terms of words. A word designating a person or an event may call forth other associated and perhaps emotionally loaded images; or it may serve as a highly symbolic phantasm representative of much potential meaning, as "energy" might for the professional scientist. Nevertheless, in the case of strictly factual knowledge, words designate or point to the concrete data itself. Hence, verbal phantasms symbolizing singular matters of fact are true instruments of understanding—potentially meaningful, in other words—only to the extent that they lead to the formation of concrete phantasms or sufficiently symbolize such images previously formed.

The importance of this point can be seen if the act of judgment in which a concrete event is understood includes not only an assent to fact but also some more universal meaning. For example, "Napoleon's downfall began when he invaded Russia." In understanding this verbal symbol, the intellect reflects to the phantasms representative of the event and understands the concrete event in the light of the downfall to which it gave rise. In the course of learning about the event, in other words, the phantasms that represent it have come to symbolize the more abstract predicated meaning. But if the verbal phantasms that designate the event have never brought about an intellectual assent to the concrete facts themselves, the predicated meaning based on the data can only be vague and tenuous. If this is the case, the actual intelligible content of judgment, in terms of our example, might read something like this: "Napoleon (an historical personage) invaded Russia (a thing which was apparently difficult to do) and this gave rise to his downfall (for some reason or other)." In contrast to this would be the depth of predicated meaning possessed by the historian for whom the verbal phantasms symbolize a meaningful inference drawn from many concrete facts, and not simply from words which express the facts.

Apart from the extremes of verbal knowledge (which we shall consider in more detail in a moment), a salient point regarding the learning of any concrete singular emerges from this discussion. In such learning, words are a *descriptive substitute for direct experience* of the fact or event; and hence they are potentially intelligible only to the extent that they describe or else symbolize and serve to recall a description already retained in the imagination in the form of phantasms. To the extent that they fail as substitutes for direct experience, concrete verbal phantasms are non-symbolic. For nothing can be symbolic unless it is potentially intelligible, and words designating singulars have no intelligibility unless there exists knowledge of the singulars in question. Verbal descriptions of past or future events can do no more than make use of one's personal experience of concrete singulars and lead the individual to weave new images from the fiber of personal experience.

ABSTRACT VERBAL PHANTASMS:
FACTS AND MEANINGS

The indifferent character of verbal symbols considered in themselves can be seen in a fuller light if, moving to the other end of the continuum of symbolic expression, we examine verbal statements in which *none* of the words designate concrete singulars. Take a statement like "man is a rational animal." From the philosopher's point of view, this proposition is a conclusion; it is a definition based on a lengthy induction and in a sense summarizes in one breath all of the experiential evidence revealed by man's activities. It is, in other words, a non-constructural scientific statement; but insofar as it is abstract and technical it is quite analogous to a statement like "chrysolite is a magnesium iron silicate." The philosopher and the chemist know what they are saying when they state these propositions. But, unlike the definition of chrysolite, the definition of man is an example of an abstract fact known by many individuals who are unaware of its technical and summary status. Now, if the philosophical induction has not been made and actually understood, what precisely does a person understand when "man is a rational animal" presents itself to the intellect in verbal phantasms? We shall use this statement as an example, but the answer to this question will be seen to apply to any abstract and technical verbal statement known in isolation from the evidence which founds it.

There would seem to be two kinds of understanding possible in this case. The first is pure assent to the truth symbolized by the words without any understanding of the meaning of the words. The intellect in reflecting to the verbal phantasms actually understands "it is a fact that" or "it is true that" man is a rational animal or chrysolite is a magnesium iron silicate. The judgmental situation is thus analogous to the type of assent given by the intellect to concrete singulars, for the words are functioning simply as sensuous materials and not as symbols. Now when the intellect assents judgmentally to concrete singulars apart from any more universal meaning, there is at least a grasp of the immediate intelligibility of the particular fact in question. Thus, the intellect actually understands *that* this desk is gray, *that* Jane is coming tomorrow, *that* Napoleon invaded Russia; and the particularities of the fact or event are filled in to a greater or lesser degree by the imagination. But in the case of pure assent to abstract words there is virtually no intelligibility unless the meaning symbolized by the words is understood, for there is little that the imagination can supply apart from the verbal phantasms themselves. The intellect's reflection to verbal phantasms terminates, in this instance, in a most empty and useless form of knowledge, since the intelligible content of the mental word is no more than "these words mean something or other." The *assent* itself is intellectual, but the *words* assented to remain sensory and non-symbolic.

A second type of understanding associated with abstract words not known in their true technical meaning involves a vague grasp of the symbolic meaning of the words. This situation would arise in the case of abstract statements with which individuals have become familiar by hearing them often enough in different situations. Take our original example, "man is a rational animal." The reflection of the intellect to abstract verbal phantasms may result in a predicated meaning in which man is understood as a "rational (he can 'think,' in a very colloquial sense of the word) animal (men have a body with legs and arms and hair, and so on)." One might question, however, whether the content of a judgment like this is a more intelligible kind of knowledge than the pure belief in words discussed above. Certainly this vague and clearly mistaken grasp of meaning is useless as scientific knowledge; and it is doubtful that it could be of any value as practical knowledge.

There is no question here of the kind of difference in understanding that exists between two persons when one understands something better than the other—for instance, the difference between the ways in which our young student and professional physicist of the preceding chapter understand "energy." Even though the physicist in a single act of judgment understands more deeply than the novice, the latter does have a knowledge of actual meaning, and the verbal phantasms representative of "energy" do symbolize the meaning that he can at present understand about energy. In the second type of assent to abstract verbal symbols just discussed, however, the meaning actually understood differs considerably from the symbolic meaning attached to the words by thinkers who use them to summarize a great deal of data.

When abstract verbal phantasms of the denotative type found in disciplined statements are the chief instruments for judgments made in the course of a learning process, it is of course inevitable that verbal learning will result. Thus, a person either gives pure assent to words without any grasp of their meaning, and in this instance learning consists of brute memory of words that the individual has managed to associate in convenient patterns through various tricks of memory. Or else he thinks he knows the meaning of the words when actually he does not, in which case there results a kind of pseudo-learning. The first type of verbal learning is likely to occur when there is *exaggerated* insistence upon memorization of the exact wordings of definitions and the like. Such memorization, which can be very useful if actual meaning has once been understood, can take place independent of even the vaguest act of understanding; the intellect merely guides the memory process and assents in an empty fashion to what has been memorized. The second type of verbal learning, exemplified above by the understanding of man as a kind of two-layer cake, is inevitable in any case in which abstract verbal symbols *dominate* the learning process. The learner is forced to get whatever meaning he can find in or attach to the words, for his intellect has little more than the verbal phantasms themselves with which to work.

A number of further conclusions concerning the nature and types of intellectual learning emerge from a consideration of abstract verbal phantasms. The function of repetition in learning and the features of abstract facts of a practical rather than theoretical nature can be profitably discussed in the present context.

Repetition does not necessarily bring about an act of understanding. If there is no potential meaning represented in the sensory material that is more and more firmly ingrained in the memory-imagination through repetition, actual meaning cannot result. Thus, repetition does not of itself render a symbol communicative. If, on the other hand, the material represented in phantasms, verbal or otherwise, is at the first instance potentially meaningful, the intellect operating according to its nature will actually understand the meaning.

Repetition as a useful tool in the process of learning, consequently, has two basic psychological purposes. It can serve to increase the potential intelligibility represented in phantasms and thus to deepen the actual meaning *already understood* by the intellect but in a more shallow fashion. Secondly, the formal principle that determines the intellect to an actual understanding of meaning cannot be recalled from intellectual memory unless there are phantasms to serve as the sensory instruments necessary for any such recall. Hence, repetition can reinforce memory of suitable phantasms for the ready recall of a meaning *once actually understood*. If actual meaning has not been grasped in the first place, this process of embellishing and reinforcing phantasms cannot really be called repetition; it is rather a question of "let's try again."

Even in the case of knowledge of concrete facts and events, which as singulars exist only in the power of imagination and not in the intellect, repetition does not in itself guarantee the emergence of a more universal meaning based on the concrete data. Although knowledge of facts is an obvious requisite for a real intellectual grasp of meaning drawn from the facts, the general meaning cannot be revealed unless the intellect has controlled the organization of phantasms in a proper way. For instance, random appearance of phantasms representative in some way of Napoleon's invasion of Russia will not necessarily cause actual understanding of the fact that this action initiated his military and political downfall. *Reinforcement* of phantasms in memory, consequently, is profitably accompanied by suitable *organization* of phantasms, by a presentation that will enable the discursive sense and imagination, working under rational control, to prepare phantasms for an actual grasp of meaning.

Now an analogy can be seen to exist between intellectual assents to concrete and to abstract facts. Just as knowledge of concrete events does not necessarily result in a grasp of the larger meaning implied in the facts, neither does intellectual assent to abstract facts necessarily imply any understanding of meaning. We have seen how purely verbal assent to *theoretical* or more strictly scientific facts of an abstract character is ultimately a vacuous form of knowledge. It is often either grossly misleading or simply useless to have learned such summary truths apart from the evidence that gives them meaningfulness as well as scientific validity. However, intellectual assent to abstract facts of a *practical* nature brings other learning factors into play.

When the intellect understands that a certain rule or norm applies in a given situation, the knowledge can be eminently useful even though there is no understanding of *why* the rule applies. Consider, for instance, a simple rule for addition like the following: in order to add numbers of more than two digits, arrange the numbers vertically, add the figures in the far right column first, and carry all but the last figure of any sum over 9 into the addition of the next column. After sufficient concrete illustrations of a rule like this, a child will know *how* to add columns of figures. Now let us assume that the child has not reached the point where this process can be done quite automatically. Perception of a situation requiring such addition calls forth from his memory abstract phantasms, perhaps verbal, which are in some way representative of the rule; perhaps he will also use some example previously learned as a kind of model for the process to be performed here and now. Now in the act of judgment the child understands simply *that* this process is to be executed. His knowledge is heavily sensory, for there is as yet no actual understanding of the reasons why such a rule is valid and helpful. To this extent, the rule exists only in phantasms, and it rises above the particularities of sense knowledge only inasmuch as the intellect understands *that* the rule is to be applied in this situation.

Although we have already considered conscious knowledge of rational order as a distinguishing characteristic of a real intellectual habit when we contrasted this with motor learning, some further elaboration of this point will prove fruitful. In the light of the above analysis, it may be seen that much of our knowledge of *methods of procedure* is knowledge of a more or less purely verbal type. True, the intellect does assent to the norm or principle represented in verbal phantasms. But the rational meaning that gives the rule scientific intelligibility remains unknown to the intellect, much as the actual meaning "these events brought about Napoleon's downfall" can remain unknown in spite of judgmental assent to the concrete events of the Frenchman's invasion of Russia.

Though the problem of *transfer of training* is considerably nuanced and would more properly be discussed in a formal consideration of habit, the psychological basis of transfer emerges in the present context and is worth noting briefly. Transfer of training with regard to method can occur only when there is grasp of the intelligibility of the method. For instance, if the concrete data of an experiment in chemistry has been presented to the intellect in such a way that the phantasms reveal the actual meaning of the method of experimentation being used, one might expect transfer when an analogous experiment in, say, physics is performed. Though the latter involves different concrete data and hence different *practical* procedures, the two experiments employ the same general method of reasoning.

Psychologically speaking, then, and apart from the complexities of the problem of transfer, transfer of training consists essentially in distinct patterns of phantasms giving rise to generally the same actual meaning. Thus, when the intellect wishes to understand the meaning again in some concrete situation, or when it recognizes the situation as involving this larger meaning, it can readily organize, through the discursive sense, the concrete phantasms that make possible a practical application of the meaning. It is important to note the fact that the concrete data themselves do not transfer, and that the actual meaning must involve more than an understanding *that* this procedure applies; for immediately practical procedures are as particularized as the concrete data. It is also clear that if there is no similar meaning potentially represented in two patterns of phantasms —no rational method, for example, common to two sets of concrete data—transfer cannot occur. On this basis, one would not expect much transfer (if indeed any) between the areas of, say, literary study and experimental science. The point here is that there is no psychological reason why there *should* be any such transfer.

Whether or not the rational order underlying principles of method should be actually known will depend, of course, upon the goals had in mind for a particular learning process. But if a principle is learned apart from its rational basis, the problem of memory becomes especially prominent, since such learning is largely a question of sensory memory. People who are not mathematicians, for instance, readily forget the more complex procedures for solving practical problems simply because, never having actually understood the meaningful basis for the procedure and fortified this understanding with suitable phantasms, the practical methods have slipped away from the imagination simply through lack of exercise. Conversely, if an individual has once understood the rationale of a science, even though immediate procedures have been forgotten, the intellect is able to prepare other new phantasms suited to the concrete situation. Thus, when a person who does not entertain the idea of becoming a scientist has at some time devoted himself to learning the fundamental *meanings* of a science, there can remain a useful as well as broadened attitude of mind, even though concrete details have been lost to memory.

There are instances in which actual understanding of the meaning of norms is a requisite for man. For example, individuals who have learned ethical principles without ever getting at the rational basis and actual meanings underlying them will not readily make use of this knowledge in intensely emotional situations or in the face of adversity, when sensory recall of verbal phantasms is impeded; for there is no particular reason why a difficult situation should lead to the recall of a norm of morality that has been only verbally learned. However, it is also evident that much of our knowledge of method must remain at the level of simple assent. We cannot all be mathematicians and physicists, though we all need at least some practical, everyday knowledge of arithmetic and simple mechanics. Moreover, a child clearly cannot form a scientific habit of thinking by a single induction; a good deal of knowledge of practical principles, especially in the sciences, must often precede knowledge of rational order.

However, in addition to the problem of memory, it is important to note that learning methods apart from meanings can be a distinct *hindrance* to subsequent learning on a higher intellectual level. Take another example from arithmetic. If a child has over a period of time acquired patterns of phantasms that represent number as something "abstracted out of" sensible objects—as though a concept of "three" were gotten by looking at, say, three apples—he may gradually and ineradicably confirm in his mind a false notion of number. He does not abstract the concept of "three" out of three apples any more than he can abstract the concept of "forty-seven" by a glance at the forty-seven slats in a picket fence. He has to *count* the slats first, just as he has to know that there actually *are* three apples before he knows "three." Arithmetic is essentially a matter of counting, and, as Peter Geach puts it, the "doctrine that 'abstract numbers' are understood by abstracting from the special nature of the things numbered puts the cart before the horse." Thus, it is suggested that "what has to be mastered here is the establishment of one-one correspondence between the numerals and the things or performances being counted— e.g. one gets the child to go on to the next numeral when and only when it goes up another stair of the staircase."[4]

Now a pedestrian knowledge of arithmetic would not be hindered by a fallacious idea of number implicit in the abstractive phantasms that are instrumental in judgments involving number. But if complex phantasms of this sort have become deeply imbedded in the imagination, the difficulty that a person meets in understanding such things as algebra in later years may be due more to already existent phantasm-constructs than to a lack of native ability. Or, to take an example from another method that has been criticized in recent years, the procedure of learning to read simply by recognizing whole words and phrases without ever attacking a word phonetically is an instance of method built into phantasms that subsequently hinder the child's ability to get at the construction of more complex words.

The essential point of this analysis is that the *simplification* often necessary for primitive learning dare not be converted into a *distortion* of the object of knowledge. When they are acquired apart from solid grasp of meaning, verbal phantasms symbolic of abstract but practical facts *can* be misleading. But when they are combined with misrepresentative phantasms of a more concrete character and ordered directly to practical knowledge, it may be virtually impossible ever to *un*learn the phantasm patterns and thus to achieve more profound knowledge of the intelligible object that they misrepresent.

APHORISTIC VERBAL PHANTASMS:
THE CULTURAL AND MYTHICAL
FUNCTIONS OF WORDS

The abstract verbal phantasms that have thus far been the object of discussion are of a strictly denotative type. The connotations associated with technical definitions, methods of procedure, and the like are minimal. Not that a person will never associate verbal phantasms of a purely denotative character with other images. Just as one word becomes associated with another quite indeliberately, so we often consciously associate verbal phantasms with the concrete situation in which they were learned in order to be able to recall them more readily; this is simply an aspect of association as controlled through the intellect and the discursive sense. But strictly denotative words are intended by their user to have (and, if taken in context, invariably do have) only one meaning, which an individual more or less deeply understands, does not understand at all, or else misunderstands.

Consider on the other hand, a verbal symbol like "democracy is the government of free people." The words here clearly do not designate concrete singulars as in "Caesar crossed the Rubicon"; they are as abstract as the words in the definition of man or chrysolite. But the meaning of the words, both in themselves and in the total symbol, is much less definite and more connotative. Though the statement is a summary of a certain body of knowledge, of certain more concrete facts, it is not the conclusion of a scientific demonstration. It symbolizes a meaning, but its meaning is not precise. Summary and general statements of this sort, whose meanings can range from the loose to the equivocal, may for the sake of a term be called *aphoristic* symbols.

It is of course possible that, when a person understands an aphoristic proposition presented to the intellect in verbal phantasms, he can

give the type of mere vacuous assent to words discussed above—
for instance, "it is a fact that" democracy is the government of free
people. The assent itself is intellectual—"these words mean something"—but the verbal phantasms for this person are not symbolic
of any further meaning and thus remain sensory shapes or sounds.

However, it is a feature of the aphoristic symbol that, unlike the
purely scientific proposition which for the uneducated person often
remains a pure verbalism, some sort of meaning is invariably attached to the words. Verbal phantasms of this type generally call
forth other associated phantasms which then become instrumental
in the act of understanding. But since the statement itself is so very
loose, the potential meaning represented in phantasms and symbolized aphoristically can be quite different for each person. Phantasms, of course, are always personal. But while a verbal phantasm
representative, for instance, of "rational" or "energy" can lead two
people to conceive essentially the same meaning in spite of differences
in depth of understanding, a single verbal phantasm aphoristic in
character might cause two individuals to conceive two entirely different meanings.

To make use of our original example, by "democracy is the government of free people" one individual (say, a political scientist)
might understand the precise and qualified way in which the statement is true, while for another person it might merely be a rhetorical
and emotionally effective way of calling up a vague idea. For example, if an individual conceives the meaning of "democracy" as
nothing more than "the American government"; and if his only real
intellectual conception of "free people" is "the kind of people Ameri-
cans are," the actual intelligible content of the mental word conceived might be equivalent to "the American government is the government of the American people." The real effect of the symbol,
for this person, is found in the emotional reaction caused by the phantasms rather than in intellectual assent. Odd as an example like this
may sound, it does illustrate the relative vacuity of actual meaning
that *can* be caused by aphoristic symbols.

Owing, then, to the vagueness of aphoristic words, it is difficult to say what an individual has learned when he has acquired knowledge of this sort. If verbal phantasms of an aphoristic character—together with whatever more concrete images may have become associated with them—dominate the sensory side of one's learning in some area, it is safe enough to say that an intellectual act in which such phantasms are instrumental will produce a vague and tenuous meaning. An immediate illustration of this point can be found in the experience of hearing a talk which at the time seemed extremely inspiring and pregnant with insight, but of waking the next morning and asking oneself, "What exactly *did* the man say?" Aphoristic symbols deal with broad meanings, which would seem to be more intellectual than the assent to concrete facts. But, although knowledge of facts does not in itself constitute knowledge of the larger meanings that emerge from the facts, purely factual knowledge does possess a definiteness that knowledge of an aphoristic nature in itself lacks.

Because of the emotions and the emotionally loaded phantasms that aphoristic symbols can arouse, a person can be led to think that he knows more about the matter at hand than he actually does know. A psychological result of this sort can be seen in "lip service" being given to a meaning. The above example concerning the statement about democracy illustrates this point. In a similar vein and one more immediately pertinent to formal learning, consider aphoristic symbols like "literature forms the mind" or "a truly liberal education trains the whole man." While such truths may be operative, for instance, in constructing a balanced curriculum, they may be intellectually useless for the student who is as yet only vaguely aware of the wealth of meaning upon which they are based. Presented to the intellect in verbal phantasms, symbols of this sort may be given a type of intellectual assent which, though not purely verbal, is nonetheless thin enough to be quite useless for any practical or motivational purpose.

It is sometimes the case that aphoristic words that are intended to have a more or less definite meaning lose virtually all of their original meaning, owing to other images that a person has associated with the words. In our discussion of abstract verbal phantasms, we observed

how strictly denotative words can be vaguely and inaccurately understood—for instance, how "man is a rational animal" can be
implicitly understood to denote a ghost-in-a-machine view of man.
Now although aphoristic symbols can certainly be totally misunderstood, any number of meanings often can be accurately applied to
them, owing to their vague nature. Thus, a word like "science" can
call forth a large variety of ideas, the accuracy of which no one would
really contest as long as the meanings had something to do with "a
disciplined body of knowledge."

However, because of the phantasms that may have become linked
with a word like this, the verbal phantasms may eventually cease to
represent in potential intelligibility much denotation and acquire for
some individual a different potential meaning that has nothing to do
with the denotation of the word. Thus, for a religious-minded person
who is unaware of the relationship between true science and religion,
"science" and its derivatives may have come to symbolize an evil
form of knowledge; while, at the other end of the scale, another
individual may have learned to understand it as the only form of
valid knowledge. If these are the potential meanings attached to the
phantasms, they will necessarily affect and distort the actual meanings understood in any intellectual act in which they serve as instruments.

This is also the realm of the "magic word" used for rhetorical purposes. The patriotic emotions aroused by a symbol like "freedom"
or "my country"; or the consumer-reaction elicited by a product
that contains "*laboratory*-tested, *scientific* ingredient *x*"—responses
of this type are obtained, psychologically speaking, by adding to or
changing the potential meaning of an aphoristic symbol. Words that
are objectively indifferent are thus given special emotional values.
It is of course clear that the rhetorical effects of aphoristic words can
be beneficial as well as harmful to the intellectual and to the moral
individual; emotions can and should be brought to the service of
human action. As we have already noted, psychological difficulties
arise chiefly when phantasms guide behavior and emotional reactions
apart from rational control.

While it is true that our knowledge of things often remains more or less vague—the normal human being cannot master every object of intellectual knowledge—still, there is a difference between learning a vague meaning and learning a distorted one. Thus, just as simplification at a primitive level of learning may possibly hinder higher learning through the formation of phantasms concretely representative of incorrect method, so can distortion of meanings that contain some grain of objectivity lead to slanted attitudes and prejudices. The cause of such distortion is found in complex patterns of phantasms, often verbal and aphoristic, imbedded in the imagination.

Many of the features of aphoristic symbols as they function in the intellectual knowledge of an individual who has never really searched into the meaning of the symbols can be summarized in terms of societal tradition and *myth*. Loose statements of the type we have been discussing are heavily instrumental in the communication of a whole group's attitudes toward things. The habits of mind characteristic of a nation or of a particular group within the society are learned, and the learning of them brings into play the unique cultural history of the societal group. Thus, a cultural tradition becomes built into the phantasms of the individual, and complex combinations of concrete images with aphoristic symbols create potential meanings representative of a societal spirit. The actual meaning tangent upon an individual's conception of national tradition or spirit is almost necessarily broad if not actually vague, since such a spirit, at least for the person who is not a cultural historian, is barely tangible as a whole. Moreover, the meanings are distorted, to the extent that a person views his group's outlook on contingent things and events as exclusive of all other perspectives.

Much of a society's tradition guides *group* behavior at a subrational level, in somewhat the same way that images can control *personal* behavior apart from the direct guidance of reason. Thus, there exist judgments common to a group or a whole people—implicit judgments that affect ways of doing things, values to be attached to things, "group heroes" or the type of person to be given communal acclaim. At this level of implicit judgment, culture becomes embodied in *myth,* owing ultimately to the symbolic meanings that have become built into phantasms. Myth can be considered "benevolent" insofar as it constitutes the personality of a culture, like subconscious images that go to make up the self-concept of an individual. It becomes "malevolent" and contributes to decadence when the culture loses sight of its reasons for maintaining certain attitudes, much as images can become totally *un*conscious and still guide individual behavior. For example, the American concept of freedom and all that it entails has become embodied in benevolent myth. The subordinate place given by society to the scholar or teacher, on the other hand, might be an instance of malevolent myth, insofar as personalities of less real value to the society are raised to the status of communal heroes. Thus, cultural historians' criticisms of this or any other matter can be construed as a kind of group therapy, intended to bring aspects of the societal myth to the rational level where it can be examined and re-evaluated.[5]

This discussion emphasizes another characteristic of intellectual learning. We have seen that the exercise of an intellectual habit requires conscious and deliberate attention, and that repetition is not in itself essential for grasp of meaning, even though it can build and stabilize the meaning. Now, to the extent that cultural tradition is embodied in myth, it is not fully intellectual knowledge; for the learning of myth in the sense discussed above does not require the full attention of the intellect. Nor will repetition of things and events connected with societal tradition ever necessarily reveal a more precise meaning underlying these things and events.

Hence, if learning in the general area of culture—this would include literature as well as the historical and social sciences—is oriented purely toward imparting culture and cultural attitudes, it will not necessarily result in intellectual knowledge of history or literature or social science. For, in the case of such an orientation, phantasms are not directly formed and organized to produce an intellectual habit of "thinking historically" or "thinking literarily" and the like. And the knowledge of culture that is learned in this fashion, though it calls for awareness of meaning, need not function subsequently at a fully rational level. Thus, a careful distinction must be drawn between learning strictly for cultural purposes and learning for the sake of understanding literature and history and the like. Learning an object of knowledge for cultural reasons alone can be analogous to the tenuous type of meaning instrumentally caused by verbal phantasms of an aphoristic character.

VERBAL PHANTASMS AS MEANINGFUL:
REAL AND NOTIONAL ASSENT AND
THE FINAL DEFICIENCY OF WORDS

The different kinds of intellectual learning that can occur through the instrumentality of verbal symbols suggests both the impersonal and the personal features of words. Whether the words be symbolic of concrete singulars, definite notions, or more or less vague ideas, the potential meaning represented in the verbal phantasms can range from varying degrees of emptiness to the accurate and pregnant intelligibility of a scientific conclusion. Words that are personal owing to emotional associations rather than to precision of meaning would seem to fall somewhere between these two extremes.

Our approach to verbal phantasms has been somewhat negative, in order that the shifting qualities of these instruments of thought and learning be brought to light. However, it is also a matter of experience that verbal phantasms can be definite aids to thought. The experiences of the lecturer or the writer afford ample testimony to this point. When one is attempting to express an idea that has real scope, verbal phantasms are the natural instruments that the intellect calls upon not only for communicating the idea, but also in the very communication of it for developing it further and for seeing new implications and relationships not actually seen before. Thus, we find that when we are attempting to explain a rather abstract idea to someone else, our verbal elucidations simultaneously bring about a clarification of our own grasp of the matter. And sometimes, in the course of such explanations and in a quite unexpected way, some new meaning will break through to us. This phenomenon of consciousness is often due, psychologically speaking, to a new organization of verbal phantasms presenting a different potential meaning to the intellect.

The instances in which we discover verbal phantasms to be most helpful seem to be cases of personal thinking—acts of thought, that is, in which we are working out our own understanding of some matter and in which we have full control over the wealth of past experience represented whether concretely or symbolically in phantasms. When on the other hand some extrinsic agent—say, a teacher—is at the moment controlling the presentation of phantasms to the intellect, revelation of meaning is often a question of tackling the same matter from different points of view or, psychologically, disposing phantasms in different ways. Owing to varied past experiences as well as to differences in ability, verbal symbols that are personally meaningful to a teacher will not necessarily be the causal instruments of actual understanding for all of his students. In a process of controlled learning, consequently, verbal phantasms, even when effective, have a character somewhat different from the purely personal use of these instruments of thought.

Though more will be said about the precise causal role of the teacher in learning in the next chapter, a glance at verbal symbols that *are* genuinely instrumental in intellectual learning will pave the way for a final discussion of the learning process as a whole.

Let us call upon the concept of "energy" once again, and suppose that an individual has worked through the intricacies of this notion in such a way that he has really learned the scientific meaning of it. He has read voraciously, he has attended many lectures, and he has laced all of this abstract study, most of which has entailed the use of verbal phantasms, with personal reflection on relativity theory and the like. He has learned, more or less deeply, the actual meaning of a statement like "energy can be understood in terms of mass and the velocity of light." His intellect assents to this kinematic consequence of the theory of relativity, and the assent is a firm one. The intellect sees this simply as an intelligible fact, however abstract.

Now our friend can also assent to the fact that the desk before him is gray, and the assent will be no different if the fact is represented verbally, since the words merely symbolize a concrete fact of immediate perception. His intensive study, however, has enabled his knowledge of the way energy can be validly understood to be as rigorous as his knowledge of the concrete fact that his desk is gray. But is the assent connected with an *abstract fact,* logically and intelligibly obtainable through verbal phantasms truly symbolic of the fact, quite the same as the assent given to an immediate *fact of sense experience?*

John Henry Newman's analysis in the *Grammar of Assent* is helpful in the present context. Following Newman's lead, we shall call the assent made to abstract facts, presented to the intellect largely through the instrumentality of the verbal phantasms whose meaning is truly understood, *notional assent;* and the assent made to the concrete data of immediate experience *real assent.*[6]

It may be noted that the *act* of assent in either case is essentially the same. The intellect undergoes an intelligible commitment, in one instance to the truth of an abstract fact, in the other to a truth of direct perceptual experience. The difference between notional and real assent thus lies on the side of the intelligible object rather than of the judgmental act itself; and in either case the intellect must reflect to phantasms in some way representative of the object of knowledge.

Let us suppose now that our friend who has become interested in the concept of energy has supplemented his intensive notional study with scientific experimentation. He actually performs a scientific induction; he integrates his mathematical and other constructural knowledge with the experimental evidence that in fact contributes to the verification of the scientific concept; and in so understanding the concrete data proper to his quest, he exercises real assent upon the data. In seeing the *notion* of energy actually realized in nature, his judgmental knowledge has been complemented and deepened by *real* assents. We are met here with another form of the analogy of predicated meaning discussed at the end of the last chapter: the same abstract fact is actually understood in either type of judgmental assent, but the notional assent itself has been made deeper and the same abstract fact exhibits a fuller intelligibility owing to the real assents. For in understanding the concrete data of experience or experiment, the intellect's commitment to the abstract notion—logically obtainable, at least by the learner, apart from real experience—is now made, not only on the basis of logical rigor, but in the light of concrete singulars. In a word, the notional assent has itself been converted into a real assent.

From the example used above it can be seen that a real assent does not necessarily involve *practical* knowledge. The scientist who sees a difficult and abstract construct realized in nature, the philosopher who finds the truth of a metaphysical principle expressed in the real existence of some being, the historian who sees a general pattern realized in the actions and thoughts of a particular era—none of these men are concerned with immediately practical knowledge. But even though they are dealing with the type of abstract notions proper to their own disciplines, the real assents of these men are as uniquely personal as the concrete experience or experiment itself.

In learning abstract meanings, consequently, the communication of the meanings takes place almost necessarily through abstract verbal symbols. For *notions* constitute that part of any body of knowledge which is common to all men. Notions can be communicated, and the abstract meanings can be grasped with genuine intellectual understanding in notional assents. But learning is in a sense incomplete until the notions have become personal; and real assents, because they *are* personal, cannot be fully communicated. Hence, there is that part of any process of learning which lies beyond and in a way defies communication.

As an illustration of the incommunicable character of real assent, consider the work of the poet. His whole effort is directed toward communicating an experience, which he embodies in words and rhythms and images—symbols of emotions and situations as well as of larger meanings. Through the music and meaning of words, he builds up one whole symbol intended to convey one total meaning, and that meaning a personal one. Assuming that the poet has succeeded in articulating the richness of his experience, we find ourselves in the area of verbal symbols that are pregnant with potential meaning; the symbols are certainly as meaningful to the person who perceives them as are the more abstract verbal phantasms that the intellect may use to come to genuine notional understanding. Now it would seem that the person who reads the poetic symbol and understands meaning gives more than a notional assent, for the meaning of the poet is clothed in the most concrete of images that seem to call forth a fully real assent. However, consider Newman's reflections on this point. Consider

how differently young and old are affected by the words of some classic author, such as Homer or Horace. Passages, which to a boy are but rhetorical commonplaces, neither better nor worse than a hundred others which any clever writer might supply, which he gets by heart and thinks very fine, and imitates, as he thinks, successfully, in his own flowing versification, at length come home to him, when long years have passed, and he has had experience of life, and pierce him, as if he had never before known them, with their sad earnestness and vivid exactness. Then he comes to understand how it is that lines, the birth of some chance morning or evening at an Ionian festival, or among the Sabine hills, have lasted generation after generation, for thousands of years, with a power over the mind, and a charm, which the current literature of his own day, with all its obvious advantages, is utterly unable to rival. Perhaps this is the reason of the medieval opinion about Virgil, as if a prophet or magician; his single words and phrases, his pathetic half lines, giving utterance, as the voice of Nature herself, to that pain and weariness, yet hope of better things, which is the experience of her children in every time.[7]

A magnificently expressed tribute to classical literature, Newman's statement also touches the salient point of real assent. It is not enough that one assent to the intelligibility of concrete things and events as they are described and symbolized to the intellect in verbal phantasms. However concrete the images formed in accord with the symbols may be, *real* assent is not actually complete until there has been a non-symbolic contact with *reality* itself. Hence, verbal phantasms, whether they be concrete, abstract, or aphoristic, never constitute the fullness of learning. Words can do no more than indicate the direction in which real assent may be found. They can only map the path of conversion from notional to real assent.

A notional assent is intelligible; otherwise it would not be an intellectual act. But notions simply lack the force possessed by immediate experience, the force of *things,* which give depth to understanding as no abstract meaning in itself can. For, the object that is naturally proper and proportioned to the human intellect is the intelligibility directly revealed by concrete things.

Hence, the type of understanding from which everything that is learned gets its final fullness and depth of meaning is the immediate, intelligible, and personal experience of concrete things. Real assent, in other words, presents itself as the *primary analogate* or point of focus for any form of learning. This central fact underlies and in a sense embraces all of the characteristics of intellectual learning that have been isolated and investigated in the course of this chapter. No matter what the knowledge, no matter how abstract or elaborate or profound the meaning learned, no matter how instrumental verbal phantasms may have been in learning the matter, *learning* is essentially incomplete until there has been a return in some way to the immediacy of sense experience.

In the light of these facts, we shall go on to examine the learning process as a whole and to see what the return to experience means, in terms of the type of learning that is natural to man.

NOTES

1. Perception is only one of the factors that enters into response to a stimulus. As Woodworth has emphasized, S–R should be revised to read S–O–R; for, the whole organism with its individual differences in structure, present physiological and emotional condition, etc., falls between the stimulus and the response. See Robert S. Woodworth, *Psychology* (3d ed.; New York: Henry Holt & Co., 1934), pp. 3–15.

    We are prescinding for the most part from the physiological factors affecting behavior.

2. Attention should be called to the fact that the analyses conducted in this and the following chapters are totally dependent upon and completely presuppose the work of chaps. 2 to 4. If thorough cross-references were to be given to the pertinent conclusions that evolved in these chapters, every other sentence would perhaps have to be footnoted. Hence, references will not ordinarily be made to our prior analyses, even though they alone give philosophical validity to the conclusions drawn here.

   It is also important to recall the theme of chap. 1, that our analysis of learning is a philosophical one. The conclusions drawn here are reached on the basis of *experiential* rather than experimental evidence, and they are made in terms of the ontological structure of knowledge and the human knower. The conclusions will in a number of instances be seen to be parallel to (not exactly the same as) the conclusions reached through *experimental* evidence and the hypothetico-deductive procedures of scientific psychology. However, references are not made to these analogous experimental conclusions, primarily because brief references do not reveal the real meaning of a higher-order experimental law. A genuine integration and objective comparison of scientific and philosophical conclusions would require a separate study, one lying outside the scope of the present work.

3. We prescind here from a philosophical analysis of habit, i.e., from consideration of the formal causes of habits within the human structure.

4. Peter Geach, *Mental Acts: Their Content and Their Objects* ("Studies in Philosophical Psychology," ed. R. F. Holland; New York: Humanities Press, 1957), pp. 31–32. Analyses of formation of different kinds of concepts, with criticisms of theories proposing a form of "drawing concepts out of" things, appear throughout *ibid.*, esp. pp. 18–44. On the psychological meaning of "abstraction," cf. above, pp. 64–65.

5. For a fuller discussion of the question of myth, in the context of the phantasm's role in judgment, see F. D. Wilhelmsen, "The Philosopher and the Myth," *Modern Schoolman*, XXXII (1954), 39–55.

6. Newman develops these ideas chiefly throughout the first part of the book, though this analysis is fundamental to his whole study; see *An Essay in Aid of a Grammar of Assent*, ed. Chas. F. Harrold (New York: Longmans, Green & Co., 1947), pp. 3–74. Although Newman elaborates these ideas for purposes of his own, his analysis has suggested a good number of the ideas developed in the present

section of this study. It is to be noted, however, that Newman does not conduct his analysis in terms of the psychology employed in our study. Hence, in integrating his notions with the psychology involved in the intellect-phantasm relationship, it is possible that I may have distorted his original ideas in some way, perhaps by limiting the scope they are meant to have in the *Grammar*.

On *assent* as St. Thomas uses the term, see below, chapter 6, note 6.

7. Newman, *Grammar of Assent,* pp. 59–60.

6

THE ANALOGY OF LEARNING

WHEN ONE looks at a color spectrum of the sort found among the illustrative plates in technical treatises on light, he sees colors ranging from red to violet. If someone should ask at what specific point the red ends and the violet begins, he would be at a loss to answer. He might indicate certain definite points on the spectrum and say that this spot represents what we usually call "red" and this particular point is definitely "violet." But since the spectrum is actually a continuum of color, his verbal isolation of specific places in the continuum would be somewhat artificial.

Human knowing, like the color spectrum, is a continuum. In discussing judgmental and conceptual knowledge in Chapter Four, we isolated definite instances of each of these acts of intellect in order to bring to light the chief characteristics of each and especially to illustrate the distinguishing marks of judgment. But the analysis must be taken precisely as an analysis, for human acts of knowing do not take place in an isolated fashion. Now, taking judgment as the distinctively human act of understanding—for it is the act that brings the intellect into contact with concrete things—we can place it at either end of the continuum of knowledge. Thus, looking at the spectrum from one end, acts of judgment gradually give rise to the moment of pure conceptual knowledge, that suspended instant of insight in which a meaning is grasped apart from predication; and conceptual knowledge, found somewhere in the middle of the spectrum, quickly gives way once again to judgment, in which the new conceptual meaning is seen in relation to another meaning or to things.

Just as color of some sort is the common factor throughout the gradations found on the spectrum, so are there common elements in every act of knowing. At the conclusion of Chapter Two, we saw what is common to cognition in general and what it means to speak of an analogy of cognition. Thus, one can analytically distinguish the common and the differing elements among ways of knowing and the cognitive powers themselves; but in the existential order each *mode* of knowledge and each knowing *power* differs from another in the very act of being similar to it. For, as things actually exist and as operations actually take place, they cannot be univocally classified with respect to their total reality.

Again, in Chapters Three and Four, we observed that both the phantasm and the intellect are common factors in intellectual knowledge. They make possible the continuum of human knowing, much as actual color makes the spectrum possible. But, to use again the somewhat artificial descriptive terms of Chapter Four, whether the intellect sees the meaning *in* phantasms and thus has purely conceptual knowledge; or whether it reflects *to* phantasms and thus judgmentally understands a meaning *of* something, each act of knowing is existentially unique, just as each point on the color spectrum is unique even though it shares the quality of color with every other point.

In developing the analogy of predicated meaning toward the end of Chapter Four, we saw how it is psychologically possible for the same meaning to be more or less fully realized by different persons or by the same person in different stages of learning. The significant point in this analysis was that the depth of actual predicated meaning is dependent upon the potential meaning represented in phantasms. Approaching the nature and types of intellectual learning by way of different sorts of verbal phantasms, we were able to illustrate in Chapter Five the psychological nuances of potential and actual meaning—from purely verbal knowledge, through various kinds of knowledge of facts and more tenuous meanings, to the fullness of actual meaning found in disciplined theoretical knowledge. In this elaboration of different types of judgmental and conceptual understanding, a further analogy comes to light. For, while images of some sort are common to all learning, from the mechanical to the speculative, the kind of assent given by the intellect and the extent to which it actually understands what is presented to it in phantasms has wide variations.

In Chapter One, it was noted how the inductive moments of philosophical or experimental procedure give way to the stage of judgmental organization, in which concrete evidences are read in the light of scientific principles. This interplay between the evidential and the demonstrative moments of reasoning was observed throughout our study of different forms of knowing and learning, to the extent that experiential evidences pertinent to a particular issue were integrated with the nature of human understanding, once we had actually determined the real structure of knowledge and the human knower. Now at this point, having seen real, non-symbolic assent to concrete things as the primary analogate of all learning; and having concluded for the most part our gathering of evidence from varied types of learning experience, we can round off our study with a consideration of learning as a total process. Thus, the present chapter, to be concluded with a definition of learning in its cognitive aspects, will serve as a final integrated exposition and summary organization of the meaning of human learning.

THE EXPERIENTIAL FOUNDATIONS
OF LEARNING

It is evident that learning must begin somewhere, and it has already been suggested that the infant can be said to "learn" with his very first cognitive acts. Jean Piaget's work on the origins of intelligence in children, summarized in terms of his "theory of assimilation," traces experimentally the earliest phases in the development of intelligence. Piaget emphasizes especially the *dynamic* part played by the child's mind in this growth. Learning, even in its primitive stages, is not simply a question of mechanically determined connections made between new stimuli and old responses. It is a real activity, one in which the child actively assimilates objects to his cognitive self.[1] Thus, learning how to put a watch chain into a very small box and figuring out how to enlarge the aperture in the box in order to remove the chain again requires an active process of this sort. From the very first, learning is a matter of cognitively extending and building naturally upon previous experience. "Just as sensori-motor assimilation of things to the subject's schemata extends biological assimilation of the environment to the organism, so also it presages the intellectual assimilation of objects to the mind, such as is proven to exist in the most evolved forms of rational thought."[2]

It may be noted, in terms of the cognitive structure of man, that the infant's primitive learning *can* be a matter of pure sense knowledge. That intellectual knowledge is not *required* for behavior of the type illustrated above by the watch chain and box is indicated by similar activity in animals. The rat learns to find his way through a maze to the cheese, and an ape manages to stack boxes one on the other in order to reach a bunch of bananas. These various activities entail the apprehension of *concrete* relations, and thus they find their psychological roots in the power of memory-imagination and the animal estimative sense. The complexity of concrete relations that the more intelligent animals can actually apprehend indicates the perfection that these internal senses can reach apart from intellect. We have already noted how the estimative sense of an animal is supplied with highly sensitive "instincts" of various sorts, innate cognitive equipment which man's senses in fact lack.

Whether or not the intellect of the infant *is* actually operative in the type of concrete learning suggested above—one can make only educated guesses in answering this question, since the infant clearly cannot tell us. The general principle is that, if the internal senses have become sufficiently developed to form a potentially intelligible phantasm and not simply an image which guides behavior apart from rational operations, then there is some grasp of meaning—initially, of course, extremely vague. But at some point in the process of the development of intelligence, there does occur a real intellectual apprehension of some object in the ken of the child's experience. This primitive judgment (the act must be judgmental and not purely conceptual, since the intellect is in contact with real objects only in judgment) does contain actual intelligibility, confused and vague as it may be. If the child had any command of language, he would say "that object is something" or whatever the verbal expression of this first vague judgment might be. But the intellect now has meaningful content with which it can work.

THE NATURAL HABIT OF REAL ASSENT

Let us take a closer look at this primitive foundation of intellectual learning. When the infant first understands that an object which he perceives is, say, "something" (and we may recall that the judgment need not be verbalized in order to be a true act of the mind), he understands an actual meaning. For even when he understands a meaning as vague as this one, the intelligible content of his act excludes all possibility of the fact that the object which he perceives is "not nothing." The fact that the object is there before him and that he intellectually assents to its presence precludes all possibility of the object's *not* being there in the same respect in which it *is* there. Rudimentary as this analysis may sound, it does emphasize the distinguishing mark of *any* act of intellectual knowledge. No matter what the intellect may know, whether in a very confused or highly precise fashion, it knows the thing as actually intelligible in some respect. Or, in terms of the human cognitive structure, no matter what a phantasm may represent in potential meaning, the cognitive intellect in virtue of the principal causality of the agent intellect always knows a thing as actually meaningful in some respect. In short, man can be said to have a *natural intellectual habit* by which he is immediately able to grasp some intelligible aspect of things, even in the first act of intellectual knowledge.[3]

To speak of a natural habit of this sort is really nothing more than to express, in terms of the nature of the intellect itself, the fact that man can understand things. The consequences of this habit in the perspective of learning are significant. For, owing to the natural ability that the intellect has to grasp the direct intelligibility of things, real assent as discussed in the preceding chapter is rendered causally possible. Let us examine this point further.

To use one of Aquinas' favorite examples, once a person actually understands what a whole is and what a part is, he can immediately understand that the whole is always greater than any of its parts. Whether or not the individual expresses this knowledge in verbal symbols, the point is that his judgment is itself an intellectual expression of the meaningfulness of things. For, whatever words be used to designate part and whole, any real whole and real part are of such a nature that the whole is *in reality* greater than any of its parts. A house is always necessarily larger than any of its rooms; a razor with its blade is always necessarily larger than the blade itself. These facts, one might say, are so obvious that they are banal. But this is the precise point of the whole analysis. Propositions such as these *are* self-evident because the real facts that they symbolize and the things to which the intellect judgmentally assents are themselves directly intelligible. Hence, once the intellect actually directs its attention to the immediate facts of sense experience, it assents to them without any further reasoning. In the example of whole and part, the knowledge obtained is more precise than the child's first intellectual awareness of "something," but it is no less immediate. For it is impossible to reason logically to the direct intelligibility of sense experience.

It may be noted that the child's meaningful experience of an object as "something" and hence "not nothing," or a person's realization that a whole is always greater than any of its parts, can be *logically* summarized in terms of the principle of noncontradiction: a thing cannot simultaneously be and not be in the same respect. As a matter of fact, this principle could be "deduced" from or is implied in *any* given act of intellectual knowledge, for it is simply a logical statement of the meaningfulness of any object of any sort which is known: a thing cannot be intelligible and unintelligible in the same respect and at the same time. Now when a person first understands a self-evident principle, he cannot give to it a notional assent; owing to the fact that such a principle is of its very nature an intellectual expression of the intelligibility of immediate experience, it can be given only a real assent upon first being understood.

We must distinguish carefully, then, between man's natural power to know things as in some way intelligible and an act of intellect in which a self-evident *abstract meaning* based on the direct intelligibility of things is actually being understood—for instance, an abstract meaning like the principle of noncontradiction. Whether or not a person verbally formulates self-evident principles in the course of learning (and symbolic formulation is itself learned) is quite irrelevant. The point is that there are times when we are confronted with some immediately meaningful aspect of things or events; and it is this confrontation, naturally assented to in judgment, which provides the intelligible material for future learning. Thus, when a person actually assents to the fact that Napoleon invaded Russia, this fact functions as a kind of first principle or starting point for any further knowledge he may gain about the matter. He does not question the basic intelligibility of this historical fact any more than the mechanical physicist speculates on whether or not bodies move. In either case, there is a real assent to concrete data, made in virtue of the intellect's natural habit of grasping the direct intelligibility of concrete singulars.

In the light of this analysis, it can be said that man's natural intellectual habit is a *natural habit of real assent*. For, once it has attended to some meaningful aspect of concrete things, the intellect cannot but assent to it: it cannot deny that what is intelligible is not intelligible in the same respect in which it *is* intelligible. Owing ultimately to this natural habit, the first principles that function as the logical foundations of disciplined forms of knowledge can be formulated. But sense experience of some kind is prior to any such symbolic formulation. Hence, there are two kinds of first principles in all knowledge and learning—the first intelligible principles of an organized body of knowledge and sense experience itself.[4]

THE FIRST PRINCIPLES OF LEARNING

From direct experience of concrete data, the primary analogate of learning, learning can branch off in many directions and take on innumerable forms. We have already noted how disciplined scientific knowledge entails as its first principles both sense data and the fundamental logical principles of the science itself. Thus, the organized stage of disciplined knowledge, whether philosophical or empirical, involves a resolution to the first principles of the science that give the conclusions their final logical validity; and to the data of experience or experiment, which are not only the ultimate source of the first principles themselves but also make possible a real assent to an abstract conclusion. At the far end of the knowledge scale, we find abstract sciences like pure mathematics, in which sense experience (apart from some basic experience of existence) plays no direct role at all and in which the first principles of the science have no direct relationship to concrete reality. At this level, real assent in the proper sense of the term is neither possible nor necessary; or one might say that seeing a mathematical conclusion in the light of the principles or set theory from which it is deduced constitutes a kind of real assent, insofar as such an insight in an a priori science is analogous to the return to sense data in other forms of knowledge.

Apart from these highly sophisticated forms of learning, however, most of our learning involves as first principles simply the concrete data from which larger meanings are drawn through thinking and reasoning of a more informal character. This is true of any type of knowledge that does not constitute a disciplined science possessing definite organizational principles of its own. Literary and historical forms of knowledge, for instance, are not in themselves philosophical or experimental sciences; and hence the intelligible basis for any more abstract meaning as well as the basis for real assent lies primarily in the concrete data itself. Most of our ordinary learning, which combines reasonable certitude regarding facts with a good deal of opinion about the meaning of the facts, belongs in the area of learning where the first principles are simply the data of experience. It is also clear that any form of mechanical learning finds its place in this realm, for such learning is thoroughly dependent upon concrete situations.

Now along with the different types of concrete data that function as the fundamental sources of learning goes a certain difference in real assent. The assent given to a bald historical fact that functions as first principle in some area of historical knowledge, for example, is in a way no less *real* than the assent to the immediate data of perception; for in either case the intellect is confronted with an intelligible aspect of concrete singulars, a meaning to which it does not reason. But within the similarity of assent lies a diversity of *perception*.

Here McKellar's discussion is helpful, in the context of his distinction between primary and secondary perceptions:

To illustrate *primary perception* we may instance seeing a table, hearing a bomb fall, and feeling the pain of being scratched by a cat or stung by a bee. Corresponding *secondary perceptions* would be seeing a picture of a table, hearing a sound recording of a bomb falling, and listening to a description of the event by one who has been scratched or stung. In the case of a primary perception there is immediate, direct experience of the object or situation; in secondary perception there is something intermediate between the subject and the object or situation perceived.[5]

It is in the realm of secondary perception that the true descriptive function of words discussed in the last chapter comes into play, as well as the innumerable other media of our day—photographs, movies, television, radio, sound recordings, and so on. To the extent that the many sources of secondary perception substitute for direct experience, they lead the way to real assent in many areas of learning where a direct return to experience would otherwise be impossible. They supply, in other words, phantasms of a concrete character which make possible some limited conversion from notional to real assent in a given area of knowledge. Thus, secondary no less than primary perceptions can function as first principles in learning. To the extent that a medium of secondary perception involves hearsay or an incomplete, arbitrary, and possibly biased arrangement of concrete data, it falls short of the objectivity and immediacy of direct experience. But it would not be disputed that such media are on the whole much more operative in broadening an individual's experience far beyond the scope that his own personal means could possibly provide.

Primary perception, however, remains an ultimate. It results in a completely personal, non-symbolic assent to the concrete; while secondary perceptions, since they entail "something intermediate between the subject and the object or situation perceived," remain in a certain sense symbolic. Thus, one who has seen an impressive movie of sociological conditions in the Far East lacks the final impression that direct experience could supply. Or, in spite of Thucydides' brilliant and vivid narration of the expeditions in the Peloponnesian War, one can never equal the Greek historian's own witness. We may also recall Newman's remarks, quoted in the last chapter, that the real meaning of a poet's insights, couched as they may be in the most concrete and emotionally connotative of symbols, often does not fully and personally strike us until we have gone through an experience similar to that of the writer. For it is at the level of direct experience that the natural habit of real assent exercises itself to the fullest degree.

THE NATURAL PROCESS OF LEARNING

We might use again our analogy of the color spectrum and compare any learning process to the spectrum. At either end lies a judgment—ideally, and if the learning process is truly complete, a judgment of real rather than notional assent. Between these points lies the learning process itself, involving all of its acts of judgmental and conceptual understanding together with the sensory material represented in phantasms which make these acts possible. The judgment of real assent initiating the process springs from the intellect's natural habit of grasping the immediate intelligibility of things. The judgment ideally concluding the process brings us once again to the situation of our art lover of Chapter Four who, once he has seen the larger whole of the mural, brings the depth of his total experience to any judgment he makes about the part. The first judgment is a commitment of the intellect to direct meaning. The last is a commitment to larger meaning, seen however in the light of direct meaning.[6]

This is the learning process that is *natural* to man because it is the process that is directly proportioned to the natural structure of human understanding. Ultimately, it is a consequence of the fact that the object proper and naturally proportioned to the human intellect is a directly intelligible aspect of sensible things.

Any given learning process is only analogous to and never identical with any other; for, the moments and stages that constitute it as well as the concrete data and principles with which it is concerned differ according to various types of knowing and learning. But in any case the process of learning natural to man is a process of *discovery*. Discovery never divorces itself from the concrete; for it is precisely the wealth of meaning latent in things that the learning process brings to light in various ways, thus leading the intellect gradually to depth of predicated meaning.

We can at this point integrate the matter of discovery with the role of the phantasm in thinking. Recall that the intellectually controlled formation of schematized phantasms for more abstract thinking depends ultimately upon concrete experience, upon more immediate data which is gradually and symbolically refined. Thus, the poet builds his artistic symbols in terms of concrete images which reflect his unique experience of the world of men and things and thoughts contemporary to him. The philosopher conducts his speculative thinking in terms of the concrete problems that emerge in the world of his own day. The scientist has always found it convenient to make use of model analogies in his construct-formation, models which in fact have varied according to the spirit and emphases of a given era. Thus, the strict mechanical models and the "billiard-ball universe" of earlier centuries have given way to the more complex and highly developed mathematical models of our own day.[7] In short, it is natural for man to discover meanings—to get at the intelligibility of things—to develop the symbolic phantasms necessary for thought and invention—in terms of his own personal experiences with the world about him, in terms of real assents.

Pursuing the same theme, we may at this point note the real status of symbolic expression and communication in learning. Expression, as we have seen, involves the clothing of actual meaning in the sensuous materials provided in phantasms; thus, verbal symbols as they exist in phantasms are highly schematized and refined patterns of of sensory matter. But, in the strict psychological order, symbolization is posterior to actual understanding. Hence, when one learns through symbols, when the symbols are for the learner prior to actual meaning, a kind of *tension* arises between the natural process of learning through discovery and learning through communication or teaching. For words, in having become prior to actual meaning, have also become prior to things, the natural and final storehouse of meaning for man.

The tension that exists between learning through teaching and the natural learning process can also be seen in a broader perspective. The teacher, it may be noted, is a true cause of learning. Just as the phantasm specifies the content of a particular act of understanding, so does the teacher specify what the pupil learns here and now; and as the agent intellect is the cause of the actual intelligibility of what is known, so is the pupil himself the one who actually learns what is presented to him. The teacher, then, is an instrumental cause of learning. But the student is always the principal cause, for the teacher can never learn for the student.[8]

Now the teacher is interested in organizing his subject matter in such a way that the pupil will acquire a reasonably well-ordered body of knowledge in some area. He does not simply teach arithmetic or literature or chemistry; rather, right now he is teaching long division or lyric poetry or the notion of valence. But, as we have seen throughout our analysis, judgmentally organized knowledge of any kind and in any area of learning is posterior to the process of discovery itself. Hence, there can exist a tension between the organizational or specificative function of the teacher and the natural process of inquiry that the learner might otherwise work through on his own, a process of investigation whose order would be determined by the immediate interests and background of the individual learner.

Recognizing the genuine though supplementary role played by the teacher in learning, St. Thomas does not hesitate to remark that "knowledge is acquired in two ways: without teaching, through discovery; and through teaching." But almost in the same breath he adds, "The teacher therefore begins teaching as one who discovers goes about discovering." Conscious that the teaching-learning situation is more artificial than natural, Aquinas suggests two ways in which the teacher proceeds. First, he offers to the pupil's consideration principles that he already knows and guides him in drawing further conclusions from these principles. Here we are in the order of intellectual knowledge that is tangent upon the teacher's organizational function. For although the pupil is working from previous knowledge, lest the learning process take place in a vacuum, the teacher nevertheless guides his learning by way of judgmental exposition. The teacher takes the student in an *ordered* fashion through the rigors of long division or chemical valence, beginning with the arithmetical or scientific principles that the student already knows. But, in order to assure that the organized teaching procedure does not break away from the natural process of learning through discovery, the teacher also proposes "sensible examples from which the phantasms necessary for understanding may be formed in the pupil's mind."[9]

Thus, it is by calling upon the learner's natural habit of real assent that the teacher is able to resolve the tension between formal organization of subject matter and natural discovery, the tension between words and things. In this light, the use of "sensibile examples" —and here all the tools of primary and secondary perception offer themselves to the teacher—is not just a helpful supplement in pedagogical method. Rather, it is a *necessary* part of any learning process if, in Aquinas' words, learning is really a matter of discovery and teaching a matter of helping the student to discover; or if, in Newman's language, notional assent is ever to give way to real assent. The completeness of a learning process proportioned to the real nature of human understanding depends upon the personal experience of things in much the same way that the organism depends for its growth upon food. For concrete experience is in a sense the natural food of the intellect that *really* learns.

DEFINITION OF LEARNING

A final summary can be made in terms of a definition of learning in its cognitive aspects, of learning as it entails the unique intentional union described in Chapter Two.

Apart from the operative powers themselves which contribute to the unity of the human cognitive structure and hence to the unity of knowing and learning, the element that is common to all learning activity is the *image,* whose function is analogous in different types of learning. In mechanical learning, images, which may be more or less precise and which are for the most part kinesthetic, can guide behavior without the conscious and deliberate attention of the intellect. They can also function at a subconscious level in much habitual behavior, and, in abnormal behavior, often at an unconscious level. In the case of intellectual knowledge, whether of a practical or theoretical nature and whether the actual meanings be precise or vague, images or, technically speaking, phantasms serve as the potentially intelligible instruments of the intellect in every act of understanding; but the different acts of the intellect are only analogously alike in form and in content.

While every image is the product of the operative power of imagination, the *acquisition* of images is different in the various types of learning, for the perceptual situation determines the kind of images that are actually acquired. Thus, verbal and other symbolic phantasms can be acquired perceptually, as well as simple concrete images involving the modes of external sense; working with any of this data, the imagination can form new patterns of images or phantasms. Moreover, some images are acquired only for the purpose of guiding concrete behavior, while others are acquired and formed explicitly to present potential meaning to the intellect.

The *organization* of images also differs according to the learning situation. The formation of complex image patterns is determined sometimes by sense perception, as in the case of images which function in motor skills and other concrete behavior; and sometimes by the intellect which, making use of the gross data of sense, guides the imagination in forming the more abstractive and symbolic phantasms suitable for higher forms of understanding. The sensory emotions also contribute in different ways to the formation and recall of image patterns; and the discursive sense enters into the process of organization especially in situations entailing practical judgment, though it is also operative in focusing attention and interest upon any situation. The internal unifying sense, finally, enters into the organization of images through its unification of the disparate data of the external senses; when it does not operate concomitantly with the power of imagination, the organization of images can take place at a nonconscious level.

Hence, *in the perspective of a philosophical psychology of knowledge, learning may be defined as the acquisition and organization of images.*

Since, we have just recalled, the image as well as its acquisition and its organization all entail analogy, the definition is analogical. We are not simply designating the feature that is common to all learning. Rather, the point of this definition is that each type of learning is different from another in the very act of being similar to it. Rational life, for example, is essentially different from biological life, even though both forms of life entail immanent activity. Similarly, consider the differences between intellectual and motor learning. In the case of the former, the intellect enters actively into the process of acquiring and organizing images or phantasms, which represent in potential intelligibility something that the intellect actually understands. In motor learning, on the other hand, images are acquired and organized not because they represent potential meaning, but only because they are cognitively necessary for guiding concrete behavior. And yet, there can be neither actual meaning nor organized sensory behavior without phantasms or images. Thus, intellectual learning differs from mechanical learning—both in the operations involved and in the resultant content of knowledge—in the very act of being similar to it.

The same definition also applies to differences and similarities *within* a given type of learning. Thus, while all motor learning entails images, the precision of images, the complexity of image patterns, and the degree of attention required in the mechanical exercise vary according to the skill in question. And while every act of the intellect is dependent upon phantasms, the intelligible content of the mental word differs according to the character of the phantasm as it is formed through the complexus of internal sensation and emotion.

Now, the definition of learning given above is only a general or *material* definition. Suppose we were to define an engine as an apparatus constructed to produce a mechanical reaction from some form of energy. Although it may be sufficient as a general description, this definition can be further specified. Thus, an internal-combustion engine produces the motion of a piston from the explosion of a fuel-air mixture. A steam engine produces mechanical power from energy created by steam. And an engine modeled on the jet principle produces its forward thrust as a result of a rearward discharge of energy. The latter descriptions of different types of engines do not negate the general, material definition of an engine. But they are more specific, more formal; for they suggest the formal features of different types of engines.

Since intellectual learning is the most fully human type of learning, a *formal* definition of intellectual learning will be very much in place here. The essential difference between intellectual and sensory forms of cognition, too, calls for a separate definition of this sort. Now, three things must be kept in mind in formulating this definition: the general definition which embraces all learning; the distinguishing or formal features of the intellective process; and the characteristic which identifies the truest and most complete form of human intellectual knowledge.

First, in order to take into account our material definition of learning, we need merely refer to intellectual learning as a "process of learning"; for any such process entails the acquisition and organization of images, in the analogous sense explained above. Secondly, noting the distinctive features of intellectual knowledge, we may call intellectual learning a judgmental-conceptual process, since any rational procedure involves judgmental references to an object of knowledge together with the conceptual insights obtained through acts of judgment. Finally, we may recall that judgments of real assent alone give intellectual learning its final validity and completeness.

Hence, *intellectual learning is a judgmental-conceptual process of learning which ideally finds both its principle and its term in judgments of real assent.*

Like the general or material definition of learning, this formal definition of intellectual learning is analogical. Without a knower there can be no object of actual knowledge. But, owing to the analogy of predicated meaning found in human knowledge, no two acts of knowing an object are identical in every respect, even though the cognitive operations and the powers from which they proceed are similar. Furthermore, a judgment of real assent involves an existential situation, for such a judgment touches some concrete reality. But, though they may be similar, no two existential situations are in every respect identical. In short, one process of intellectual learning differs from another in the very act of being similar to it.

We might well end this chapter with a note of caution. The analogical definitions of learning given here are conclusions drawn from our entire study. As such, they are meaningful only if read

strictly in the light of the evidences gathered and the analyses conducted throughout the course of the study. In itself, a definition is an
abstract notion. Its intellectual force flows only from personal, real
assent.

NOTES

1. Jean Piaget, *The Origins of Intelligence in Children*, tr. Margaret
   Cook (New York: International Universities Press, 1952), p. 409;
   on the theory of assimilation and the theoretical conclusions of
   Piaget's experimental data, see pp. 407–19.
2. *Ibid.*, p. 409. Cf. the order found among the powers of the soul,
   above pp. 73–74.
3. Generally speaking, a *habit* is an acquired modification (quality) of
   an operative power that does not require the loss of any other perfection of the power. Thus, adaptation of a biological organism to
   its environment is not usually construed as a habit for reasons that
   are in fact philosophically sound; such adaptation modifies the
   structure of the cell itself and hence (philosophically) involves the
   loss of a previous qualitative perfection. The habit spoken of above
   is called a *natural habit* because it is the very nature of the human
   intellect, in every act, to know whatever it does know as intelligible;
   individual differences, consequently, do not affect this natural habit.
   Thus, the passivity of the intellect is totally overcome as it were by
   an active principle, namely, the intelligible *species* which always determines the intellect to knowledge of an object that is intelligible in
   some respect. But, as Aquinas emphasizes, no habit is totally natural,
   since some sensible apprehension is required to generate the habit;
   hence, the habit with which we are concerned here is not properly
   speaking *innate*. For further details on these points, see *S. T.* I–II,
   q. 51, aa. 1–3.
4. For some detailed statements on sense as the first principle of knowledge, see e.g., *Commentary on the Sentences*, Bk. IV, dist. 9, a. 4,
   qa. 1; *De Veritate*, q. 12, a. 3 & ad 3.
   As was indicated in the bibliographical survey in the Introduction
   to this study, St. Thomas' teaching on the matter of first principles
   has often been grossly misunderstood. The chief error seems to
   arise in confusing his *psychological* treatment of the natural habit
   (cf. above, note 3) with the *logical* first principles of organized

science. Thus, Aquinas' teaching has not infrequently been converted into a rationalism.

Thomas does not formally state the principles of *noncontradiction and identity* (the latter is the positive side of the former, i.e., "what is, is" or "being is being") as they are found in logic texts; he rather gives examples of self-evident knowledge (like the whole-part example used above). See Louis-Marie Régis, O.P., *Epistemology* (New York: Macmillan Co., 1959), pp. 379–81, where the author lists the statements given by Aquinas as illustrations of first principles; on first principles considered especially as the foundation of the truth of knowledge, together with discussions of ontological, epistemological, and psychological aspects of noncontradiction and identity and the ontological and epistemological aspects of the principles of efficiency and finality, see pp. 369–402.

The principles of *causality* do not have the same universality or the same function in knowledge as do noncontradiction and identity (*ibid.*, p. 395). As universal principles, efficiency and finality are hardly self-evident; e.g., the child, working by analogy, attributes his own purposeful activities to non-intelligent beings. "Wherever the world is young, the movements and changes of physical nature have been and are spontaneously ascribed by its people to the presence and will of hidden agents, who haunt every part of it, the woods, the mountains and the streams, the air and the stars, for good or for evil;—just as children again, by beating the ground after falling, imply that what has bruised them has intelligence. . . ." Newman, *Grammar of Assent*, p. 51. Cf. Jean Piaget's remarks on imitation and transfer in the development of causality in the child's mind; *The Construction of Reality in the Child*, tr. Margaret Cook (New York: Basic Books, 1954), pp. 137–39, 219–319.

As to the principle of *sufficient reason*, there is no basis, in the works of Aquinas at least, for asserting this as a self-evident principle or as a psychological first principle of knowledge. See Régis, *Epistemology*, pp. 369–402.

5. Peter McKellar, *Imagination and Thinking* (New York: Basic Books, 1957), p. 77.

6. In Aquinas' works, the act of understanding that concludes a disciplined reasoning process (*ratio*) is very often called an act of *intellectus*—"understanding" or "insight." It is the determination of the intellect to a conclusion seen in the light of first principles. The act of assent to first principles is also *intellectus*, and thus this act is the principle and term of any reasoning process. For the textual bases

of these very summary remarks, see J. Peghaire, C.S.Sp., *'Intellectus'*
et 'Ratio' selon s. Thomas d'Aquin ("Publications de l'Institut
d'Etudes Médiévales d'Ottawa," VI; Paris: J. Vrin, 1936), pp.
184–280.

Thomas also uses the term *assensus* to designate either of these
acts. The essential point of the whole matter is that the intellect is
really determined to its intelligible object. For an investigation of
assensus in the Thomistic texts, see Patrick J. Burns, S.J., "St.
Thomas and Judgment: Selected Texts" (unpublished Master's
thesis, Dept. of Philosophy, St. Louis University, 1957), pp. 66–94.
Our use of the term *assent* is an analogous extension to assents other
than those of philosophy or of faith with which Aquinas is primarily
concerned.

7. On mental models in abstract thinking, see McKellar, *Imagination*
and Thinking, pp. 74–76. For detailed discussions of the historical
factors influencing imagination in scientific thinking and the constructural development of science, see Mary B. Hesse, *Science and*
the Human Imagination (New York: Philosophical Library, 1955).

8. On the principal-instrumental analogy, see above, p. 105. As
the analogy is applied to the teaching-learning situation, see e.g.,
S. T. I, q. 117, a. 1; *De Veritate,* q. 11, esp. a. 1; but see the remarks
on these texts, above, Introduction, note 23.

The discussions above will tackle the problem of the teacher
strictly from the point of view of the learner. For further development of the teacher's role in learning, the following may be suggested as the most accurate and best of the studies available:

Francis C. Wade, S.J., "St. Thomas Aquinas and Teaching,"
Some Philosophers on Education, ed. Donald A. Gallagher (Milwaukee: Marquette University Press, 1956), pp. 67–85.

Etienne Gilson, "The Eminence of Teaching," *Truth and the*
Philosophy of Teaching ("McAuley Lectures," 1953; West Hartford, Conn.: St. Joseph's College, 1954), pp. 5–15. Reprinted in
A Gilson Reader, ed. Anton C. Pegis (New York: Hanover House,
1957), pp. 298–311; also as the second selection in *Disputed Ques-*
tions in Education (New York: Doubleday & Co., 1954).

9. For the Latin text that is quoted and paraphrased in this paragraph
(*Summa contra Gentiles,* Bk. II, end of chap. 75), see Appendix,
no. 6.

"Drawing conclusions from principles" is expressed in Aquinas'
language by *principia in conclusiones deducendo* (see the *Contra*
Gentiles text). Although the term *deducere* very rarely refers to a

strict logical deduction, it does designate the judgmentally organized discourse of reason which completes the process of discovery and determines the intellect to actual grasp of the meaning uncovered by investigation and inquiry. According to the mind of Aquinas, then, *deducere* or *discurrere* (other terms are used) necessarily implies and presupposes the moments of *inquirere* or *investigare*. Discovery in turn is essentially incomplete without organized discourse. See Peghaire's textual conclusions on this point, *'Intellectus'* et *'Ratio,'* esp. pp. 100–102, 104.

7

THE ANALOGY OF LEARNING
IN THE CLASSROOM

A PHYSICIST who knows the laws of mechanics is not at one and the same time an engineer. If he were to undertake, say, building a bridge, there are many more facts he would first have to know—the type of bridge to be designed, the lay of the land, the kind of materials available, and so on. Applying the laws of mass and force to a specific situation is a gradual process and one which involves consideration of many more factors.

In a similar way, a study of the learning process does not automatically yield principles of teaching. The act of teaching brings into play a number of factors that need not be considered in an analysis of learning as such, for learning can and clearly does take place apart from teaching. Hence, if the type of speculative analysis found in this book is to be applied to concrete situations, further evidence must be considered.

Taken as a whole, the act of teaching naturally involves three components, namely, the teacher himself, the student, and the subject matter being taught. Although this statement may on the surface appear overly evident, it offers a warning to anyone who wishes to examine the process of teaching and come up with workable principles and methods. Like the engineer who designs a bridge, we must examine each of the components with which we are working, one by one, step by step. For, reduction of the principles of speculative psychology to an immediately practical situation is a gradual process and cannot be handled hastily if the application is to prove sound.

Many practical considerations on teaching have been included as illustrations in our investigation of the nature of human learning. For instance, the analysis of different types of verbal phantasms in Chapter Five touched on such matters as verbal learning, the learning of methods, the psychological nature of "transfer," and emotionally loaded images leading to distortion of meaning. The place of the teacher in the learning process was precisely located in Chapter Six, and the teacher's symbolizing function was analyzed in the light of the act of discovery which constitutes fully natural learning. In the present chapter, we shall continue the process of practical application by looking at a few of the academic subjects ordinarily taught in American schools. Our purpose will be to consider the nature of each subject in terms of the nature of the learning process. Thus, the psychological conclusions reached inductively throughout the preceding chapters will be brought into contact with new data; and this analysis will yield an initial set of principles governing the act of teaching.

The analysis here is not intended to be exhaustive. Rather, our aim will be to raise some of the more important problems tangent upon teaching in accord with the nature of human learning. The following discussions will also indicate some of the directions in which a philosophical psychology of learning can profitably be taken.

FACTUAL SUBJECTS

Many of the subjects taught at the high-school and particularly the grade-school level are principally factual in nature. History, general science, and the social sciences, for example, are initially taught to give students a general factual background in these areas. Now factual knowledge, as the reader will recall, is heavily sensory. The intellect does little more than assent to the truth of the fact represented in phantasms. This is not to say that factual knowledge is unimportant. Though the intellectual content of an act of assent to concrete facts is minimal, factual knowledge supplies the foundation for any higher type of cognition. It is here that the mind gradually builds up a store of phantasms which will be the instruments for future intellectual knowledge.

In this context, the importance of an organized presentation of factual materials in a classroom situation shows itself. Broader meanings cannot emerge from a body of concrete singulars, even in an adult mind, unless the factual materials have been organized in such a way that they carry a potential meaning. Thus, organization of phantasms is an essential part of our general definition of learning. A young mind, of course, cannot be expected to grasp a larger scientific principle from a single experiment in general science, even if the experiment is conducted in the most orderly of fashions. Nor will an immature student discover a theory of politics in his first study of history or grasp the spirit of a given culture in his first glance at geography. However, a body of facts that is initially acquired in an organized way can be most effective for future learning. An organized pattern is cohesive. It is more easily seen as a whole and hence more easily recalled from the memory-imagination. Thus, we find in our own experience that, if we have once mentally organized a body of facts, a whole factual pattern can be recalled by a glance at a brief outline which in fact only symbolizes the body of materials in a very general way.

Even though a basic factual framework may be quite scanty at first, once it is erected in a child's mind it can be filled in as the years go on, until at some point the intellect begins to find larger meanings in the facts. But if the factual materials were scattered around the imagination in disorderly array, a whole area of intellectual learning could be left undeveloped, perhaps indefinitely. For the intellect would be unable to find the sensory materials necessary for its operation. We may add, too, that the immature mind is as yet unable to organize facts for itself. The quality of seeing things "as a whole" or "in a broader light" which we attribute to a truly adult mind is largely the result of learning to order facts, to see facts and ideas in relation to one another rather than in isolation. The ability to organize things mentally must be learned. And the younger and more inexperienced the student, the more organization is demanded of the teacher.

In a classroom situation, facts are imparted principally by means of verbal symbols. Hence, it would be well to recall here that words representative of concrete facts are only symbolic substitutes for direct perceptual experience—and they are not the best possible substitutes. In a completely natural process of learning through discovery, the mind perceives and assents to the concrete facts of perception before it symbolizes these facts in verbal phantasms. Consequently, it is more in accord with human nature to teach concrete facts by supplying pupils with direct perceptions than by filling their memories with words. Although primary perceptions are clearly impossible to achieve in many areas of learning, there still remain the many tools of secondary perception discussed briefly in Chapter Six. Non-verbal symbolic diagrams that teachers will often devise for schematizing subject materials and thus aiding the memory can also be included among the instruments of secondary perception. Words too can be perceptual tools since the purpose of any narrative is to create non-verbal images in the mind.

The use of any perceptual tool, of course, is conditioned by the resources of the school, the time allotted for a given set of facts, and the relative importance of the factual data. Moreover, the teacher cannot hope to let a movie, a tour, a demonstration, a diagram, or even a good story do his teaching for him. In whatever way sensory materials may be presented, they must be organized and pointedly explained if a student is to derive from them anything more than a vague meaning. It is not difficult to supply a youthful mind with images, especially when the images are picturesque or dramatic. But if the images are to serve as phantasms, as true instruments of intellectual meaning, the presentation of images must be thoroughly prepared. In short, the use of any non-verbal perceptual tools rarely simplifies the teacher's job. Their effective use will frequently demand much more preparation than will a merely verbal presentation of the factual materials.

The importance of the concrete, the non-verbal experience in learning cannot be overemphasized. An immature mind thirsts for and thrives upon the concrete; it is naturally curious about *things*. Words, on the other hand, mean little to the youthful mind. Anyone who has ever tried to teach poetry, even to a college student, has experienced the difficulty of getting his pupils interested in the word for its own sake. Although the adult mind has developed a greater sophistication toward the phenomena of direct experience and tends to move more rapidly from particular facts to broader meanings, it too thrives upon things. For even an effective adult process of learning begins and ends with judgments of real assent, which always in some way involve the concrete, the non-verbal. Thus, insistence on supplying perceptions in the presentation of factual materials is merely a practical consequence of the fact that the object most naturally proportioned to the human intellect is the intelligibility directly revealed by some concrete thing.

Many subjects make use of more or less *abstract* facts even at a basic level. It is difficult, for instance, to restrict a general-science or social-science course to the level of mere particulars. Generalizations almost necessarily arise. When the purpose of the course is primarily to acquaint students with the basic facts of a given subject, such generalizations might lead to merely verbal learning. Scientific terminology at this basic level might be misleading or meaningless jargon. And the type of generalization used in social sciences might result in a student's learning distorted meanings of the sort described in our discussion of aphoristic verbal phantasms. It is during his grade-school and high-school days that a person picks up much of the cultural myth and traditions of his own society—the American "way of life," for example, or a particular group's ideas of success, ideals, and attitudes toward life. But, as we have seen, myth can be malevolent as well as benevolent. Hence, hasty generalizations made without sufficient factual background might lead to unfortunate prejudices and uncritical acceptance of many cultural generalizations that may hinder a person's intellectual objectivity in later years. Knowledge and the actions that flow from knowledge are never divorced from the personal history of the knower.

Now the assent given to a set of verbally learned facts is intellectual. The intellect acknowledges the *truth* of the fact; but the fact itself is not understood, for merely verbal learning does not render words symbolic or capable of carrying a true meaning to the intellect. In any case, though, the intellectual assent must rest on some basis. Otherwise the assent would not be made; the intellect would remain uncommitted to the fact in question. In the case of verbal learning, when intellectual assent does not rest on a factual or evidential basis, it must rest on authority—often the authority of a teacher. It is this basis of authority rather than evidence that a process of indoctrination seeks. Consistent verbal learning of factual materials, particularly those of an abstract or aphoristic character, can dull a person's mind to the point where he will accept anything on the word of another rather than go to the trouble of examining facts and evidence. When this point has been reached, indoctrination has succeeded.

There is no doubt that the normal human being, adult and adolescent alike, must accept many things on the authority of another. No one can master every field of knowledge. But an intelligent acceptance of authority is always accompanied by an awareness that, even though the facts upon which a generalization rests are not within the ken of one's own knowledge, they *are* available to another person, and he has made valid use of them. Thus, there is a difference between an intelligent nod to an authority more competent than oneself and a naive, blind acceptance of unexamined fact. Meaningful acceptance of authority is a conscious recognition of another's competence. Indoctrination, however, involves an habitual and perhaps even subconscious attitude of mind in which a person has lost awareness that objective evidence must underlie any generalization. Thus, it is possible that a series of teachers who are overly concerned with "covering the matter," in spite of the danger of verbal learning, have indeliberately indoctrinated rather than taught their students. For they will have aided in creating an uncritical attitude of mind, the type of attitude that can eventually destroy one's natural sensitivity for concrete evidence.

Now, to look at the problem of verbal learning in a more positive light, how can a teacher avoid intellectually harmful consequences of this sort when he is teaching a basic factual subject? Aside from the fact that a teacher must be truly interested in *teaching* his students, there is only one final answer to this question: the teacher must be competent in his subject. When a more abstract fact or generalization arises, he will be able to explain it—and, more important still, he will be able to *recognize* it as something that *needs* explanation. He will see to it that his students have built a sound factual foundation beneath the generalization, according to their present capacities. When he quizzes or tests his students, the competent teacher, who knows an abstract fact or generalization for what it is, will not force his pupils to parrot a proposition that they are now incapable of handling. Behind all this must lie an attitude of mind that it is far better for students to be ignorant of a more abstract idea at their present stage of training than to possess an idea which they misunderstand.

The notion of competence implies that a teacher cannot simply be given a textbook or a methods book and told to teach a course. Two teachers, one who really knows his subject and one who knows little more than the facts contained in the textbook, may end up teaching exactly the same basic facts. But the teacher who understands his subject will know far better how to organize the facts intelligently, how to handle generalizations, how to balance a generalization with the facts necessary for his students to understand it, and thus how to avoid verbal learning. A more mature mind can recognize incompetence and thus make judgments on the teacher's statements accordingly. An inexperienced student, on the other hand, will in this situation base his intellectual assents on an authority which itself has no basis.

Abstract facts learned at a basic level of schooling do not always give rise to the problem of distorted meanings or verbal learning. There are many times when a student gets an initial grasp on some abstract fact or generalization; the primitive insight is then deepened as his intellectual capacities increase. A young mind, for instance, is quite capable of seeing a simple cause-effect relationship in history or human events or nature even though he lacks a deeper understanding of causality. Learning is a gradual process, and grasp of meaning necessarily begins in a primitive fashion. Hence, in a classroom situation, students will often receive a basic and very general introduction to some more abstract fact or principle. In future years the abstraction will take on a deeper meaning—perhaps much sooner than would have been the case if the student had never before been introduced to the idea. A teacher's effort here will be to see that the idea is not misunderstood, and that the simplification necessary for primitive learning does not lead to a distortion of the object of knowledge.

The teaching of religion and morals to the young is a very good example of a situation where many facts of a more abstract character are learned without optimum understanding. A child does not understand the attributes of God or the real meaning of grace. Still, he can become acquainted with the basic facts of faith and morals, and his initial knowledge can be deepened as he matures.

But, since the facts of religion and morality are in themselves rarely concrete, a number of problems are bound to arise. There is the danger of merely verbal learning and hence of indoctrination. This may be the case especially when the content of a young person's religious knowledge is largely restricted to the question-and-answer catechism, which is more concerned with terse definitions than with clear explanations meaningful to an immature mind. Any religious symbolism or moral principle learned in terms unfamiliar to a young mind can result in distorted if not vacuous meanings. Thus, phrases like "temples of the Holy Ghost" or "heirs of heaven" or "full consent of the will" might be thoroughly useless to one who has no real concept of a temple, of what it means to inherit, or of an act of free will. Phrases like these are quite typical of the verbal content of many basic religion courses. In an effort to avoid verbal learning, a teacher could slip to the other side of the scale and turn religious or moral instruction into mere exhortation. But a person whose religious training has been pervaded, through "inspiring" exhortation, with sentimental images of Christ or the saints may find his faith severely shaken in later years when emotions are not sufficient to carry him through a moral crisis.

Teaching moral and religious facts at a basic level of learning sharply exemplifies the type of problem that arises when abstract facts are learned at a primitive stage of training. The teacher clearly cannot lead immature minds through the lengthy inductions of moral philosophy, nor can he delve very deeply into the religious facts or principles that are known through faith alone. And yet the young student must be given some basic instruction in morals and religion.

One effective means of handling a problem of this sort lies in the type of judgment of real assent available to a student. If the facts of faith and morals are presented as much as possible in the light of a pupil's concrete experiences, the dangers of verbal learning and mistaken meanings can be minimized to a large extent. As a person progresses through childhood and adolescence into adulthood, his moral concerns shift in perspective. Consequently, a teacher who is alive to his pupil's particular problems and interests will teach the more abstract truths of morality and religion in terms of their personal experiences and present awareness of human living. He can in this way lead them to real assent, to judgmental reference of an abstract principle to a set of concrete circumstances. Even the more doctrinal and less practical truths of faith can be handled in this way. For there is generally *some* referent in a young person's experience of people and things in terms of which religious facts and symbols might be explained.

By leading his students to judgments of real assent in accord with their present maturity, the teacher will be helping them to develop a habit of relating moral and religious principles to real situations. An early development of this attitude of mind can be instrumental in aiding one to avoid the divorce of moral principles from everyday actions—a divorce so often seen in adults' actions. Genuine moral and religious convictions are impossible without some form of real assent to the principles in question; for a person cannot will what he does not really understand, any more than he can be hungry for a steak if he has never before seen a steak. It may be noted that, in the context of real assent, the problem of whether the end of education is intellectual or moral might be a pseudo-problem. True intellectual learning always involves real assent, and true moral convictions are always based on real assents. Thus, neither the intellectual nor the moral can be truly taught apart from real assents; and, conversely, real assents achieve the goal of intellectual learning and lead naturally to true moral convictions.

Leading a young mind to judgments of real assent in religious matters—or, for that matter, in any area of learning where abstract facts or generalizations are introduced to immature minds—is no easy task. This aspect of teaching demonstrates the amount of thought and imagination and even creative genius required of a teacher. A good amount of time in the course of a teacher's training could profitably be spent in getting him to devise *for himself* various methods of presenting his subject matter. Though he may later discover in an actual classroom situation that the methods he so carefully planned in college are not very practical, he will at least have been made aware of an approach necessary for effective teaching proportioned to the nature of human learning.

SCIENTIFIC SUBJECTS

At many points throughout this book, the procedures of science and the types of knowledge yielded in science have been discussed in detail. Enough has been said on these matters to warrant brevity in handling the problem of teaching the sciences. As in our treatment of factual subjects, we shall be concerned more with basic psychological principles and the nature of science than with the details of teaching a specific science.

The easiest way to teach a scientific subject, one that will require the least possible imagination and preparation, is to present the conclusions of the science and to impress them firmly upon the students' memories through frequent repetition and drill. The trouble with this method is that pupils are not really learning *science*. Rather, they are memorizing a handful of abstract facts that they understand vaguely or not at all. Nor are they really being *taught* science. The whole natural inductive process that makes a science scientific is reversed, and the possibility of real assent is virtually destroyed. Hence, as has been implicit throughout our study, the only way to teach science as science is to teach it inductively, leading the student from observation of concrete data to higher-order conclusion.

Performance of experiments in a classroom or school laboratory is, of course, limited by the equipment available to the teacher. It is the rare high school that would be equipped with a cyclotron for teaching atomic theory. But the greater majority of scientific principles taught in basic secondary-school courses are readily demonstrable, often with very simple equipment. The science teacher who spends an hour planning and setting up an experiment which takes only a few minutes to perform during class may feel that the whole business is not worth the time and effort. Still, one might suggest that his students will learn more science from a well-conducted, three-minute experiment than from an hour of verbal explanations. When equipment is not available for demonstrating a particular principle, the problem of performing an induction might be solved by a *concrete* explanation, perhaps assisted by film strips or other visual aids, of how the principle has been established through experimentation. Young minds like a good story, and this liking is a natural one. If the students remember nothing but the story of an experiment, they at least have a solid experiential basis for learning the conclusion meaningfully through future repetitions of the conclusion.

Perhaps the largest problem facing the teacher of basic science courses is: When is a pupil ready for anything more than basic facts and descriptions? When is he ready for broader principles and actual scientific theories? Only the individual teacher, of course, can answer these questions; and his answers will differ according to the caliber of individual classes. A beginner in science has to build up a large store of factual knowledge—basic descriptions, classifications, terminology, definitions. Moreover, he will invariably need a good deal of drilling in these matters, for any real assent to broader conclusions is quite dependent upon knowledge of such facts.

On the other hand, the capacity of, say, a high-school junior or senior should not be underestimated, even if his training in science is only beginning. The teacher of science has a unique advantage. He is able to teach with the assistance of things, objects, which the student can see and touch and observe in motion. Experimental paraphernalia naturally pique a young imagination; they stimulate interest and serve to keep attention closely focused on the matter at hand. Now, given the interest that a concrete experiment can arouse and a fairly decent knowledge of basic factual material, a student might be curious enough to push his way through to a more abstract meaning in science much more readily than he will in another academic subject. It would be unfortunate to restrict a pupil's scientific knowledge to the popular-mechanics level when he is actually ready for more than this.

Use of an inductive method may also enable the teacher to set as one of his objectives for a basic course some knowledge of scientific method. If throughout the course of a year the teacher performs a large number of experiments, using the same general procedure and always explaining carefully what it is he is doing, a student could be made to see a scientific *modus operandi,* a procedural pattern for handling scientific questions. Toward the end of the year, the teacher could begin to talk about the experimental method as such. Thus, the year's experiments (including a student's own lab work, carefully directed) would serve as so many patterns of phantasms, eventually organized to yield a primitive but still meaningful insight into the nature of science. If a pupil left high school with a very basic grasp of this matter, we could surely say that he has learned some *science* and that the objectives of a basic science course have been attained.

Once again, careful planning and foresight are called for. The teacher will have to see this knowledge of method as an ultimate goal of his course, start teaching it implicitly from the very beginning of the course, and persist in focusing his pupils' minds upon procedural matters long before he actually lectures on science as such. It is a sad fact that people who have "taken" college courses in science leave college without ever having received any solid notion of what science is all about. Teachers' inadvertence to the real method of science may well be a primary source of many a college graduate's personal confusion and pseudo-problems concerning science versus philosophy and especially science versus religion.

MENTAL SKILLS AND LANGUAGE STUDY

A large body of the material taught particularly in primary and secondary schools may be grouped under the heading of "mental skills." Included here are such things as reading, writing, grammar, language, and the methods of computing used in arithmetic and mathematics. These skills are neither purely sensory nor purely intellectual; both patterns of images and intellectual control of the imagination are required. The intellect does enter into the more complex motor skills, such as watchmaking or any mechanical skill requiring precision and concentration. However, *mental* skills can be distinguished from *motor* skills for two reasons. First, while motor activity can enter into a mental skill—such as the movement of the eyes in reading or the formation of sounds in speaking a language— the activity to be performed in a mental skill is primarily immanent, taking place chiefly within the mind. Secondly, a mental skill is oriented directly toward serving an intellectual purpose. Thus, computing techniques are meant to assist mathematical thinking; reading serves the communication of ideas; and language skills along with grammar and writing aid the expression of thought.

Some mental skills involve a patterned activity or use of method which does not change with different concrete data. The computing techniques of arithmetic and mathematics, for example, are regular. Once a given technique has been decided upon for handling a particular set of data, the method is carried through with little or no variation. Owing to the strict rigor of methods of this type, computers can be constructed to perform the operation much more rapidly and accurately than the human mind, which is capable of handling only so much data at one time. Reading, too, involves a very regular technique. It is simply a method of perceiving a written symbol, and we do not need different reading skills for ordinary data any more than we need different ears to hear the different sounds of ordinary experience. Concerning the learning of regular mental skills or methods, the reader is referred to our lengthier discussions on repetition and knowledge of methods in Chapter Five, in the treatment of abstract verbal phantasms. The major problem here is to avoid teaching regular methods in such a way that they become a hindrance to subsequent, more advanced learning.

Many of the techniques learned in such subjects as algebra and geometry are ordered toward the attainment of mathematical ideas rather than toward developing an ability to handle the figures of everyday experience. Thus, when a student learns the mental skills necessary for handling algebraic ratios and proportions or geometrical construction, he is not learning techniques primarily for practical use in later life. Use of these skills gradually leads him to see necessary mathematical relationships, to develop mathematical concepts, to learn the *science* of mathematical construction. As time passes, a person will forget the details of using a given skill. But, if he has once conceived the ideas toward which the skills are ordained, the intellectual values that touch upon mental clarity and sharpness in perceiving relationships can remain, even though the heavily sensory techniques have slipped from the memory. The intellectual purpose of a mathematical skill, then, has significant implications for the teacher. Once a student has grasped the idea toward which a mental skill is ordered and strengthened his grasp through sufficient use of the skill in solving problems, it could be a waste of time to keep him busy doing more and more problems. The faster student would profitably be led into new areas of mathematics rather than made to repeat what he already clearly *understands.* Even though such repetition might perfect his use of a *skill,* this perfection is quite unnecessary if the real *purpose* of the mental skill has been achieved.

Other mental skills entail patterned mental activity that is considerably less regular than the type of operations we have discussed so far. This is true especially of the skills connected with the expression of ideas. There is no one way of articulating a thought, either in writing or in speaking. Hence, although quite regular patterns of verbal phantasms are established in the memory-imagination, the use of language patterns requires more than the general, over-all guidance that the intellect exercises in methodical skills like computing or reading. Since the intellect is expressing its own thoughts (if we may be pardoned the reification), it must exercise the most precise control over the imagination in any deliberate and fully *conscious* use of language. Careful self-expression thus calls for a very close interplay between intellect and imagination.

The teaching of grammar brings into focus both the sensory and the intellectual side of language. Learning grammatical principles (and these would include matters of spelling and vocabulary as well as the rules of correct usage) has as its most basic goal the correct use of verbal phantasms. Before all else, the imagination must be supplied with conventionally correct verbal patterns. Hence, even though grammatical rules like any other idea require the attention of the intellect, they are basically oriented toward a sensory function. And, because a knowledge of practical rules is useless without an habitual readiness to apply them, grammar must be persistently drilled until it is second nature to a student.

One danger arising in the teaching of grammar is that memorization of rules might be insisted upon and drilled apart from application. Some sort of practical exercises entailing concrete application will generally meet this danger. Thus, precise knowledge of *rules* will in the course of time be forgotten; but a habit of correct *usage* will remain. The teacher's real problem here is to keep his students interested enough in language so that they will pay sufficient attention when grammar is taught or drilled. Hence, a reading program or, at a more advanced level of schooling, a study of literature will ordinarily accompany grammar training.

In an effort to keep young minds interested, however, it is possible to err in another direction, by letting wide reading suffice for language training. A person cannot learn to build a gas engine simply by looking at a lot of automobile motors through a glance beneath the hoods of cars. Neither can an immature mind pick up correct usage simply from reading good writing. Grammar involves detail. And the details of basic grammar must be *taught*—that is, the student's mind must be directly focused upon the details, one by one—if correct usage is ever to be learned properly.

The same facts hold true with regard to the teaching of writing, which goes indefinitely beyond merely correct use of language into the realms of more effective and more mature expression. On the one hand, mature writing is not just a matter of learning a handful of rules. Rules for effective writing are a kind of practical conclusion initially reached by observing how good writers express themselves. Hence, just as a scientific conclusion cannot be learned effectively apart from the data of experience or experiment, so the teaching of effective writing cannot be divorced from a concrete study of good writing.

But, once again, an immature mind will not learn how to write well simply through contact with great authors. Good writing is not a matter of general impressions. Although effective writing brings into play techniques and rhetorical principles that are different from the rules of merely correct writing, effective writing like correct usage involves attention to detail every step of the way. Consequently, one cannot learn to write effectively unless he is made conscious of detail through analysis. Getting students to imitate brief excerpts from great authors is one way of making this analysis personal to them; it enables them to see a technique or rhetorical device for themselves. But whatever method may be employed to teach effective writing, careful preparation and explanation is required of the teacher if a student is to learn anything positive. The teaching of writing is too easily reduced to a series of red-pencil marks on compositions, leaving the student without any clear notion of what effective self-expression really is.

Although the study of grammatical principles initially pertains more to the memory-imagination than to the intellect, there is a distinctively intellectual side to grammar study. Concepts of tense, voice, mood, and the like, begin to emerge gradually from the concrete expressions of language. The student begins to see more or less definitely what a noun or a verb or an adjective *is*. Thus, we find that a child speaks in simple terms of subject-verb-object. But as a person matures, he subordinates one thought to another, links ideas in different ways, uses different word positions. This is more than a matter of increased vocabulary. Experience with language brings about a greater intellectual awareness of linguistic concepts or categories, a greater awareness of the structure of language. This awareness in turn can result in greater fluency in the use of verbal materials, for the intellect comes to possess greater control over the verbal functions of the memory-imagination. A mature person, for instance, will know more than one way to express an adversative notion. Since he has become somewhat aware of an idea precisely *as* adversative, he can express it in other ways than simply to introduce it with "but." Fluency and variety in expression by no means come automatically with the emergence of linguistic concepts, but the latter does *aid* the former.

Intellectual grasp of broader linguistic concepts can be speeded up and made more definite through study of a foreign language. When one consciously notes two different ways of expressing essentially the same idea—or, psychologically speaking, when the intellect possesses as sensory instruments two different verbal phantasms symbolic of essentially the same thought—a person rather naturally becomes more language-conscious. In fact, it may often be the case that a pupil never becomes really aware of words as words until he does study another tongue. But language-consciousness, like any other process of learning, is personal. It is consciously and not indeliberately acquired. A passing glance at an oak and a birch tree will do little more than make a person aware that there is more than one kind of tree. Similarly, mere exposure to a foreign tongue may result in little more than an awareness that different people say things differently.

Language-consciousness seems to break down into two principal types. The first type may be called *conceptual*. It involves an awareness of general linguistic concepts or functions, like voice and mood or noun and verb, which are particularized in different verbal symbols. As was mentioned above, conceptual language-consciousness is achieved to some extent through familiarity with the grammatical principles of one's own tongue. However, studying a foreign language with attention to its grammatical structure provides an effective way of prodding the mind to look at general structures and not merely at the sensory symbols of thought. In the process of translating back and forth between two languages, the intellect is led to cross-compare two verbal symbols and thus to discover the broader function common to both symbols.

A strictly inflected language like Latin or Greek serves this purpose best in our Western culture, both because these languages form much of the basis for English and other modern tongues, and because cross-comparison of an inflected with a non-inflected language leads the mind more rapidly beyond the sensory particularities of verbal symbols. For example, the intellect can be forced to grasp the function of a possessive more readily when it compares the symbols "of the man" and "viri" than when it compares the English expression with one like "de l'homme." Similarly, the notion of passive voice can be made to emerge more readily in comparing "is established" with "constituitur" than in comparing it with "est établis." These, of course, are only isolated examples. But they do point to the fact that modern languages are *in general* too similar *symbolically* and hence are not as efficient as the classical languages for prodding the mind to look at linguistic categories and functions.

The second type of language-consciousness we may, for sake of a term, call *literary*. It involves learning a classical or modern language for its own sake, learning it as another distinctive body of symbols for the expression of thought. Although verbal symbols are arbitrary and conventional, one language differs from another in much the same way that one artist's work differs from that of another. Just as an artist cannot avoid including himself and his personality in his work of art, so a language embodies the personality of a people. Many of the peculiar interests, attitudes, and ways of thinking common to a particular culture or nation find their way into language. Thus, once we look beyond the level of literal meaning or denotation, we find that different languages like different people have different personal traits. The Greek's *logos,* the Roman's *res publicae,* the Frenchman's *raison,* the German's *Weltschmerz*—it is almost trite to remark that these and innumerable other symbols are ultimately untranslatable.

Now, a person cannot have studied any two languages *thoroughly* without having imbibed both conceptual and literary values. These two types of language-consciousness have been distinguished because, owing to different methods of *teaching* languages, it is possible for these values to be acquired separately or in exclusion of each other.

Thus, if one wishes to learn as rapidly as possible how to read or speak a foreign language, he will not study it analytically and compare it with his own tongue, moving from simple nouns and verbs to their various modifiers and on into the greater subtleties of phrases, clauses, voices, and moods. Rather than follow this grammatical order of procedure, he will by-pass comparison with his own tongue, learning the new words and expressions by hearing them and by referring as far as is possible and convenient to the realities which the new words symbolize. This more direct method of learning a new tongue has the advantage of enabling a student to spend more time on the symbolic expressions of the new tongue than on a cross-comparison of verbal symbols. However, since the student is acquiring a set of symbols for practical use rather than analyzing the language, he *could* end up in a position comparable to that of the accomplished tourist who can speak many tongues but who knows very little about language. Conversely, one who takes a strictly analytic approach to foreign languages and thus comes to know a great deal about language *could* be unable to read or speak any other language than his own with any facility.

These remarks imply that there can be two extremes on the scale of language methods. One extreme would be the type of analytic approach that has nothing but grammatical or conceptual values in view. The other would be a purely direct method of the type often used to give travelers abroad a strictly pragmatic knowledge of some foreign tongue in as short a period of time as possible. In an academic course, these extremes will invariably shade into each other to some extent; and the more intelligent student will gradually find both conceptual and literary values in his study of foreign language, no matter how he has been taught. However, in order to see more sharply the psychological principles underlying language studies, let us compare the "analytic" and the "direct" approaches. These terms will for the moment designate the two extremes just discussed, rather than any method which, while emphasizing one approach, still attempts to impart both conceptual and literary values.

Learning a language through a purely direct method and learning it through grammatical analysis *initially* involve different mental skills. The direct method attempts to provide the memory-imagination with patterns of verbal phantasms that will function by themselves and apart from the verbal patterns of any other language which may happen to be stored in the imagination. The analytic method, on the other hand, builds new verbal patterns in terms of verbal phantasms already existing in the imagination. Because phantasms of the new language are linked with those of the vernacular, verbal knowledge tends to be more detailed than contextual knowledge. The mind is almost forced to compare the languages, to think of one in terms of the other, to translate and often to transliterate the less familiar into the more familiar, to go through the familiar language in order to express something in the new tongue.

A purely direct method, therefore, initially develops a skill of recognition, auditory or visual or both. It is primarily oriented toward immediate use of the new tongue. Since it stresses grasp of over-all meaning, its danger is that a person may think he knows what is being said when actually he does not, and thus that the vague knowledge had of the language is useless for literary ends.

The method of learning a language strictly according to grammatical structure, on the other hand, initially develops a skill of analysis. It is oriented more directly toward an intellectual study of language as such than toward a practical use of any particular tongue. It stresses precise translation, which sometimes tends to become transliteration, rather than paraphrase or contextual grasp of meaning. Its drawbacks are that a person might never acquire a working knowledge of the language for use in literary study, and that he may never become conscious of the new tongue as a unique body of symbols for the conveyance of thought.

The teacher of classical or modern languages at a basic level of learning ought to keep in mind the general principles that were stated prior to the above discussion of language methods. Both conceptual and literary language-consciousness hold an important place in learning. From a psychological point of view, there is no valid reason for teaching language *as an academic subject* in such a way that the ability to read or possibly to speak a tongue becomes divorced from the analytic study of language—or vice versa. Language learned purely for use is primarily a sensory skill and may never yield any sound conceptual or literary values. Language learned purely for analytic purposes may deepen one's knowledge of linguistic categories and grammatical functions; but this is not really a study of language in its total reality.

Hence, if language study is to be a fully valuable part of the learning process, a spot on the scale of linguistic methods must be found which will combine the virtues of the two extremes without at the same time incorporating their distortions. More recent methods attempt to combine the analytic and the direct approaches. The student begins his study of the new tongue by acquiring rather vague verbal phantasms through simple but extensive reading of the language. When this primitive knowledge is brought into contact with formal grammar and analytic comparison of the new language with the vernacular, analysis can be made in such a way that the mind will recognize the languages as *similar* but not *identical*. An early acquaintance with the new tongue made apart from a comparative structural analysis can create an awareness of this language as a distinctive body of symbols. Thus, verbal knowledge of the new language can in the long run be more accurate than it would be if acquired through a purely analytical approach; for the latter extreme, as we have noted, tends to treat two languages as equivalent rather than as only similar. And, since the features of a purely direct method are balanced by formal linguistic analysis, the initially vague and highly sensory knowledge of the language can be made more precise and meaningful. The potential intelligibility of the primitive verbal phantasms is thus enriched through further direct contact with the language; and the phantasms are at the same time set into a linguistic framework through formal grammar study.

Although this note concerning recent language methods is hardly a thorough psychological analysis, it does illustrate the type of approach that has to be taken if one is to study *language as language*. In its complete reality, any language embraces both conceptual and literary elements; a dichotomy artificially created between these elements will ultimately be a distortion of the nature of language. The study of foreign language is profitably being introduced early in grade school when the child's memory for words is quick. It does not seem possible to avoid an artificial split between conceptual and literary values, or to hope that students will derive any really permanent value from their study of foreign languages, unless they are introduced to these studies earlier than is now generally the case.

LITERARY SUBJECTS

A useful psychology of the art symbol, including both symbolic expression and perception, can be worked out of the psychology of judgment presented earlier in this book. This, however, would take us far beyond the purposes of this chapter, where we are interested only in outlining some of the problems that arise in teaching various subjects at an initial rather than advanced stage of training. Our discussions on the teaching of literature, then, will be restricted to the more basic objectives of literary training.

One purpose of teaching literature has already been mentioned, namely, the use of literature to provide an experiential basis for learning how to write effectively. However, using literature to teach writing is in some respects extrinsic to the purpose of literature as literature.

In itself, literature is an expression of life. The literary artist has through his personal experience achieved some insight into one or another of the many aspects of life. This insight he goes on to communicate verbally, and for this end he can call to his aid all the power that a word possesses—its sound and its rhythm as well as all of the connotations associated with the word in itself and in context. Although the poet more than any other literary artist depends upon the power of each *individual* word, verbal symbols clearly remain the principal source of expressing an impression of life in any form of literature. Thus, the novelist or story writer uses words to present plot, character, and setting. The literary journalist employs words to present facts, psychologically arranged to yield the broader meaning he finds behind facts. A teacher of literature will profitably keep in mind the fact that some of the art forms ordinarily included in a literature course are not exclusively literary. The dramatist, for instance, uses words and actions to present his artistic idea; and the ballad has melody as well as words. Thus, "literary" forms of this sort cannot really be taught without reference to or reproduction of the non-verbal aspects of the whole symbol.

Whatever the literary form, any piece of true literature is integral. For, behind the disparate verbal symbols lies a guiding matrix, namely, the insight into life which the literary artist is striving to communicate. Thus, as we saw in our discussion of symbols in Chapter Two, a total piece of literature is in the last analysis but *one* symbol, expressive of one more or less complex insight. The literary symbol must therefore be taken as the author presents it. This implies, of course, that the study of foreign literature in translation is only second best; for, the personality of the language along with each artist's unique and untranslatable way of handling the tongue is an integral part of the total symbol.

A piece of literature is like a sentence. Just as one cannot clearly understand a sentence unless he knows the meaning of the words in the sentence, neither can a literary symbol be grasped as a whole unless its parts are intelligible. This means that a student will need more than the ability to read with reasonable speed and general comprehension, for a *careful* reading habit is more than a matter of imbibing large bodies of printed material and knowing roughly what is being said. If a student is ever to get at great literature, he needs a basic knowledge of the literary techniques used by great writers, such as rhetorical devices and the body of material customarily grouped under the heading of figures of speech. This is not to say that learning literary skills is an end in itself. Since the author presents his work as a whole and not as something to be minutely dissected, classroom analysis of rhetorical techniques is somewhat artificial. But unless a person's attention is at some time called explicitly to details, he may never learn to see parts well enough to understand a whole. Thus, detailed literary analysis can aid in the development of the careful reading habits that a person needs in order to handle anything more than a Sunday supplement intelligently. With this aim in view, the teaching of the many kinds of literary techniques can be seen as an effective means rather than as a somewhat picayunish end.

Analysis of the parts of a literary symbol, however, tends to magnify certain parts out of proportion to their importance in the literary work as a whole. Hence, the work must finally be taught as an integral whole and discussed in its total reality. Toward the end of our treatment of aphoristic verbal phantasms in Chapter Five, we noted how learning about culture and cultural traditions through literature is not the same as studying literature as such. The goals of each study are different, and phantasms acquired with different ends in view will carry different potential meanings.

However, knowledge of the way different people in different ages think and act is closely related to literary knowledge. In fact, some cultural knowledge is essential if the whole meaning of a literary classic is to be grasped. Homer, Virgil, Milton, Racine, Goethe, Cervantes—none of the art of these men can finally be understood apart from some knowledge of the age in which they lived. Thus, study of a literary work as a whole will necessarily embrace some cultural study—study of the *spirit* of an age, not just memorization of historical facts. And, conversely, genuine cultural knowledge will naturally stem from a study of literature. It may happen that a pupil's first real assents to the meaning of historical facts will occur through literary rather than formal historical studies, since literature presents personal contact with great minds of the past.

The teacher of basic courses in literature occupies a rather precarious position. Too much analysis leaves Jack a dull boy, and he may lose all desire to continue reading good literature when he finishes his formal schooling. But synthesis without analysis leaves Jack just as dull, for the vague and sometimes quite empty meanings he acquires in such a process surely do not pique his appetite for good reading. Still, though a secondary-school teacher may earn dislike for tipping the balance a little too heavily on the side of literary analysis, the college teacher would then be able to teach real literature. For, his students would already have acquired the skills that are absolutely necessary for an intelligent study of better literature.

Teaching literature of a higher quality offers a special difficulty to the high-school teacher. In many instances, his students will not have sufficient maturity and experience with life to understand what the author is really saying. In the first years of high school, for example, many students find it very difficult to grasp the point of stories built more on character than on plot. Hence, a teacher should not be ashamed to cater rather often to his students' tastes. He desires to improve their tastes, but this cannot be done unless he is willing to build on their own interests rather than on his. For, literary training, like any form of intellectual learning, is a matter of personal knowledge, of judgmental assents made in accord with one's own experience of reality.

Hence, much of a student's basic literary training, even in grade school, can profitably be devoted to increasing his breadth of experience vicariously. Good stories will often serve this purpose much better than more profound literary works which, though they may be greater works of art, are ill suited to the student's present experience and level of maturity. It is difficult to say which is more damaging to literary attitudes—reading too far beyond one's level of experience, or lacking any form of acquaintance with human life beyond one's own ken of experience. A wide reading program directed more immediately toward youthful tastes and intended primarily to build up reading experience can minimize both of these dangers; such reading broadens one's experience of people and knowledge of literary forms, and in so doing it paves the way for an intelligent study of more difficult literature. A reading program of this sort is also a good supplement to analytic training and the learning of literary techniques. Wolfing down a good number of light books purely for experience's sake will perhaps compensate for the discomfort felt in analytically digesting the heavier materials.

A final remark on the teaching of literature brings into play the uniqueness of artistic knowledge. In scientific forms of knowing, the intellect uses sensory phantasms only because they are psychologically necessary instruments for making judgments and conceiving meanings. In any form of artistic knowledge, however, sensory images are inseparably associated with intellectual meaning. The artist does not make an abstraction and then proceed to clothe it in concrete symbols. Rather, he experiences life in a way that is at once intellectual and emotional. Thus, when he communicates his experiential insights in an artistic form, he articulates a complex impression that plays both on the power of intellect and on the powers of sense and emotion. An artistic meaning or "idea," then, is neither intellectual nor sensory. It is both.

Consequently, if a student is to learn a work of literature as the author presents it, he cannot be taught to divorce intellectual notions latent in the literary work as a whole from the sensory aspects of the literary symbol. Children are often taught to extract a moral from everything they read. Thus, when they grow older, they read a piece of literature, are told by their teacher to state the "theme" of the work, and promptly proceed to summarize the work in terms of a *personal application* to themselves. A student who has read *King Lear,* for instance, might state the theme of the whole drama as, "Lear hastily partitions his kingdom and thus brings ruin upon himself." As a very general summary of the play, this statement is reasonably adequate and perhaps helpful for purposes of discussion. But if he says, "You must not act rashly or you will bring ruin upon yourself," then he has moralized. Application of a literary insight to one's own life may be morally or religiously fruitful, but it is not literature. And a teacher who gets students into the habit of extracting messages from literature may be well-intentioned, but he is distorting the true nature of literature.

Even having students state the "theme" of a play or novel or poem has its dangers. Formulating a theme can be helpful for pinning down the over-all structure of a work and particularly for making certain that the pupil has really grasped what the work in general is all about. But knowledge of the theme is not in itself literary knowledge. A music teacher, for example, does not content himself with having a pupil tell in *intellectual* terms what he thinks a particular composition means; the instructor is satisfied only when the pupil's understanding of the composition is *concretely* expressed in his own performance of the work. A teacher of literature cannot have his pupils express their understanding of a work in quite the same way. But unless a student is made to realize that a theme statement of any sort gives only the abstract skeleton of a literary work and strips the work of its real flesh and emotional-sensory force, he may never understand the purpose of literature or learn to experience the pleasure of artistic knowledge. For, the material with which literature works and which gives literature its distinctive place in human knowledge is the meaningfully concrete and not the pure meaning—Hamlet and not *homo*.

THE ACT OF TEACHING

At the beginning of this chapter, we observed the relatively evident fact that, as a real act performed in a definite situation, teaching involves the teacher and the student as well as the subject matter. So far we have looked primarily at subject matter and considered various academic subjects in the light of the nature of the human learning process. The conclusions emerging from this analysis of only one of the components of the teaching act are practical as opposed to speculative. That is to say, the conclusions are ordered to action. They raise problems. They bring into focus a number of facts that must be kept in mind if these subjects are to be taught in accord with their own nature and the nature of human learning.

However, the reduction of the psychological principles governing the learning process to practical procedures is far from complete. A teacher does not teach literature or science in general; here and now he is teaching a particular novel or a particular law of motion to a specific group of students who possess distinctive cognitive histories. In other words, when one explicitly combines two components of the teaching process, the subject matter and the student, he cannot speak in quite so general terms. A specific teaching situation emerges from the combination, and further application of psychological principles becomes more particularized. Now, the more general analysis conducted in this chapter is hardly complete. There are many aspects touching the nature of a given academic subject that we have not considered. Moreover, it is difficult to determine the point at which such an analysis *would* be complete, since general consideration of subject matter shades into the study of a specific teaching situation. But it is at the level of the specific teaching situation that *immediately* practical methods of teaching can be devised.

This chapter has deliberately attempted to avoid stating immediately practical principles. We concerned ourselves with the teaching of factual subjects or science or language rather than the history of the Civil War or chemical valence or the Latin third conjugation.

One obvious reason for this concern is that thorough analysis of any specific teaching situation would require a volume in itself.

However, there is another more important reason for the rather general type of discussion found above, and that reason is methodological. When one turns his attention to any specific teaching situation, he finds himself in an area where philosophical knowledge of the nature of the learning process and the nature of an academic subject is insufficient. This knowledge is necessary for really effective teaching, but at the concrete level it must be joined with experience and experiment. For, while the nature of human learning and of a given subject remains essentially unchanged, different approaches for teaching the matter in accord with human nature are entirely possible. Hence, the experimental method of devising laws and methods through trial and error is most effective at the level of a specific teaching situation.

This does not mean that the philosophical approach must be dropped when one turns his attention to an immediately practical situation. It is here that a philosophical psychology of learning can serve its heuristic function. Negatively speaking, if a practical method of teaching a certain subject does not square with the nature of the learning process or the nature of the subject as these things are known through philosophical analysis, then it would not seem fruitful to spend time testing the method experimentally. In a more positive light, a philosophical learning theory can direct the experimenter to possible approaches, point the way toward new methods that may be fruitful where others have been found barren. Thus, if an educational psychologist or an individual teacher is alive to the real nature of human learning, he may be led to find practical and effective methods for further experimental testing or for immediate use in the classroom—methods that will be proportioned to the way man naturally learns. To create this awareness of the nature of human learning has been a principal purpose of this book.

A brief glance at the final component of teaching, the teacher himself, will enable us to locate the place of practical methods in the teaching process.

Telling a person how to teach is very much like instructing a young artist to be a good painter. The professional artist can tell his protégé about the techniques of balancing colors, using different brushes for different purposes, developing various brush strokes. He can, in short, teach the novice effective methods, both general and specific. But the part of artistic work that entails self-expression cannot be communicated through a method, for this is a question of personal history—temperament, emotional make-up, unique background and interests. Methods are notions, in the technical sense discussed in Chapter Five. They are impersonal; they can be directly communicated or imitated. But personality, as the word clearly implies, *is* personal; it cannot be adequately symbolized or exhaustively communicated to another.

Similarly, methods of teaching—even the most practical methods adapted to the most specific situations—are impersonal. They can be shared by different teachers, they can be written down, they can be taught in training courses. They are ways of telling a teacher how to symbolize, how to lead his students to form the phantasms that will be most effective as instruments of the intellect. But a method, however workable, is never employed in an impersonal vacuum. An individual teacher uses methods and a group of individuals learns through them. Thus it is that different masters can teach the *same* subject in different ways to different people living in different cultures. As a real act, then, teaching is personal. And the most practical methods devised and tested by human genius will not finally tell a person how *he* should teach, any more than Picasso can be told how to paint like Picasso.

Thus, when subject matter, student, and teacher are looked at in the real situation in which they are actually found, teaching, like learning or being, becomes a matter of analogy. It cannot finally be conceptualized into univocal categories or regulated with univocal rigor. In this existential perspective, principles or methods of teaching are like an unformed mass of molten ore. They are not finally practical until they have been pressed into the mold of the individual teacher. Though all of the images may be made of the same metal, each mold yields a different image. Our hope is that the principles presented throughout this book may help to form images made, not of dross, but of true gold.

APPENDIX:
TEXTS TRANSLATED IN
THE BODY OF THE WORK

1

Respondeo. Dicendum quod impossibile est intellectum secundum praesentis vitae statum, quo passibili corpori coniungitur, aliquid intelligere in actu, nisi convertendo se ad phantasmata. Et hoc duobus indiciis apparet. Primo quidem quia, cum intellectus sit vis quaedam non utens corporali organo, nullo modo impediretur in suo actu per laesionem alicuius corporalis organi, si non requireretur ad eius actum actus alicuius potentiae utentis organo corporali. Utuntur autem organo corporali sensus et imaginatio et aliae vires pertinentes ad partem sensitivam. Unde manifestum est quod ad hoc quod intellectus actu intelligat, non solum accipiendo scientiam de novo, sed etiam utendo scientia iam acquisita, requiritur actus imaginationis et ceterarum virtutum. Videmus enim quod impedito actu virtutis imaginativae per laesionem organi, ut in phreneticis, et similiter impedito actu memorativae virtutis, ut in lethargicis, impeditur homo ab intelligendo in actu etiam ea quorum scientiam praeaccepit. Secundo, quia hoc quilibet in seipso experiri potest, quod quando aliquis conatur aliquid intelligere, format sibi aliqua phantasmata per modum exemplorum, in quibus quasi inspiciat quod intelligere studet. Et inde est etiam quod quando aliquem volumus facere aliquid intelligere, proponimus ei exempla, ex quibus sibi phantasmata formare possit ad intelligendum.—Huius autem ratio est quia potentia cognoscitiva proportionatur cognoscibili. Unde intellectus angeli, qui est totaliter a corpore separatus, obiectum proprium est substantia intelligibilis a corpore separata; et per huiusmodi intelligibilia materialia cognoscit. Intellectus autem humani, qui est coniunctus corpori, proprium obiectum est quidditas sive natura in materia corporali existens; et per huiusmodi naturas visibilium rerum etiam in invisibilium rerum aliqualem cognitionem ascendit. De ratione autem huius naturae est quod in aliquo individuo existat, quod non est absque materia corporali; sicut de ratione naturae lapidis est quod sit in hoc lapide, et de ratione naturae equi est quod sit in hoc equo, et sic de aliis. Unde natura lapidis, vel cuiuscumque materialis rei, cognosci non potest complete et vere, nisi secundum quod cognoscitur ut in particulari existens. Particulare autem apprehendimus per sensum et imaginationem. Et ideo necesse est ad hoc quod intellectus [L. + actu] intelligat suum obiectum proprium, quod convertat se ad phantasmata, ut speculetur naturam universalem in particulari existentem. Si autem proprium obiectum intellectus nostri esset forma separata; vel si formae rerum sensibilium subsisterent non in particularibus, secundum Platonicos, non oporteret quod intellectus noster semper intelligendo converteret se ad phantasmata.

[*S. T.* I, q. 84, a. 7. Ed. Ottawa I, 521b4–522a20. Translated above, pp. 96–98.]

2

Effectus autem sensibilis per se habet quod ducat in cognitionem alterius, quasi primo et per se homini innotescens, quia omnis nostra cognitio a sensu oritur. Effectus autem intelligibiles non habent quod possint ducere in cognitionem alterius nisi inquantum sunt per aliud manifestati, idest per aliqua sensibilia.

[*S. T.* III, q. 60, a. 4. ad 1. Ed. Ottawa IV, 2811b26–34. Translated above, chapter 3, note 15.]

3

Phantasma est principium nostrae cognitionis, ut ex quo incipit intellectus operatio, non sicut transiens, sed sicut permanens, ut quoddam fundamentum intellectualis operationis, sicut principia demonstrationis oportet manere in omni processu scientiae, cum phantasmata comparentur ad intellectum ut obiecta, in quibus inspicit omne quod inspicit vel secundum perfectam repraesentationem vel per negationem. Et ideo quando phantasmatum cognitio impeditur, oportet totaliter impediri cognitionem intellectus etiam in divinis. Patet enim quod non possumus intelligere Deum esse causam corporum sive supra omnia corpora sive absque corporeitate, nisi imaginemur corpora, non tamen iudicium divinorum secundum imaginationem formatur.

[*In librum Boethii de Trinitate,* q. 6, a. 2, ad 5. Ed. Paul Wyser, O.P. (Fribourg: Société philosophique, 1948), p. 65. Translated above, chapter 3, note 16.]

4

Respondeo. Dicendum quod sicut ad unitatem motus requiritur unitas termini, ita ad unitatem operationis requiritur unitas obiecti. Contingit autem aliqua accipi ut plura, et ut unum; sicut partes alicuius continui. Si enim unaquaeque per se accipiatur, plures sunt; unde et non una operatione, nec simul accipiuntur per sensum et intellectum. Alio modo accipiuntur secundum quod sunt unum in toto, et sic simul una operatione cognoscuntur tam per sensum quam per intellectum, dum totum continuum consideratur, ut dicitur in III *De An.* Et sic etiam intellectus noster simul intelligit subiectum et praedicatum, prout sunt partes unius propositionis; et duo comparata, secundum quod conveniunt in una comparatione. Ex quo patet quod multa secundum quod sunt distincta, non possunt simul intelligi; sed secundum quod uniuntur in uno intelligibili, sic simul intelliguntur. Unumquodque autem est intelligibile in actu, secundum quod eius similitudo est in intellectu. Quaecumque igitur per unam speciem intelligibilem cognosci possunt cognoscuntur ut unum intelligibile; et ideo simul cognoscuntur. Quae vero per diversas species intelligibiles cognoscuntur, ut diversa intelligibilia capiuntur.

[*S. T.* I, q. 58, a. 2. Ed. Ottawa I, 351b45–352a24. Translated above, pp. 116 and 118.]

5

Intellectus enim possibilis, sicut et quaelibet substantia, operatur secundum modum suae naturae. Secundum autem suam naturam est forma corporis. Unde intelligit quidem immaterialia, sed inspicit ea in aliquo materiali. Cuius signum est, quod in doctrinis universalibus exempla particularia ponuntur, in quibus quod dicitur inspiciatur. Alio ergo modo se habet intellectus possibilis ad phantasma quo indiget, ante speciem intelligibilem: et alio modo postquam recepit speciem intelligibilem. Ante enim, indiget eo ut ab eo accipiat speciem intelligibilem: unde se habet ad intellectum possibilem ut obiectum movens. Sed post speciem in eo receptam, indiget eo quasi instrumento sive fundamento suae speciei: unde se habet ad phantasmata sicut causa efficiens; secundum enim imperium intellectus formatur in imaginatione phantasma conveniens tali speciei intelligibili, in quo resplendet species intelligibilis sicut exemplar in exemplato sive in imagine. . . . Unde videmus quod illud cuius scientiam semel accepimus, est in potestate nostra iterum considerare cum volumus. Nec impedimur propter phantasmata: quia in potestate nostra est formare phantasmata accomoda considerationi quam volumus.

[*Summa contra Gentiles,* Bk. II, cap. 73 ad fin. Ed. Leonine manual (Romae: Apud sedem Commissionis Leoninae, 1934), pp. 175–76. Translated above, chapter 4, note 19.]

6

In eo enim qui docetur, est principium activum ad scientiam: scilicet intellectus, et ea quae naturaliter intelliguntur, scilicet prima principia. Et ideo scientia acquiritur dupliciter: et sine doctrina, per inventionem; et per doctrinam. Docens igitur hoc modo incipit docere sicut inveniens incipit invenire: offerendo scilicet considerationi discipuli principia ab eo nota, quia *omnis disciplina ex praeexistenti fit cognitione* [I *Poster.* I, 1; 71a], et illa principia in conclusiones deducendo; et proponendo exempla sensibilia, ex quibus in anima discipuli formentur phantasmata necessaria ad intelligendum.

[*Summa contra Gentiles,* Bk. II, cap. 75 ad fin. Ed. Leonine manual, p. 181. Quoted and paraphrased above, p. 183.]

BIBLIOGRAPHY

I. *PRIMARY SOURCES*

Saint Thomas Aquinas, O.P. *In Aristotelis librum De Anima commentarium.* Ed. A. Pirotta, O.P. 2d ed. Taurini: Marietti, 1936.

————. *In librum Boethii de Trinitate: Quaestiones Quinta et Sexta.* Ed. Paul Wyser, O.P. Fribourg: Société Philosophique, 1948.

————. *In Metaphysicam Aristotelis commentaria.* Ed. M.–R. Cathala, O.P. 3d ed. Taurini: Marietti, 1935.

————. *Quaestiones Disputatae* 2 vols. Ed. R. Spiazzi, O.P. 8th ed. revised. Taurini: Marietti, 1949.

————. *Quaestiones Quodlibetales.* Ed. R. Spiazzi, O.P. 8th ed. revised. Taurini: Marietti, 1949.

————. *Scriptum super libros Sententiarum Magistri Petri Lombardi.* 4 vols. Ed. P. Mandonnet, O.P., and M. Moos, O.P. Paris: Lethielleux, 1929–33.

————. *Summa contra Gentiles.* Ed. Leonina manualis. Romae: Apud sedem Commissionis Leoninae, 1934.

————. *Summa Theologiae.* Vols. I–IV. Ed. Ottawa-Piana. Ottawa: Impensis Studii Generalis O. Pr., 1941–44.

II. *WORKS ON AQUINAS AND EDUCATIONAL THEORY*

This is an alphabetical listing of the works reviewed more or less chronologically in the Introduction; studies that were not located (and indicated as such in the Introduction) are also given here, in order to keep the list as complete as possible.

BOOKS

Alves de Siqueira, A. *Filosofia da educação.* Petrópolis: Vozes, 1942.

Barthélemy, A. L., O.P. *L'éducation: Les bases d'une pédagogie thomiste.* Bruxelles, 1925.

228   *The Analogy of Learning*

Boullay, P., O.P. *Thomisme et éducation.* Bruxelles, 1933.

Casotti, Mario. *Maestro e scolaro: Saggio di filosofia dell' educazione.* Milano: Soc. ed. "Vita e Pensiero," 1930.

————. *La pedagogia di s. Tommaso d'Aquino.* Brescia: Soc. ed. "La Scuola," 1931.

————. *Pedagogia generale.* 2 vols. Brescia: La Scuola, 1947–48.

Chevalier, J. *L'habitude: Essai de métaphysique scientifique.* Paris: Boivin, 1929.

García Vieyra, Alberto. *Ensayos sobre pedagogía según la mente de s. Tomás de Aquino.* Buenos Aires: Desclée, 1949.

Guzzo, A. *Tommaso d'Aquino: Il maestro.* Firenze: Vallechi, 1930.

Leoncio da Silva, C., S.D.B. *Pedagogia speciale practica.* Vol. I: *L'educando.* Torino: Soc. ed. internaz., 1948.

Maritain, Jacques. *Education at the Crossroads.* "Terry Lectures," 1943. New Haven: Yale University Press, 1943.

Mayer, Mary Helen. *The Philosophy of Teaching of St. Thomas Aquinas.* Milwaukee: Bruce, 1929.

McCormick, John F., S.J. *St. Thomas and the Life of Learning.* "Aquinas Lecture." Milwaukee: Marquette University Press, 1937.

Muzio, G. *S. Tommaso d'Aquino: Il maestro.* Torino: Soc. ed. internazion., 1928.

di Napoli, Giovanni. *De Magistro.* Torino: Soc. ed. internaz., 1954.

Navarro, B. *Commentario filosofico-teologico a la carta de s. Tomás sobre el modo de estudiar fructuosamente.* Almagro: Dominicos de Andalucia, 1925.

Roland-Gosselin, B. *L'habitude.* Paris: Beauchesne, 1920.

ARTICLES

de Beaurecueil, S., O.P. "S. Thomas d'Aquin et la pédagogie," *Cahiers, Cercle thomiste,* II (1949), 3–30.

Bednarski, F., O.P. "Animadversiones s. Thomae Aquinatis de iuvenibus eorumque educatione," *Angelicum,* XXXV (1958), 375–411.

Busnelli, G., S.J. "Filosofia e pedagogia," *Civiltà Cattolica,* LXXXII (1931), III, 413–22; IV, 30–40, 229–38, 309–25.

Calà-Ulloa, Guglielmo. "Il concetto della pedagogia alla luce dell' aristotelismo tomistico," *Sapienza,* III (1950), 28–45.

Casotti, Mario. "La neoscolastica e la pedagogia," *Rivista di filosofia neoscolastica,* suppl. spec. XXVI (1934), 241–47.

————. "Pedagogia e metafisica," *ibid.,* XLI (1949), 137–52.

Castiello, Jaime, S.J. "The Psychology of Habit in St. Thomas Aquinas," *Modern Schoolman,* XIV (1936), 8–12.

Chabrol, J. "Habitus et éducation," *Cahiers, Cercle Sainte-Jeanne* (1932), 60–67.

Chiochetti, E. "La pedagogia di s. Tommaso," *S. Tommaso d'Aquino: Pubblicazione commemorativa del sesto centenario della canonizazione* (Milano: Vita e Pensiero, 1923), 280–93.

Corbishley, Thomas, S.J. "St. Thomas and Educational Theory," *Dublin Review*, no. 424 (Jan., 1943), 1–13.

Devy, V. "La pédagogie de s. Thomas d'Aquin," *Revue de l'Université d'Ottawa*, II (1932), 139*–62*.

Dufault, L., O.M.I. "The Aristotelian-Thomistic Concept of Education," *New Scholasticism*, XX (1946), 239–57.

Engert, J. "Die Pädagogik des hl. Thomas," *Pharus*, VI (1925), 321–31.

Gilson, Etienne. "The Eminence of Teaching," *Truth and the Philosophy of Teaching* ("McAuley Lectures," 1953; West Hartford, Conn.: St. Joseph College, 1954), 5–15. Reprinted in *A Gilson Reader*, ed. Anton Pegis (New York: Hanover House, 1957); also as the second selection in *Disputed Questions in Education* (New York: Doubleday & Co., 1954).

Grabmann, Martin. "Die Psychologie des Lehrens und Lernens nach dem hl. Thomas von Aquin," *Die Christliche Schule* (1910), 145–51.

Jacobs, J. F., O.P., and Bishop, J., O.P. "Learning Humanly," *Reality*, I (1950–51), 37–43.

Keller, L. "Lehren und Lernen bei Thomas von Aquin," *Angelicum*, XIII (1936), 210–27.

Kocourek, R. A. "St. Thomas on Study," *Thomistic Principles in a Catholic School* (St. Louis: Herder, 1943), 14–38.

Kuničić, Jordanus, O.P. "Principia didactica Sancti Thomae," *Divus Thomas* (Piacenza), LVIII (1955), 398–411.

Leoncio da Silva, C., S.D.B. "Il fine dell' educazione secondo i principi di s. Tommaso," *Salesianum*, IX (1947), 207–39.

Mangieri, G. A. "Presupposti di un' educazione nel pensiero di s. Tommaso," *Sapienza*, IV (1951), 309–24.

Maloney, C. L. "Dualism in Education," *Cath. Educ. Review*, XLIV (1946), 335–41.

Morando, D. "Sul 'De Magistro' di s. Tommaso," *Rivista Rosminiana*, XXV (1931).

Pace, E. A. "St. Thomas' Theory of Education," *Cath. Univ. Bulletin*, VIII (1902), 290–303.

Rung, R. "Studio sulla Quaestio disp. *De Magistro* di s. Tommaso d'Aquino," *Rivista di filosofia neoscolastica*, XIV (1922), 109–65.

Schwalm, M. B., O.P. "L'action intellectuelle d'un maître d'après s. Thomas," *Revue thomiste,* VIII (1900), 251–72.

Shannon, G. J., C.M. "Aquinas on the Teacher's Art," *Clergy Review,* XXXI (1949), 375–85.

di Sisto, Rosa T. "El concepto de pedagogía según s. Tomás," *Anales del Instituto de Investigaciones Pedagogicas* (San Luis, Argentina), II (1952–53), 234.

Slavin, Robert J., O.P. "The Essential Features of the Philosophy of Education of St. Thomas," *Proceed. Amer. Cath. Philos. Assoc.,* XIII (1937), 22–38.

―――. "The Thomistic Concept of Education," *Essays in Thomism,* ed. R. E. Brennan (New York: Sheed & Ward, 1942), 311–31.

Tauzin, S., O.P. "S. Tomás e la pedagogía moderna," *Revista Brasileira de Pedagogía,* XXXVIII–IX (1937), 118–29.

Tincani, G. "L'azione intellettuale del maestro secondo s. Tommaso," *Scuola cattolica,* ser. 5, vol. XIX (1920), 37–50, 115–29, 173–85.

Todoli Duque, Jose. "Los fundamentos de la educación en s. Tomás," *Sapientia,* V (1950), 89–111.

"Traité sommaire d'éducation d'après la psychologie thomiste," *L'ami du clergé,* LII (1935), 593–601.

Van Acker, L. "S. Tomás de Aquino e a escola nova," *A ordem,* XII (1931), 138–45.

Wade, Francis C., S.J. "Causality in the Classroom," *Modern Schoolman,* XXVIII (1951), 138–46.

―――. "St. Thomas Aquinas and Teaching," *Some Philosophers on Education,* ed. Donald A. Gallagher (Milwaukee: Marquette University Press, 1956), 67–85.

Woroniecki, Hyacinth. "St. Thomas and Modern Pedagogy," *Cath. Educ. Review,* XXVIII (1930), 170–80.

Willmann, O. "Thomas von Aquin," *Lexikon der Pädagogik* (Freiburg im B.: Roloff, 1917) V, cols. 105–21.

―――. "Des hl. Thomas von Aquin Untersuchungen über dem Lehrer," *W. aus Hörsaal und Schulstube, gesammelte kleinere Schriften zur Erziehungs und Unterrichtslehre* (Freiburg im B.: Herder, 1904), 40–45.

UNPUBLISHED MATERIAL

Donohue, John W., S.J. "The Teaching-Learning Process according to St. Thomas and Henry C. Morrison." Unpublished Master's thesis, Dept. of Education, St. Louis University, 1944.

Lauer, J. Quentin, S.J. "The Art of Teaching according to the Principles of St. Thomas." Unpublished Master's thesis, Dept. of Philosophy, St. Louis University, 1943.

III. *TEXTUAL STUDIES OF AQUINAS' PSYCHOLOGY*

BOOKS

Hoenen, Peter, S.J. *Reality and Judgment according to St. Thomas.* Tr. H. F. Tiblier, S.J. Chicago: Regnery Co., 1952.

Klubertanz, George P., S.J. *The Discursive Power.* St. Louis: Modern Schoolman, 1952.

Ledvina, J. P. *A Psychology and Philosophy of Sensation according to St. Thomas Aquinas.* Washington, D.C.: Catholic Univ. Press, 1941.

Peghaire, J., C.S.Sp. *'Intellectus' et 'Ratio' selon s. Thomas d'Aquin.* "Publications de l'Institut d'Etudes Médiévales d'Ottawa," VI. Paris: J. Vrin, 1936.

Ryan, Edmund J., C.PP.S. *The Role of the "Sensus Communis" in the Psychology of St. Thomas Aquinas.* Carthagena, Ohio: Messenger Press, 1951.

Tyrrell, Francis. *The Role of Assent in Judgment.* Washington, D.C.: Catholic Univ. Press, 1948.

ARTICLES

Albertson, James S., S.J. "Instrumental Causality in St. Thomas," *New Scholasticism,* XXVIII (1954), 409–35.

Brennan, Robert E., O.P. "The Thomistic Concept of Imagination," *ibid.,* XV (1941), 149–61.

Cunningham, Francis A., S.J. "A Theory on Abstraction in St. Thomas," *Modern Schoolman,* XXXV (1958), 249–70.

Desmarais, Marcel-Marie, O.P. "L'auto-perception de la personne psychologique," *Etudes et recherches,* Vol. I, *Philosophie* (Ottawa: Collège Dominicain, 1936), 11–47.

Fearon, Arthur D. "The Imagination," *New Scholasticism,* XIV (1940), 181–95.

Geiger, L.-B., "Abstraction et séparation d'après s. Thomas," *Revue des sciences philosophiques et théologiques,* XXXI (1937), 3–40.

Klubertanz, George P., S.J. "St. Thomas and the Knowledge of the Singular," *New Scholasticism,* XXVI (1952), 135–66.

———. "The Unity of Human Activity," *Modern Schoolman,* XXVII (1950), 75–103.

Lonergan, Bernard J., S.J. "The Concept of *Verbum* in the Writings of St. Thomas Aquinas," *Theological Studies,* VII (1946), 349–92; VIII (1947), 35–79, 404–44; X (1949), 3–40, 359–93.

Meissner, William W., S.J. "Some Aspects of the *Verbum* in the Texts of St. Thomas," *Modern Schoolman,* XXXVI (1958), 1–30.

Muller-Thym, Bernard. "The 'To Be' which Signifies the Truth of Propositions," *Proceed. Amer. Cath. Philos. Assoc.,* XVI (1940), 230–54.

Phelan, Gerald B. "Verum Sequitur Esse Rerum," *Medieval Studies,* I (1939), 11–22.

Régis, Louis-Marie, O.P. "Analyse et synthèse dans l'oeuvre de s. Thomas," *Studia Mediaevalia* (Bruges: De Tempel, 1948), 303–30.

Wébert, J., O.P. " 'Reflexio': Etude sur les opérations réflexives dans la psychologie de s. Thomas d'Aquin," *Mélanges Mandonnet: Etudes d'historie littéraire et doctrinale du moyen âge,* Vol. I ("Bibliothèque thomiste," XIII; Paris: J. Vrin, 1930), 285–325.

UNPUBLISHED MATERIAL

Burns, Patrick J., S.J. "St. Thomas and Judgment: Selected Texts." Unpublished Master's thesis, Dept. of Philosophy, St. Louis Univ., 1957.

Kennard, George V., S.J. "The Intellect Composing and Dividing according to St. Thomas Aquinas." Unpublished Master's thesis, Dept. of Philosophy, St. Louis Univ., 1949.

Wade, William L., S.J. "A Comparison of the 'De Magistro' of St. Augustine with the 'De Magistro' of St. Thomas." Unpublished Ph.D. dissertation, Dept. of Philosophy, St. Louis Univ., 1935.

IV. *OTHER SECONDARY SOURCES*

BOOKS

Adler, Mortimer J. *What Man Has Made of Man: A Study of the Consequences of Platonism and Positivism in Psychology.* New York: Longmans, Green & Co., 1938.

Andrews, T. G. (ed.) *Methods of Psychology.* New York: Wiley & Sons, 1948.

Bartlett, Sir Frederic. *Thinking: An Experimental and Social Study.* New York: Basic Books, 1958.

Bode, Boyd Henry. *Conflicting Psychologies of Learning.* New York: D. C. Heath & Co., 1929.

Brett, George Sidney. *Brett's History of Psychology.* Ed. and abr. R. S. Peters. London: Allen & Unwin, Ltd., 1953.

Brown, Clarence W., and Ghiselli, Edwin E. *Scientific Method in Psychology*. New York: McGraw-Hill, 1955.

Bruner, J. S., and Others. *A Study of Thinking*. New York: Wiley & Sons, 1956.

Caldin, E. F. *The Power and Limits of Science*. New York: Harper, 1949.

Castiello, Jaime, S.J. *A Humane Psychology of Education*. New York: Sheed & Ward, 1936.

Cohen, Morris R., and Nagel, Ernest. *An Introduction to Logic and Scientific Method*. New York: Harcourt, Brace & Co., 1934.

Collins, James. *History of Modern European Philosophy*. Milwaukee: Bruce Publ. Co., 1954.

Connolly, F. G. *Science versus Philosophy*. New York: Philosophical Library, 1957.

Feigl, Herbert, and Scriven, Michael (eds.). *The Foundations of Science and the Concepts of Psychology and Psychoanalysis*. Vol. I of *Minnesota Studies in the Philosophy of Science*. Minneapolis: Univ. of Minnesota Press, 1956.

Gaffney, Mark A., S.J. *The Psychology of the Interior Senses*. St. Louis: Herder, 1942.

Gannon, Timothy J. *Psychology: The Unity of Human Behavior*. Boston: Ginn & Co., 1954.

Geach, Peter. *Mental Acts: Their Content and Their Objects*. "Studies in Philosophical Psychology," ed. R. F. Holland. New York: Humanities Press, Inc., 1957.

Gilson, Etienne. *Réalisme thomiste et critique de la connaissance*. Paris: J. Vrin, 1939.

Hawkins, D. J. B. *Causality and Implication*. London: Sheed & Ward, 1937.

————. *The Criticism of Experience*. New York: Sheed & Ward, 1945.

————. *Crucial Problems of Modern Philosophy*. London: Sheed & Ward, 1957.

Henle, Robert J., S.J. *Method in Metaphysics*. "Aquinas Lecture," 1950. Milwaukee: Marquette Univ. Press, 1951.

Hesse, Mary B. *Science and the Human Imagination*. New York: Philosophical Library, 1955.

Hilgard, Ernest R. *Theories of Learning*. 2d ed. New York: Appleton-Century-Crofts, 1956.

Humphrey, George. *Thinking*. London: Methuen & Co., 1951.

Kant, Immanuel. *Immanuel Kant's Critique of Pure Reason*. Trans. Norman Kemp Smith. London: Macmillan & Co., 1950.

Klubertanz, George P., S.J. *The Philosophy of Human Nature.* New York: Appleton-Century-Crofts, 1953.

Langer, Susanne. *Feeling and Form.* New York: Chas. Scribner's Sons, 1953.

————. *Philosophy in a New Key.* 2d ed. Cambridge, Mass.: Harvard Univ. Press, 1951.

Learning Theory, Personality Theory, and Clinical Research. University of Kentucky Symposium, March 13–14, 1953. New York: Wiley & Sons, 1954.

Lee, Otis. *Existence and Inquiry.* Chicago: Univ. of Chicago Press, 1949.

Marc, André, S.J. *Psychologie réflexive.* Vol. I: *La connaissance.* Paris: Desclée de Brouwer, 1948.

Maréchal, J., S.J. *Le point de départ de la métaphysique.* Vol. V: *Le Thomisme devant la philosophie critique.* 2d ed. Paris: Desclée, 1949.

Maritain, Jacques. *The Degrees of Knowledge.* Trans. Bernard Wall. New York: Chas. Scribner's Sons, 1938.

May, Rollo (ed.). *Existence: A New Dimension in Psychiatry and Psychology.* New York: Basic Books, Inc., 1958.

McKellar, Peter. *Imagination and Thinking: A Psychological Analysis.* New York: Basic Books, Inc., 1957.

McKeon, Richard (ed.). *Basic Works of Aristotle.* New York: Random House, 1941.

Moore, Thomas Verner. *Cognitive Psychology.* Philadelphia: J. B. Lippincott Co., 1939.

Murphy, Gardner. *Historical Introduction to Modern Psychology.* New York: Harcourt, Brace & Co., 1949.

Newman, John Henry Cardinal. *An Essay in Aid of a Grammar of Assent.* Ed. Charles F. Harrold. New York: Longmans, Green & Co., 1947.

Osgood, Charles E. *Method and Theory in Experimental Psychology.* New York: Oxford Univ. Press, 1953.

Piaget, Jean. *The Construction of Reality in the Child.* Trans. Margaret Cook. New York: Basic Books, Inc., 1954.

————. *The Origins of Intelligence in Children.* Trans. Margaret Cook. New York: International Universities Press, Inc., 1952.

Rapaport, David (ed.). *Organization and Pathology of Thought.* New York: Columbia Univ. Press, 1951.

Régis, Louis-Marie, O.P. *Epistemology.* Trans. Imelda Choquette Byrne. New York: Macmillan Co., 1959.

————. *St. Thomas and Epistemology.* "Aquinas Lecture." Milwaukee: Marquette Univ. Press, 1946.

Schneider, Wilhelm. *Die Quaestiones Disputatae De Veritate des Thomas von Aquin in ihrer Philosophiegeschichtlichen Beziehung zu Augustinus.* Vol. XXVII, Part III of *Beiträge zur Geschichte der Philosophie und Theologie des Mittelalters.* Ed. Martin Grabmann. Münster: Aschendorffschen Verlagsbuchhandlung, 1930.

Stace, W. T. *A Critical History of Greek Philosophy.* London: Macmillan & Co., 1928.

Stevens, S. S. (ed.). *Handbook of Experimental Psychology.* New York: Wiley & Sons, 1951.

Stolurow, L. M. (ed.). *Readings in Learning.* New York: Prentice-Hall, 1953.

Taylor, Hugh (ed.). *Science in Progress.* New Haven: Yale University Press, 1957.

Veatch, Henry Babcock. *Intentional Logic: A Logic Based on Philosophical Realism.* New Haven: Yale University Press, 1952.

Wertheimer, Max. *Productive Thinking.* New York: Harper & Bros., 1945.

Wild, John (ed.). *The Return to Reason.* Chicago: Regnery Co., 1953.

Wilhelmsen, Frederick D. *Man's Knowledge of Reality: An Introduction to Thomistic Epistemology.* Englewood Cliffs, N.J.: Prentice-Hall, 1956.

Woodworth, Robert S. *Psychology.* 3d ed. New York: Henry Holt & Co., 1934.

ARTICLES

Barrett, Sister Mary Constance, R.S.M. "An Experimental Study of the Thomistic Concept of the Faculty of Imagination," *Studies in Psychology and Psychiatry: Catholic Univ. of America,* V (1941), no. 3.

Collins, James. "Toward a Philosophically Ordered Thomism," *New Scholasticism,* XXXII (1958), 301–26.

Feigl, Herbert. "Scientific Method without Metaphysical Presuppositions," *Philosophical Studies,* V (1954), 17–29.

———. "Some Remarks on the Meaning of Scientific Explanation," *Readings in Philosophical Analysis,* ed. H. Feigl & Wilfred Sellars (New York: Appleton-Century-Crofts, Inc., 1949), 510–14.

Guzie, Tad W., S.J. "Evolution of Philosophical Method in the Writings of St. Thomas," *Modern Schoolman,* XXXVII (January, 1960), 95–120.

Henle, Robert J., S.J. "Existentialism and the Judgment," *Proceed. Amer. Cath. Philos. Assoc.,* XXI (1946), 40–53.

Klubertanz, George P., S.J. "The Doctrine of St. Thomas and Modern

Science," *Sapientia Aquinatis* (Rome: Catholic Book Agency, 1955), 89–104. (Presented at the 4th International Thomistic Congress, Rome, September 13–17, 1955.)

————. "The Psychologists and the Nature of Man," *Proceed. Amer. Cath. Philos. Assoc.*, XXV (1951), 66–88.

Wilhelmsen, Frederick D. "The Philosopher and the Myth," *Modern Schoolman*, XXXII (1954), 39–55.

INDEX

Consult the bibliography for the authors whose works are reviewed in the Introduction, and for those proper names mentioned only in the footnotes.